ISOCRATES AND CIVIC EDUCATION

EDITED BY

TAKIS POULAKOS AND DAVID DEPEW

Isocrates and Civic Education

UNIVERSITY OF TEXAS PRESS, AUSTIN

This book has been supported by an endowment dedicated to classics and the ancient world and funded by the Areté Foundation; the Gladys Krieble Delmas Foundation; the Dougherty Foundation; the James R. Dougherty, Jr. Foundation; the Rachael and Ben Vaughan Foundation; and the National Endowment for the Humanities. The endowment has also benefited from gifts by Mark and Jo Ann Finley, Lucy Shoe Meritt, the late Anne Byrd Nalle, and other individual donors.

Material from Josiah Ober, *Political Dissent in Democratic Athens*, copyright © 1998 by Princeton University Press, reprinted by permission of Princeton University Press.

Material from Takis Poulakos, "Isocrates' Use of *doxa*," *Philosophy and Rhetoric*, vol. 34, no. 1 (2001), pp. 61–78, copyright 2001 by the Pennsylvania State University, reproduced by permission of the publisher.

Material from John Poulakos, "Early Changes in Rhetorical Practice and Understanding: From the Sophists to Isocrates," *Texte*, 1989, nos. 8–9, reprinted by permission of the publisher.

Library of Congress Cataloging-in-Publication Data

Isocrates and civic education / edited by Takis Poulakos and David Depew.— 1. ed.
p.   cm.
Includes bibliographical references and index.
ISBN 0-292-72234-6
1. Isocrates—Political and social views.   2. Speeches, addresses, etc., Greek—
Greece—Athens—History and criticism.   3. Athens (Greece)—Intellectual life.
4. Education, Greek—Greece—Athens.   5. Education, Ancient.
I. Poulakos, Takis.   II. Depew, David J., 1942–
PA4218.I746   2004
885'.01—dc22
2003021064

To *Brigittine,*
MOTHER OF DIONYSOS,
and *Mary,*
LOVER OF ALL THINGS HELLENIC

CONTENTS

ACKNOWLEDGMENTS

The origins of the essays in this volume lie in the 1998 Obermann Humanities Symposium, "Civic Education in Classical Athens and Humanities Education Today." The symposium was held at the University of Iowa under the sponsorship of the Obermann Center for Advanced Studies in October 1998. The editors are grateful to the Obermann Center, and especially to its director, Dr. Jay Semel, for his encouragement and support in every phase of this project. We are also grateful to the University of Iowa's Project on the Rhetoric of Inquiry for its cooperation and support, as well as to several cosponsoring departments in the College of Liberal Arts and Sciences: Classics, Philosophy, Rhetoric, and Communication Studies. We are grateful finally to Humanities Iowa for their grant in support of our symposium, and to Ray Heffner for his thoughtful report to Humanities Iowa.

The volume has benefited greatly from the remarks of those who served as respondents at this interdisciplinary Humanities Symposium. These colleagues include Professors Eve Browning Cole, Philosophy, University of Minnesota, Duluth; John Finamore, Classics, University of Iowa; Kenneth Cmiel, History, University of Iowa; the late Michael Calvin McGee, Communication Studies, University of Iowa; Thomas Williams, Philosophy, University of Iowa; Dennis Moore, Rhetoric, University of Iowa; Diana Cates, Religion, University of Iowa. We also wish to thank Professors Helena Dettmer, John Garcia, Peter Green, and Robert Ketterer for chairing the panels and leading the conversation during the symposium. We wish to acknowledge our special debt to John Finamore and Mary Depew who were there for us from the start and through every logistical step on the way.

Much credit is due to the contributors to the volume. Their willingness to amplify and revise their work to assure a high degree of integration and mutual illumination among the essays is praiseworthy, as is their patience during the volume's long process of gestation. We are grateful to the steady hands guiding that process of gestation, the Humanities editor of University of Texas Press, Jim Burr, our anonymous reviewers, and especially Professor Michael Gagarin, Classics, University of Texas, who believed in and guided this project from the very beginning.

We are most thankful to all the people who helped us finalize various aspects of this project, Bonnie Bender and Lorna Olson for their administrative assistance with the symposium, David Banash, Brian Lain, and Danna Prather for their research assistance, Sandy Mast for her technical support, and especially Adam Roth for his tireless assistance with copyediting.

Introduction

Isocrates as Civic Educator

CIVIC virtue, and the sort of public education that was supposed to inculcate it, became something of a theme in American political discourse during the nineteen eighties. In this context, appeals were often made to the ancient Greeks as having had a deep commitment to educate their citizens with a view to virtues of character and devotion to public life. Among Greeks who wrote on political matters, it is Aristotle who seems to have received the lion's share of the attention. That is partly because philosophers such as Alasdair MacIntyre have singled out Aristotle's *Politics* and *Ethics* as a compendium of good talk about civic virtue and civic education (MacIntyre 1981; Garver 1995).

Prominent rhetorical scholars too have cast Aristotle in the role of civic educator (Kennedy 1963; Farrell 1993). From the perspective of measurable influence on public debates rather than mere scholarly reflection, the current prominence of Aristotle can be traced to the efforts of William Bennett, then chairman of the National Endowment for the Humanities and later author of a best-selling *Book of Virtues* (Bennett 1993). Bennett promoted Aristotle as a model of public-spirited, virtue-centered civic education.

Partly in consequence of these efforts, the theme of civic education became something of the possession of conservatives. Such preaching may have had a point as a counter to purely procedural liberalism, which declares all values and most behaviors to be private matters and thinks of our public life as devoted simply to providing economic, legal, and political machinery calculated to get everyone the best possible deal. They may also be of some use in blunting the nativism of the Christian right. But virtue talk, especially when it is so closely tied to the elitist Aristotle, has elicited consider-able resistance from rhetors who have been arguing for a more diverse, less sexist, less "republican" vision of democratic life. The discourse of dead white European males in the radically sexist, militarist, and imperialist cul-ture of ancient Athens has seemed in this context to be worse than irrele-vant. Its reinvocation can be perceived as constituting a coded attack on the values that progressives, liberals, and democratic radicals have been trying to instill in our democratic life for a long time and which seem as important as ever to defend today.

This said, we must report that the contributors to the present volume are in agreement with at least one assumption of today's "virtuecrats." They are willing to consider the possibility that those who value democratic plu-ralism need not entirely dismiss our old, and perhaps still useful, habit of thinking about ourselves by thinking about the ancient Greeks. We need not tell ourselves that ancient Greek males were a whit less miserable on questions about women, foreigners, and the fate of the lower classes than they have been shown to be. But many of our authors suspect that the theme of civic education in a democratic culture, and especially its relation to humanistic educational practices, might be advanced more surely if we take not Aristotle, but Isocrates, as a focal figure—not for imitation, as he was an elitist too, but as a whetstone for our own reflections on contempo-rary humanistic education and its relation to the theme of civic virtue.

For one thing, this is a matter simply of setting the historical record straight. In his own time, and well into later classical antiquity, Isocrates was a more central figure in discussions of civic education, and especially the role of rhetorical training in civic education, than Aristotle ever was. Isoc-rates, too, arguably makes a more plausible foil for Plato than Aristotle. Like Plato, his near contemporary, Isocrates founded a school in Athens. (Isocra-tes was born in 436, Plato in 429.) Unlike Plato's, though, Isocrates' school did not elevate the status of philosophy by disparaging rhetoric as an edu-cational medium for civic education. A hallmark of Isocratean civic educa-tion is that it recast philosophy *as* rhetoric precisely in order to introduce an element of reflective, aesthetic deliberation into the discussion of rhetorical training and practice. Isocrates undercut his rival's identification of rhetoric with the ignoble ghostwriting and ambulance chasing that he too disdained. He did so without repudiating, as Plato certainly did, a principle that was to be taken up repeatedly by humanistic educators in centuries to come— that good speaking (*eu legein*) and good, prudential action (*eu prattein*) are closely allied. In consequence, Isocrates stands somewhere between the flashy Sophists of an earlier day, whose giddy sense of human autonomy seems to a number of writers to resonate with postmodern themes (Too 1995), and Plato and Aristotle, who, as Harvey Yunis (1996) puts it, hoped to "tame" democracy, if they could not eliminate it.

By positioning Isocrates first in relation to the Sophists, then Plato, and finally Aristotle, the contributors to this volume attempt to demarcate the place he occupies between sophistical rhetoric and Platonic philosophies, as well as between sophistical and Aristotelian rhetorics. They articulate this place as a space of critique. Such a space issues a number of challenges against the normative claim that civic virtue in classical Athens must be thought of and talked about in monolithic terms, that discourse on civic education can lend itself unproblematically to a stable, non-agonistic perspective, and that the contestation of civic norms—when unavoidable—can ensue productively only from a certain angle. Some of these challenges become apparent as contributors track Isocrates' fidelity to sophistic principles of relativism. Others run in the other direction: toward his clear commitment to a unitary vision of the common good for the community. Others still delimit Isocrates' dual participation in discourses that uphold both elitist and democratic values. On the one hand, Isocrates portrays a leader he would create through his educational program both as a sovereign ruler and a selfless servant of the people, while on the other hand he shows a strong commitment both to stable principles of collective deliberation and to an open-ended notion of individual *doxa* (reputation).

As some contributors to this volume point out, this constant shuttling back and forth between conflicting discourses about civic values, this ongoing vacillation between disparate ends for civic education, registers as an inherent paradox in Isocrates' thinking, even an internal contradiction in his civic educational program. But it also registers, as other contributors insist, as a sign of the diverse stances and plural positions available to an intellectual in the fourth century B.C. A focus on Isocrates that acknowledges his contradictory commitments and paradoxical positions can act as a powerful reminder that the discourse on virtue, along with the type of education designed to inculcate the appropriate civic values, was not the exclusive property of the consistency-obsessed Plato and Aristotle. In his efforts to revise, redirect, and recast sophistical rhetoric and to confirm and uphold some of its principles while distancing himself from others, Isocrates manages to create doubts about his rival Plato's portrayal of sophistical discourse as a thing of the past, no longer creating any conflict for or substantive opposition to the dominant philosophical discourse on civic virtue.

The variety of individual perspectives taken up by the contributors will no doubt encourage readers of this volume to reach their own conclusions about whether Isocrates made a substantive or only a tangential contribution to fourth-century notions about civic education—and whether our own discussions about the humanities today are best served by examining his program in rhetorical education from a dominantly critical or dominantly endorsing lens. Readers of the volume are invited to adopt a lens of their choosing. But the overall structure of this volume asks that one reach conclusions about Isocrates on the basis of multiple comparisons to other intellectuals of the times. For the strands traversing his work are diverse and contradictory. To pursue one in isolation of the others and in disregard of the larger intellectual context is certain to lead to one-sided conclusions.

Two relatively recent works are a case in point for cultivating historical accuracy as an antidote for one-sided anachronism. We refer to Victor Vitanza's *Negation, Subjectivity, and the History of Rhetoric* (1997) and Kathleen Welch's *Electric Rhetoric* (1999). To Vitanza, the strand in Isocrates' writing of political unification by rhetoric, along with his advocacy of a panhellenic expedition against the Persians, is taken as the paradigmatic gesture of all imperialistic impulses. Isocrates is shown to advance a politics that becomes actualized in Nazi Germany. At the other extreme, the strand in Isocrates' writings of earnestly directing education toward the needs of the *polis* is taken by Welch as a paradigmatic critique of formalistic education and an anticipatory gesture toward post-Marxist notions of critical pedagogy. These vastly different uses of Isocratean rhetoric in today's classroom demonstrate the ambiguous and indeterminate place that Isocrates still occupies in our intellectual tradition. While this volume does not set out to assign him to his "proper" place in the history of rhetoric, it does aim to convey complexities and subtleties that only the study of Isocrates situated among his rivals and supplanters can reveal.

Isocrates' Literary Rhetoric and Literary Genres

Isocrates' medium for advancing his conception of rhetoric as deliberative philosophy was the beautifully written speech circulated for reading. It is the topic of aesthetic polish and its relation to deliberative excellence that forms the strongest link between Isocrates and the emergence of humanistic education in the Italian Renaissance, in particular in the republican city-state of Florence. There are many mediating figures involved in this reception—Cicero, but also Quintilian, whose complete works were only discovered in the fifteenth century, as well as Longinus. Ever since early modernity, the tie between civic education, virtue talk, and republican principles has scarcely been conceivable outside a framework of humanistic education. Under the imperative for pluralistic democracy, the structure and aims of humanistic education are as deeply contested today as ever. So we have one more reason for training our reflections on Isocrates, who of all the ancient Greek writers is closest to the textualist, aestheticist, and ethical impulses of the humanist tradition.

Isocrates regarded the beautifully written speech, disseminated by the powerful technology of writing, as having immense potential to transform all aspects of the existing landscape of civic education and political life. Speaking generally, his tactic was to transform already developed genres of praise and blame into instruments of reflective deliberation by circulating published speeches. Conscious of his own efforts to tap into this potential through experimentation, he tested out in the *Evagoras* the possibility of entering into the poet's privileged terrain of encomiastic praise (T. Poulakos 1987). Later, in the *Philip*, he deployed this same form of encomium in conjunction with explicitly political ends, trying out the extent to which an orator might use this newly created form to exert maximum influence on a leader. Isocrates also experimented with the *epainos* of Athens, seeking to lift the laudatory praise of the city's excellence out of the rigid structures to which it had been confined in the *epitaphios*, or funeral oration, and to liberate it from the formulaic treatment it had continued to receive in the burial speeches of orators (which Plato either satirized or imitated in the *Menexenus*).

Resituated in the more spacious texture of the *Panegyricus*, the *epainos* was brought into contact with political action. As a result of that contact, it acquired new vitality and took on a new purpose. The older function of the *epainos* was to display Athenian excellence for the enjoyment and education of spectators. In Isocrates' hands, it was given a deliberative turn. The form of the *epainos* assumed the new mission of articulating the city's past commitments in such a way as to make the proposal for concrete action seem historically justifiable and ethically desirable. These self-conscious experimentations with formal combinations and generic mixtures, whose deployment created new venues for rhetoric, can be traced back to the *Helen*. Here

Isocrates first tried his hand at investing clever showpieces of self-display with a serious undercurrent of political sentiments that were familiar to his contemporaries.

Throughout these experimentations, the beautifully written speech carried on the sophistical tradition in rhetoric by sustaining its familiar claim to aesthetic appeal and its recognizable display of an orator's eloquence and dexterity. But Isocrates also broke away from that tradition by setting it on a search for ethical and political content. Joined with the important ethical and political questions of the day, the aesthetic impulse of eloquent discourse thus presented itself as a new, explicitly, and self-consciously literary site for civic education. Here a variety of possibilities for participation in public affairs could be explored. The citizenly conduct Protagoras had once connected with Athenian practices of deliberation in the assembly appeared now to be too restricted. It was opposed by another aspect of citizenly conduct that written and circulated speech was now making possible.

The participation of citizens in the affairs of the *polis* no longer needed to be thought of as exclusively speaking before an inflamed or an indifferent crowd gathered to address the contingent demands of a particular situation. Political deliberation could also be committed to writing, circulated to the reading public, and so disseminated to a wider audience. But if it were possible to participate in the affairs of the *polis* by taking a step back and by distancing oneself from the assembly, then we must also see that distance and that step as the creation of a new space that transformed political deliberation proper—and, as a result, put in place alternative notions of civic education. Had Isocrates used the analogy of a flute-playing city to address civic education in Athens, as Protagoras did, he would have not merely parceled out that city into expert and novice players, but would have included a third category: composers of musical scores for the flute.

We see that the various combinations of oratorical forms that Isocrates experimented with can be understood only as part and parcel of a larger effort to transform the existing landscape of civic education, to give it wider scope, and to connect rhetoric with every aspect of that enlarged discursive sphere. Isocrates used the open form of educational contest and debate in *Against the Sophists*, as in the introduction to *Helen*, to disarticulate his perceived association with sophistical civic education, to contest the relevance of current eristic practices to the affairs of the city, and to claim for his own rhetorical practices, against the Academics, the title of "true" philosophy.

In the *Antidosis*, he employed the form of *apologia* to promote his own educational activities as a necessary prerequisite for training orators who would be willing to devote their skills to the service of the *polis*. And he took up various combinations of epideictic and political oratory to work out an interdependence between the domains of values and action, which he considered to be the basis of deliberation proper. By blending forms of oratory, he carved out a deliberative practice that attached moral choices to political questions and addressed ethical concerns as they could be realized concretely, in contingent action. A deliberative process that implicated political questions with ethical concerns and moral values with concrete action required orators-to-be to discern, at one and the same time, the politically possible and the morally desirable, and to serve their *polis* by proposing courses of action in line with the city's historical commitments.

Isocrates himself admittedly did not realize the radical possibilities of his own innovations with forms of oratory and notions of civic education. On the contrary, he poured the content of his own conservative politics into the novel forms of oratory he himself had charged with reformist potential. The promise made by the blending of celebratory and political oratory in the *Panegyricus*—to produce a revisionary history of Athens that might influence the future treatment of other city-states—was drowned out by the conservative voice of the moralist assumed in the *Areopagiticus* and *On the Peace*. Similarly, whatever potential had been conveyed through the artistic innovations of the *Evagoras* was left unrealized in the *Nicocles* and the *To Nicocles*. The effort to influence the *physis* of the king through education was abandoned in the face of the more lucrative pursuit of advising the king how to control the way he was perceived and, in the process, how to produce the most obedient subjects.

Isocrates and His Democratic *Polis*

The gap between the innovations of an artist and the politics of a particular person goes some way toward explaining the diversity of assessments of Isocrates rendered by the contributors to this volume. Above all, Isocrates' notions about civic education are marked by the contradiction of wishing to tame democracy by creating perspectives that might very well be used to strengthen it.

Josiah Ober deals with this issue in his theme-setting analysis of Isocrates' *apologia pro vita sua*, the *Antidosis*. Ober (1989) builds on themes that he set out in his pathbreaking *Mass and Elite in Ancient Athens*. After the terrible but transient crisis at the end of the fifth century, Athens recovered and even strengthened its participatory democracy. So strong was the *dēmos* that it could tolerate and sometimes even learn from the elite dissidents it sheltered in its midst (Ober 1994). In the very act of allowing its critics free speech, the *dēmos* found a way to exhibit its power, confidence, solidarity, and legitimacy. At the same time, its critics showed themselves to be free-speech democrats in spite of themselves. For like it or not, they were forced to occupy a subject position of critic that had been graciously left open to them by the many (Euben 1994).

Isocrates' *Antidosis* circulates in this paradoxical space—and, according to Ober, makes better use of it than Plato. Isocrates takes upon himself the mantle of the martyred Socrates and, like him, makes a speech of self-defense. According to Ober, Isocrates explicitly misperforms the Platonic defense of Socrates with the purpose of wresting the mantle of *philosophia* from the monopoly of Academics and other sectarian post-Socratics. The Socrates of Plato's *Apology* assumes that he cannot and will not persuade the *dēmos*, and his demand to be thanked by them is ironic to the point of insult. (For a contrary, and contrarian, view, see Brickhouse and Smith 1989.) The speech delegitimates those to whom it is ostensibly addressed in order to validate the antidemocratic pretensions of its primary audience and its actual author, Plato.

Isocrates, by contrast, compliments his judges. He misperforms the Platonic *Apology* by portraying himself not as a martyr to a tyrannical mob, whom he intentionally offends, but as a citizen seeking justice from his peers and assuming he can actually get it. Isocrates presumes that he can persuade his fellow citizens of the justice of his cause and solicits their genuine gratitude for the way in which he teaches arts that actually sustain the regime. Conservative though he may be, Isocrates is at heart an Athenian, and hence a democrat.

Takis Poulakos supplements Ober's portrait of a democratic Isocrates by concentrating on the notion of *doxa*, which Plato had famously reduced to "mere opinion," as opposed to epistemically secure knowledge. By contrast, Isocrates deploys *doxa* to sustain and perhaps recover the more rooted meaning of one's glowing reputation, one's *kleos* or fame. This conception of one's *doxa* (unlike contemporary notions of one's "image") harks back to the heroic conception of virtuous deeds and words that forms the backbone of Greek poetic-performative education in all of its settings—lyric, epic, and tragic. Like Protagoras, Isocrates refers the concept not to the glory of would-be epic heroes but to the reputation of civic subjects, subjects who are willing to enter into *agōn* on behalf both of their own self-worth and their contribution to the commonweal. Acting with an eye to one's *doxa* is for Isocrates, as it is for the entire republican tradition thereafter, a noble, not a vain, preoccupation. For one cannot be practically wise without cultivating the ability to say the right thing at the right or the opportune moment; and one simply cannot achieve this skill—the skill that Isocrates wants to teach—without positioning oneself as one who appears before and is accountable to one's fellow citizens. If the democratic *polis* leaves a space for its elite critics, Isocrates avails himself of that opening in an effective way.

Isocrates and the Sophists

These considerations of Isocrates' project can but raise subtle questions about his relationship to the sophistic tradition. Like the Sophists, and unlike Plato, Isocrates is an antifoundationalist. But, as John Poulakos (1995) shows, this does not mean that Isocrates has as straightforward a connection with the sophistic movement as one might assume. Poulakos argues that it is difficult (for anyone but a Platonist) to paint Isocrates as an inheritor of this tradition at all. Using his well-known ideal-typical portrait of the Sophists as a beginning point, Poulakos takes them to be nomadic, cosmopolitan, hit-and-run, agonistic, somewhat individualistic, and prone to Gorgias' implicitly materialistic conception of language as a powerful force that bears down on an audience and causes them to behave in certain ways.

Measured by this criterion, however, Isocrates is anything but a Sophist. He demands reflection and deliberative choice, not unthinking response. He is far from a nomadic intellectual. He is a sedentary, somewhat conservative citizen of democratic Athens. His conceptual scheme does not revolve around what is powerful (*dunastēs*), as did that of the Sophists whose experience was formed by the rise of tyrants. It revolves instead around the concept of "hegemony," a term whose contemporary resonance owes much to Isocrates. He uses it to shore up Greek cultural identity by urging the various powerful *poleis* to unite against the barbarians under the presumably sweet sway of Athenian leadership. (The idea had a certain doomed ring in view of the distinctly non-Athenocentric version of panhellenism that was soon to be pursued by Philip.)

Ekaterina Haskins' portrait of Isocrates is somewhat more open than John Poulakos' to aligning Isocrates with the sophistic tradition. Haskins is keenly aware that our own contemporary demands for a racially, culturally, and sexually pluralist democracy involve a performative element that potentially subverts the hegemonic order of traditional republicanism, with its fetishization of representation in both the political and the textual spheres. She notes that, for all his differences from the Sophists, Isocrates does concur with them in attempting to appropriate the mythopoetic, performative tradition of Greek *paideia* by transposing it into a new, textualized key. The point is important because it is just this performative tradition that Plato and Aristotle, in different ways and to different degrees, refuse to accept.

In developing this theme, Haskins views Isocrates through the lens of the illuminating work on orality-literacy issues that continues to be done by classical and rhetorical scholars. The paradigmatic Sophist Gorgias, Haskins says, was positioned on the cusp between an oral and a literate world. It was in the context of orality, and not just of tyranny, that his conception of rhetoric as force (*bia*) achieved its resonance. With Isocrates we are fully, indeed constitutively, in the world of the literary. Building on the work of Yun Lee Too (1995), Haskins shows how Isocrates, using the topical excuse of having been born with a weak voice, fashions his own civic identity, and hence a general conception of civic identity itself, by means of prose textualization. Isocrates, it seems, is unwilling to concede the public sphere and public education to the fractious world of oral discourse and to disappear, like Plato, behind a set of dialogical masks. On the contrary, Isocrates meets Plato's demand for a stable self as a condition of good deliberation by constructing in his polished speeches an indexical, if still performative, "I." This "I" (Ober comments extensively on it) remains stable precisely because it can rely on the continuous reiteration of textuality itself. This "I" is deployed to bring forth hearers who are induced to inhabit a similarly reflective and consistent identity, from which good deliberation is presumed by Isocrates to follow.

Isocrates and the Academics

The mention of Isocrates' demand for stable, reflective selves as a condition of legitimate and effective political participation reminds us that we can scarcely consider Isocrates apart from his relationship with Plato. They were wary competitors, conceding important points to each other precisely in order to distinguish themselves and their pedagogical wares from the other. For his part, Isocrates concedes that the contemporary logographers, or speech writers, among whom he once made his own living, are as contemptible as Plato makes them out to be. Similarly, Plato confesses to a certain grudging respect for Isocrates. When, in a famous scene in *Phaedrus*, Plato has the discourse-addicted Phaedrus reveal to a dubious Socrates the purloined text of Lysias' latest speech, we are probably meant to read Isocrates (and his circulating texts) for Lysias. At the end of the dialogue Socrates steps out of the frame to prophesy a great future for Isocrates—with irony to be sure, but also with respect (Asmis 1986; Coventry 1990). Plato and Isocrates are joined at the hip, it seems. They both have visions of civic education, puritanical and antidemocratic in the one case, seductively aestheticist and at least controversially democratic in the other.

In their contributions to the volume, David Konstan and Kathryn Morgan address a series of puzzles that arise from the fact that Plato and Isocrates set forth rival but comparable programs for civic education. With his stark distinction between the inner landscape of the soul and its outer appearance in social *doxa*, Plato is well positioned to predicate the stable identity of the self. He demands this as a condition of wise action in his thoroughgoing rejection of democratic life. Democratic man, Plato says in the *Republic*, the charter document of the Academy, is too protean, too underdefined, and at the mercy of conflicting desires and images to be capable of any coherent action or conviction at all. Accordingly, Plato transfers the scene of public education to an imagined state that repudiates democratic self-government altogether. This is the state outlined in the *Republic* and later qualified in the less high-flying *Laws*.

Isocrates is also wary of the *dēmos*. He too projects the state of the soul onto the social structure in order to find a reflective point for criticizing that structure and demanding self-possession from the soul. Still, as Morgan points out, Isocrates does not divide the soul into parts, as Plato does, any more than the consubstantial *dēmos* to which he addresses himself is divided. Nor is Isocrates any more above currying favor with monarchs than Plato was in his doomed mission to Syracuse. That is exactly what he does with the *Nicocles*, in fact, instigating thereby the long-lived genre of the "mirror for princes." Still, Isocrates feels free to present himself as a loyal Athenian and in consequence as a loyal democrat. Wrapped in precisely this constructed and projected identity, he steps forward to give advice about the shared interests and common good of his fellow citizens. But that is just the problem. Can someone as full of mental reservations as Isocrates—and as wistfully fond of the old Areopagite constitution about which conservative Greeks had fantasized ever since the middle of the fifth century—actually share the values and commitments of his auditors? Is not Isocrates' problem somewhat like that of contemporary communitarians, virtuecrats, and small "r" republicans, who like to reassure themselves that not so long ago in the history of the democratic United States lesser folk gladly deferred to their betters?

Konstan's proposed solution to this troublesome issue begins by drawing a contrast between fifth-century discussions of competing sorts of regimes—democracy, oligarchy, monarchy—and fourth-century treatments of the same theme. In the fifth century, he claims, a regime had to be either one or the other. In the fourth century, the criterion becomes whether a regime is good or bad, not whether it is formally democratic, oligarchic, or monarchical. An indication that this shift was widely shared lies in the fact that, as Konstan points out, fourth-century Athenians increasingly predicated the most heavily value-laden aspects of their civic identity on their autochthony, or descent from time immemorial from other Athenians, and not on their democratic constitution as such. Such a shift might explain why Plato says that democracy is a combination of all regimes.

However that may be, Konstan claims that this dissociation of democracy from the very idea of a good *polis* gives a desirable explanation of why Isocrates can consistently and sincerely portray himself at one and the same time as a democrat, a critic of democracy, and a client of overbearing monarchs and princelings. As Konstan puts it, in the fourth century it was "entirely possible to be in favor of an individual king or aristocratic regime, or any mixture of the basic types, and at the same time to represent oneself as a supporter of the democracy that is one's birthright." A regime, if it is to be a good one, must exhibit certain virtues no matter what. A reflective democrat, even one who reiteratively proclaims and performs his identity as a citizen of Athens, could also admire an aristocracy or a monarchy. It is just constitutional pluralism and tolerance of this sort that Isocrates needs, Konstan argues, if he is to get anywhere with his version of panhellenism. In this project Athens is to exercise leadership in a great national crusade including *poleis* that are quite variously governed and far from uniformly democratic.

Morgan addresses the same problem from a dissenting perspective. She concedes that Isocrates aims at consistency in thought and behavior as much as Plato. Unlike Konstan, however, she doubts whether Isocrates achieves it, or could in principle even hope to achieve it. This is because, in contrast to Plato, he cleaves too deeply to his presentation of himself as an Athenian democrat. In the fourth century no less than in the fifth, to be an Athenian was to be educated by and self-defined in terms of the consubstantial *polis* itself, not by dissenting elite philosophers. *Polis* education, so construed, is as pervasive and tyrannical as Plato took it to be.

This meant that a democratic citizen—any democratic citizen—must necessarily expose himself to complicity in whatever contradictory, wavering, and ill-fated policies the city happened to become embroiled. Given the overwhelming fact that democratic Athens demanded full commitment to its assumptions, values, loves, hatreds, and decisions—a fate we moderns hope to evade by regarding our private life as constitutive of our identities, putting off our citizenly roles as lightly as we put them on—Morgan asks whether it is plausible that Isocrates' "charismatic presence and elevated style, his balanced clauses and lack of hiatus, [are] going to solve the political problems of Athens." The implied answer is No. To address the crowd in the way he does is to compromise the very political and psychological consistency Isocrates prizes. Thus, he falls afoul of the many; it is no accident that Isocrates, in defending himself in the *Antidosis*, is forced to wrap himself in the mantle of Socrates'—that is, Plato's Socrates—*Apology*. Unlike Ober's misperforming Isocrates, Morgan's Isocrates is implicated in a conservative principle that is at odds with democratic opportunism and *"polis* education."

Isocrates and Aristotle

Whether or not in the heyday of Plato and Isocrates the criteria of good government had already been distinguished from straightforward competition among monarchy, aristocracy, and democracy, as Konstan suggests—and increasingly open to the idea of good monarchies—by the time of Aristotle, Isocrates' junior by a full thirty-two years, the notion of good government was in full feather. Aristotle's famous taxonomy of constitutions begins with the idea of good constitutions and their matching deviant or malformed counterparts. Within this framework, Aristotle makes it a matter of contingent circumstance whether this or that political situation or civic tradition calls for a monarchy, an aristocracy, or a "polity" (*politeia*), that is, a law-governed semipopular regime. Which constitution is best under a given set of circumstances is a matter of judgment: of practical wisdom (*phronēsis*) in its incarnation as political wisdom (*politikē*). All that Aristotle asks is that monarchies not degenerate into tyrannies, that aristocracies not decline into money-grubbing oligarchies, and that polities strive, in their law-governed compromise between the interests of rich and poor, to remain distinct from purely populist democracies.

This studied effort to remain more or less true to Plato's antidemocratic legacy, while at the same time acknowledging that some elements of democratic thinking might well go into the making of a good, modern constitutional regime, is typical of Aristotle's habits of mind. He tends to take his opponents in and turn their views into something else. This habit of mind is especially important when we come to Aristotle's views about the art of rhetoric and his relationship to the legacy of Isocrates.

David Depew argues that Aristotle pays Isocrates the compliment of agreeing with him about one key point in the philosophy of rhetoric in order to dissent more persuasively from him on a deeper level. He suggests that Aristotle's conception of practical wisdom (*phronēsis*), as distinct from theoretical knowledge (*epistēmē*) and from craftsmanly expertise (*technē*), pays explicit homage to Isocrates' use of this term. In the *Antidosis*, Isocrates says, "They are wise (*sophoi*) who are able out of their opinions to chance upon what is generally the best course of action or speech . . . those who are able to grasp such things have practical wisdom (*phronēsis*)." Aristotle's formulation in *Nicomachean Ethics* 6.5 is very close to this. Both Aristotle and Isocrates are asserting that political and ethical affairs—constitutional issues as well as decisions about the proper roles and influence of the various arts, including rhetoric, in society—should not be governed by the same standard of certainty and truth that applies to scientific knowledge. Where they differ, Depew claims, is that Isocrates believes that practical wisdom is all we humans have, while Aristotle, true once again to the spirit of his master, believes that some human beings can ascend to real theoretical science (*epistēmē*), even about human affairs. In consequence, Aristotle, unlike Isocrates, is unwilling to identify wisdom (*sophia*) simply with *practical* wisdom (*Nicomachean Ethics* 6.12).

Depew goes on to claim that Aristotle would subordinate even the most universal of the arts (*technai*), such as rhetoric and medicine, to practical wisdom in the same way in which practical wisdom, if it is to be truly practical rather than merely clever, must pay homage to higher, purely contemplative objects and inquiries. In practice, this means that in good states practitioners of the art of rhetoric must be distinguished from (and in some sense subordinated to) practically wise political leaders. If so, it would seem that there cannot be nearly as close a link between good speaking (*eu legein*) and good thinking (*eu phronein*) as Isocrates demands. Rhetorical skill does not, by itself, confer political knowledge (*politikē*) on its possessor. Taking the argument one step further, it might seem that Aristotle's latter-day reputation as the civic educator par excellence might not be deserved. Isocrates, who proclaims the autonomy of public deliberation by linking it to a systematic form of civic education, might fill that description better.

Eugene Garver contests this interpretation of Aristotle; it does scant justice, he says, to the genuine autonomy for all sciences and arts on which Aristotle repeatedly insists. Deploying the central claim of his *Aristotle's Rhetoric: An Art of Character* (1995), Garver argues that the art of rhetoric is truly autonomous in this sense because it has internal standards of excellence to which its practitioners, insofar as they are arguing artfully, must necessarily abide. The aim of Aristotle's *Rhetoric* is to show that by conforming to its own internal standards, rhetoric ascends to the level of a practical art.

To make this argument, Garver distinguishes between the genuinely artful element of rhetoric and de facto rhetorical success. The artful element consists in observing the available means of persuasion, which for the most part consist of good arguments well and honestly proffered by speakers who project an ethical persona to audiences who are interpellated as rational judges. For Garver, this remains an adequate account of rhetorical art to this day. It is Aristotle, not Isocrates, the implication is, who should remain our guide in civic education.

The Legacy of Isocrates and Humanistic Education Today

We conclude these invitatory reflections with some remarks about Isocrates' relevance to contemporary humanistic educational norms and practices. We would like to draw attention once again to the aesthetic dimension of Isocrates' rhetorical practice. For aesthetics has been central to humanistic education since the Renaissance. Its relationship to democracy was first broached by mid-century Victorians like Matthew Arnold, John Stuart Mill, and Ralph Waldo Emerson. Like many intellectuals and artists after them, Arnold, Mill, and Emerson grudgingly accepted the rising democratic order. But they argued that it could be an object of praise or even a viable political order only if it were informed and even constrained by a sustained effort to project predemocratic norms of taste as far down into the population as possible.

Humanistic educational practices in the United States have, at least until quite recently, been predicated squarely on this vision. It is commonly recognized that what marks off the so-called postmodern condition is the erosion of the hitherto sustained effort to construct, maintain, and even police a distinction between elite and mass culture. This erosion has been accompanied, and perhaps stimulated, by the pervasive deployment of electronically mediated forms of communication and by the concomitant blurring of the distinction between nature and artifice. Such blurring also attends the expansion of biotechnology, and the erasure of the distance between the ineffable depth that was previously accorded to personal identity and the constructed identities deployed at the surface through the agency of technological interpellation.

Humanistic, aesthetics-centered educational practices can appear from this changed vantage point as inescapably complicit in constraining democracy just when it needs to expand itself universally by freeing itself from a hopefully dispensable connection to racism, colonialism, sexism, classism, and what might be called "culturism." Should it free itself from its humanistic and aestheticist legacy as well?

Seen in this connection, Isocrates can all too readily appear as an Athenian Matthew Arnold. To contest this impression, much of the most creative recent scholarship on Isocrates has concentrated on how a technology of writing (an analogue of today's electronic technologies) helped him project an identity that is invested as fully as possible in the act, as well as the art, of writing, and hence in performing a virtually constructed self rather than expressing a pre-existent "essential" one (Too 1995; Haskins this volume). That identity is projected at the surface of social presentation rather than in the coherent, consistent depths in which Plato would hide it. From this perspective, what seems to be called for and even anticipated by Isocrates is not the rejection of aesthetics, but a postmodern aesthetics that fully embraces precisely what Plato rejected about democratic culture—its mimetic prowess, its creative misperformances, its tendency to "act up." In today's circumstances, when the enlargement of democratic practice is linked increasingly to notions of performance and identity, Isocrates' creativity commends itself as a replacement for the representational culture of republicanism, old and new, which seems unable to contain the global, transcultural thrust of democratic life.

In his reflections on the contemporary resonance of the figure of Isocrates, Robert Hariman advances the view that our efforts to respond creatively to Isocratean educational initiatives must be guided by clearly identifying the kind of imitation that his educational plan projected, defended, and practiced. Against his contemporaries, who promoted (or in Plato's case rejected) the notion of imitation as a purely instrumental, merely mechanical technique for generating and responding to discourse on demand in a particular time and place, Isocrates, according to Hariman, practiced a sort of imitation that asserted the agency of speakers by exploring their identities and expanding their temporal and spatial horizons. It was a kind of imitation that drew on sources exceeding one's immediate circumstances, that aligned itself with the city's larger cultural inheritance, and that sought to support practices contributing directly to the sustainability of public culture.

Isocrates' conception of imitation enables Hariman to explain not only his commitment to a flexible, identity-sensitive model of civic virtue, but also his clear resolve to promote the themes of a single type of discourse, the discourse of panhellenism. Here the themes of an enlarged spatial realm for discourse to complement the "gift of time" for deliberation, stressed by T. Poulakos, come into view. When it comes to a contemporary analogue, Hariman names ecological discourse as functioning in something of the way that panhellenism functioned for Isocrates. Like Isocrates' panhellenic crusade, ecology promotes global concord as a way of solving problems that cannot be solved by individual states or on the basis of conceptions of the good life that are specific to one culture. Like Isocrates' flexible norms for civic education, the ecological movement and the discourses it generates and nourishes depend on a kind of education. It is inherently aesthetic and humanistic in its recommitment to an education aimed at revitalizing the threatened practices of grassroots democracy and resituating them in the enlarged space of a global unity.

Michael Leff finds that the rather idealistic image of Isocrates on display in Hariman's essay emerges from most, if not all, of the essays in the volume. Isocrates, in this collective view, wields a notion of good rhetoric that is neither applied superscience, as in Plato, nor relativistic manipulation; that is reflective even while it is opportune; that is addressed to all, but discriminating in what voices are to be heard and amplified in response; that is virtuous and technical at the same time; and that is rooted both in stable virtues and in the historical experience of a people. Assuming the accuracy of this image, Leff professes himself less worried than Morgan about how deeply his apparent inconsistencies entangle Isocrates in a forced choice between Platonic demands for consistency in both personal and policy matters and submission to the group-think of "*polis* education." In slipping between these poles, Isocrates can serve as a stimulus for contemporary thinking about "how we can conceive and devise a program of education that is sufficiently realistic to account for the sprawl of democratic practices and that is also sufficiently idealistic to promote civic virtue."

In closing, allow us to note explicitly that this volume is an interdisciplinary effort. It has arisen from conversations and interventions on the part of rhetorical scholars, classicists, ancient philosophers, and historians. The volume, as well as the Obermann Humanities Symposium at the University of Iowa from which it sprang, pays homage to the perception that much of the best scholarship done in our day results from a conscious effort to blur disciplinary lines. This approach helps our effort to burnish the image of Isocrates. For his genre-bending and his resolute effort to keep the lines between rhetoric, politics, and philosophy as open and flexible as possible, make him for us something of an icon of interdisciplinary scholarship. As a textualized being, Isocrates might even be considered a martyr to this openness and flexibility. For against his own explicit wishes, he has been extruded entirely from the philosophical canon, while among rhetorical scholars who have canonized him the seriousness with which he presents himself as a philosophical rhetorician has been downplayed. We wish to pay belated homage to Isocrates' attempt to speak earnestly and persuasively against what in his day, as in ours, were fast-hardening lines between the disciplines and the arts.

PART ONE

Isocrates and Classical Civic Education

JOSIAH OBER

I, Socrates . . .
The Performative Audacity
of Isocrates' *Antidosis*

ATHENS, in the fourth century B.C., was an interesting place for any number of reasons, and not least because of the fierce political debates among some of its most highly educated and highly articulate residents. Some of these debates were carried out in public and drew large audiences: the policy battles in the Ecclesia and the forensic contests in the people's courts were treated by Athenian audiences of assemblymen, jurors, and spectators as at once important, enlightening, and amusing.

What's at Stake?

The stakes in each major public confrontation between politicians of the likes of Demosthenes and Aeschines were high—most obviously, because of the weightiness of the decision that was being urged: war or peace, the disposition of public finance, the guilt or innocence of citizens accused of capital crimes, the disposition of public and private property. The stakes were raised even higher in that every major public confrontation was a chance for a public speaker to establish or elaborate upon his own reputation, and to undermine the reputation of his political opponents. Demosthenes seems to have made his name as a successful litigant and logographer before becoming known as a speaker in the assembly. The stakes were high, finally, because major speeches to large audiences were occasions for public deliberation on the core values that underpinned the democratic polity and the relationship of those values to practices, public and private: how individual Athenians acted and behaved in institutional contexts and in their everyday lives.

Each major public address by an Athenian rhetor had at least three intertwined aspects: each was simultaneously about "decision" (what should
we decide to do in the current case?), about "reputation" (what should you
think about me and my opponents, now and in the future?), and about
"civic norms" (how should we be conducting our public and private lives if
we are to be true to our core values?). In posing these three questions, I have
allowed the assumption that the "we" in question was well understood. Yet
arguably there was a fourth aspect underlying these public discussions, the
question of "our" identity. Who are "we," really? And if "we" are not (yet)
formed, how might "we" go about becoming our "true" selves? The problem of identity did not necessarily arise every day for each and every Athenian, but it was certainly a matter of intense concern for the members of
Athens' intellectual community.

The intellectual debates that characterized fourth-century Athens were
not limited to contests in the assembly and law courts fought by renowned
public orators. Parallel to those public speech-contests and, in a sense yet to
be determined, underpinning them, were debates among philosophers, by
whom I mean all those who claimed the title *philosophia* for their own intellectual enterprises. As I have argued elsewhere,[1] the Athenian "intellectual community" was diverse, fiercely competitive, and motivated by a
common critical agenda. The big problems for Athenian intellectuals in the
decades after 404 B.C. included: What and how to think in response to the
evident success of democracy? How to express dissenting ideas? And how
(or indeed whether) to move from critical speech to political action? The
range of proposed answers to these hard questions was wide but not in-
finitely so, and by mid-century the terms of the discussion and the competitive ground were pretty well established.

Isocrates' *Antidosis* speech is an especially skillful and complex intervention into the intellectual debates that flourished in mid-fourth-century
Athens. The audacity of the speech, to which my title refers, emerges both
in its ambition and its strategy. Isocrates' ambition is a unification of contexts, a conflation of a public (in this case forensic) speech with its mass audience of ordinary citizens, and then with the conventions of the private,
philosophical discourse associated within a closed elite, intellectual milieu.
Isocrates sought to reconcile the aims of personal betterment of the superior individual (what we might call "soul-saving") and the public good (or
"*polis*-saving"). He sought to conjoin the ends of the just *polis* with the integral soul and thereby allow for a politics that was at once personal and

public, leadership that was at once beneficial and legitimate. The presumed desirability and profound difficulty of that equation between self and state had provided much of the drama of Plato's *Republic.*

But Isocrates sought even more: he proposed to reconcile two senses of "we" available to his Athenian audience—"we the few and good" and "we the *dēmos*"—with a third, much broader conception of "we the Hellenes." And the speech has a pragmatic and didactic function. It is a *paradeigma* of what Isocrates claims is a uniquely practical form of civic education for both the many and the few. It is also a discursive form that seeks to demonstrate alike to "those who are wise" and "those who are ignorant" why it is that Isocratean rhetoric is the most suitable vehicle for achieving personal integrity and the renewed political order that could (via the most velvety of revolutions) replace the currently messy business of democratic public life.

A speech with bold ambitions indeed: the unity of the many and the one, the ordinary and the elite, the wise and the ignorant, the Athenians and the Hellenes, and all under a distinctively Isocratean vision of civic education. But we will also need to confront Isocrates' audacious rhetorical strategy in this speech: the dazzling appropriation, citation, and reconfiguration of Socrates, Plato's own chosen mouthpiece. And not just "any Socrates," but a Socrates as he appeared in his most characteristic historical moment (the trial), and in a definitive Platonic text (the *Apology of Socrates*). In the *Antidosis* Plato's "Socrates on trial" is reperformed or, perhaps more accurately, it is deliberately *misperformed*, by Isocrates on the occasion of the rhetorician's own master statement concerning himself, his *paideia*, and the rhetorician's rightful role in the democratic polis.

Isocrates' audacious citation of Socrates provides a clear example of the general phenomenon of subversive "verbal misperformance" or "alternative iteration," topics that have recently been explored in relation to modern legal discourse by Judith Butler, in the last chapter of her important book, *Excitable Speech.*[2] By conjoining Louis Althusser's conception of "interpellation" with J. L. Austin's theory of speech acts, Butler argues that the omnipresent possibility of "misperforming" conventionalized types of speech acts provides human agents with a source of resistance to what might otherwise seem to be oppressively totalizing matrices of social behavior and public institutions. One obvious example (mine, not Butler's) of subversive misperformance is that of a gay couple enacting a marriage ceremony in a state in which such ceremonies are not recognized as legally valid.

Butler's discussion of "misperformance" seeks to explain some of the ways in which human agents might resist by subverting the oppressive authority of interpellation, the normalizing process of being "hailed" into a conventional social identity by the ordinary and legal forms of speech that arise from and instantiate those conventions. Now, I suppose that Isocrates did in fact have to contend with a discursively constructed and institutionally supported social identity, a condition that I have elsewhere referred to as the "ideological hegemony of the *dēmos*."[3] But Isocrates' "misperformance" of the trial, and his alternative citation of Plato's textual representation of it, show us how highly self-conscious literary texts can participate in the subversion of a literary and philosophical canon (whether an emerging canon or an established one) by the same process of appropriation and subversive alternative citation. That subversive intervention can have educational and political effects, even if it is not performed within the confines of ordinary political institutions. Isocrates' *Antidosis*, with its combination of audacious ambitions and boldly misperformative rhetorical strategy stands (and was intended to stand) as a didactic monument to a teacher whose "little voice" and "lack of boldness" prevented him from addressing the democratic public assembly in his own person.

The Rhetorician in a Competitive, Critical Context

Isocrates' mid-fourth-century speeches, the great series in which the *Antidosis* is chronologically located within his corpus,[4] seem to transport the reader back to a mid-fifth-century environment inhabited by characters similar to the "Old Oligarch" (Pseudo-Xenophon, author of an *Athenaiōn Politeia*) and his ilk, a world of disgruntled aristocrats who find democracy distasteful. Such men spend considerable time in voicing their political dissatisfaction to one another and yet they are incapable of doing much of anything about it. Isocrates evokes this milieu in the introduction to his *Areopagiticus:*

> We sit around in the shops (*ergastēria*) denouncing (*katēgoroumen*) the current state of affairs and claiming that we have never been worse governed under a democracy (*en dēmokratiai kakion epoliteuthēmen*), yet according to our actions (*pragmata*) and the sentiments (*dianoiai*) which we hold in regard to it [the current *politeia*], we cherish it (*agapōmen*) more than that regime which was handed down to us by our ancestors (7.15).

In this passage Isocrates points to a constant level of dissatisfaction, but carefully limits its scope: "We have never been worse governed *under a democracy*"; by implication there were worse nondemocratic governments within living memory. Like Plato of the *Seventh Letter*, Isocrates implies that the current regime, however problematic, is preferable to the oligarchic interludes of the late fifth century. Yet, *unlike* Plato—and this is a key point —Isocrates did not abandon hope for democratic amelioration. The question, Isocrates suggests, is how to improve *dēmokratia*. When compared with Plato's political philosophy, Isocrates' political discourse may appear conventional. It is sprinkled with *topoi* familiar from the Old Oligarch and from Plato's caricature of democracy in *Republic* Book 8.[5] It is, we may suppose, a reasonable approximation of what had become, by the mid-fourth century, a canonical and perhaps rather desultory list of complaints, just the sort of buzzing by fat, lazy, stingless would-be gadflies that one might expect to hear on an ordinary afternoon in an Athenian shop favored by the leisure class.[6]

Yet Isocrates claims to be much more than just an epitomator of other men's ideas, more than a spokesman for the discontents of his class. He supposes that his highly developed rhetoric, a facility at manipulating words that was both innate and refined by education and practice, could transform the droning murmur of the *ergastēria* into a program of action.[7] If skill at manipulating language could be sufficient to the task of focusing the background noise of aristocratic complaints into a clear argument against popular rule, then Isocrates was surely the right man for the job. The question remained whether skillfully crafted speeches which assume the generic form of publicly performed addresses, yet are directed toward private reading audiences, can in fact be adequate to the critical project of exposing and proposing solutions to substantive problems within a system that is overtly based on genuinely public performative speech.

More explicitly than any previous Athenian political writer, Isocrates portrays himself as existing within and contending with a matrix of critical voices. Whereas Thucydides and Plato, for example, leave their readers fairly subtle traces of their own competitive struggles for primacy within the critical community of Athenian intellectuals, Isocrates is up front about the game and willingly displays his battle scars. He portrays himself as a critical commentator who concerns himself with democracy. But he also claims to be a prominent rhetorician and a famously wealthy Athenian citizen—the object addressed by other social critics, both elite and democratic. While affecting shock and indignation at attacks upon himself, upon his profession, and upon his *polis*, Isocrates clearly takes pride in adopting the role of master competitor in a contest in which he is surrounded by opponents on all sides.

It is in his finely honed orations that Isocrates depicts the attacks of his opponents. And it is his masterful deployment of the *technē* of rhetoric that he will claim allows him to answer the opposing critical voices and thereby to resolve the substantive issues that they raise. Isocrates' *logoi*—embodying his *paideia*, which is also his *philosophia*—join their author at the center of the fray. They are the putative subject of the several disputes, and they are (he claims) the means by which all quandaries can be resolved in favor of his rhetorical art. Through the same epideictic speeches in which he proves himself to be the master of *logoi*, Isocrates invites his listeners and readers to embark upon his educational curriculum (*paideia*). That curriculum presents a way of life and a mode of comprehension and expression (a *philosophia*) that will allow students to deal with the cacophony of critical speech. They will learn to counter and refute that which is slanderous or deleterious, embrace that which is meritorious, and avoid extremism of all sorts. Isocrates' *philosophia* holds out the promise of a political program (*politeia*) that will fulfill the needs and guarantee the just deserts of all decent persons, in the *polis* of Athens and in the broader realm of Hellas.[8]

Contesting *Philosophia*

Among the elite critics with whom Isocrates contended, Plato and the Academy hold pride of place. By the early decades of the century, Platonic dialectic already threatened to monopolize the term *philosophia*, reserving what had become (in educated elite circles, anyway) a prized word for an intellectual undertaking that had no sympathy for the sort of education and *technē* championed by Isocrates. Whether or not Isocrates had actually been a student of Gorgias, Plato's *Gorgias* (and the later *Phaedrus*, among other dialogues) made it eminently clear that in the view of his school, neither practitioners nor teachers of rhetoric could ever be regarded as philosophers. For the Academy, rhetoric was a branch of Sophism and as such was inevitably foreign to philosophy proper.[9] Moreover, the *Republic* had developed the metaphysical justification for an epistemology which rendered rhetoric irrelevant to the central problem of connecting ideas with words, objects, and actions. In the course of sorting out problems of ethics, ontology, and epistemology, Plato had developed an ethicopolitical program that threatened to displace as potential cultural leaders the sort of students Isocrates hoped to produce. Plato had argued in the *Republic* for a new form of moral and political education that sought to invalidate and obviate the rhetorical *paideia* Isocrates offered his own students.

This threatened philosophical monopoly might in itself have been enough of a challenge to provoke a response from Isocrates, but there was more. The content of several of Isocrates' speeches makes it quite clear that by the mid-fourth century, if one claimed to be an intellectual—a practitioner of *philosophia*—one must also be a critic of the rule of the people. Plato and his associates tried to claim as their own not only the terminology of *philosophia*, but the project of criticizing democracy from an intellectual perspective. Plato's "epic" foundationalist project provided the Academy with a distinctive and seemingly secure ground from which to challenge the hegemony, indeed the legitimacy and very reality, of "democratic knowledge." Moreover, the trial and execution of Socrates had gained for the Academy a genuine and widely acknowledged hero and martyr. Socrates had not regarded himself as the founder of any philosophical school, nor was the Socratic heritage a unique possession of the Academy.[10] But Socrates had died at the hands of the democratic Athenians for the sake of philosophy as dialectical inquiry. Those, like Isocrates, who espoused the cause of philosophy as rhetorical *epideixis* had no comparable figure to counterpoise. The democracy certainly had punished any number of public orators (sometimes with death), but it could not be said that any of them had suffered or died for the cause of philosophical rhetoric per se.[11] If Isocrates hoped to provide his *technē* with resources to stand up to the Platonic challenge, he would have to find a way to refute the claims of Platonic dialectic and education to a general superiority on the basis of a superior apprehension of the relationship between ideas, experience, and the world. And he would have to establish for himself a place in the critical spectrum worthy of his own self-image and capable of standing up to (or, better, displacing) Socrates, the martyr-hero who was so centrally important to Platonic ethics and political thought.

The Rhetorician as Patriot and Cosmopolitan

In the *Antidosis*, Isocrates asserted his superiority over his philosophical rivals on the grounds that whereas they sought to attract a few students, he focused on policies that were good for the *"entire polis"* (84–85). Yet, at the same time that Plato and his dialectical approach to problems of knowledge and power were threatening to crowd out all competitors from the realm of totalizing "external" political criticism, the real world, incremental change, "internal critic" end of the intellectual spectrum was being occupied by the practicing rhetors. Public speakers like Demosthenes and Aeschines stood up before their fellow citizens in the assembly and in the people's court and freely railed against their fellow citizens' failures to live up to the high political ideals and elevated standards of international conduct putatively established by their own ancestors. Modern Athenians, according to the rhetors, were getting soft. They cared too much for the pleasures of the moment; they were too willing to listen to those (other) public speakers who recommended policies that were sweet and easy, rather than difficult, austere, and worthy of the *polis'* traditions.[12]

Not only did the rhetors criticize contemporary slackness in their publicly delivered speeches. Some of them published certain of their major dicanic and symbouleutic speeches; the existing corpus of speeches suggests a surge in publication by working rhetors in the period ca. 355–343 B.C. By mid-century if not before, Isocrates' *epideixeis* had to compete not only with the showpiece orations of his fellow rhetoricians and with Platonic dialogues, but also with the polished written versions of actual speeches delivered in major addresses before the Athenian Assembly and in famous public trials.[13] Isocrates refers directly to the challenge of the practitioners of symbouleutic oratory when he claims that certain people claim that "those speeches are much better and more profitable which denounce (*epiplēttontas*) our current errors than those which praise (*epainountas*) our former accomplishments, and those which advise us in regard to what we ought to do (*dei prattein sumbouleuontas*) than those which dredge up ancient deeds" (*erga:* 62). What was the teacher and practitioner of epideictic oratory to say in response?

Isocrates' relationship to the working rhetors was complex. They might be his competitors for students and prestige within the elite community. On the other hand they might actually be his students (directly or indirectly), and they were the practitioners, however imperfect, of what he regarded and taught as the master *technē*. Isocrates could hardly take refuge in Platonic scorn for all forms of overtly rhetorical speech as a corrupt manifestation of a degenerate democratic political culture. Instead, if Isocrates were to find a secure and prominent niche for himself in the intellectual/critical community, he was constrained to distinguish between the speech of the public orators and his own rhetoric. That distinction could be established in large part on the basis of form and style. Yet in light of the challenges offered by both the Academy's claim to ontological rigor and the working rhetors' claim to practicality and seriousness, the content of Isocrates' *epideixeis* must be capable of convincing sophisticated consumers of critical discourse that Isocrates really had something to say, that he was more than a mere juggler of words. Hypersophisticated disquisitions "in defense of Helen" simply would not cut it in the competitive intellectual environment of mid-fourth-century Athens. If he wanted to be a player in the major leagues of Athenian intellectual life, Isocrates had to enter the critical fray and demonstrate that his *paideia* offered a distinctive and effective means for focusing and expressing the now-canonical list of elite concerns about Athenian democracy.

Dialogues emanating from the Academy and the published orations of working rhetors hardly exhaust the list of critical voices to which Isocrates felt himself called upon to respond. Panhellenism (or at least a highly developed sensitivity to a cosmopolitan Greek-speaking community that was at once much broader and much more exclusive than the citizenship of his native *polis*) is a hallmark of Isocrates' corpus. In a number of his speeches Isocrates portrayed himself as at once a loyal Athenian citizen, champion of Athens' reputation, and a cosmopolitan inhabitant of a wider Hellenic society. In the *Antidosis* he claims that his oft-proclaimed policies would be to the advantage of both Athens and Hellas (79). "Intelligent persons (*tous noun echontas*) should concern themselves for both [*polis* and Hellas], but among these, they ought to give preference to the greater and worthier cause" (80). Loyal Athenian Isocrates ultimately prefers to work for the greater good of a society that transcended *polis* affiliations. He sought to incorporate upper-class Greek-speakers into an overarching order that was both very old (harking back to Homeric and archaic antecedents) and a "postmodern" product of the new post–Peloponnesian War international situation.[14] Isocrates' Hellas was simultaneously culturally expansive and socially delimited. It offered no pride of place to an ill-educated lower class. Yet the polyphonous complexity of aristocratic society, which embraced elite Greeks from a variety of old *poleis* (with their strong commitment to the ideal of "similarity" among aristocrats) [15] as well as the autocratic kings of Macedon and Cyprus (among others), required special talents of those who would claim to speak for it. Few men were worthy to do so; those (like Isocrates) capable of rising to the occasion should, he claimed, be regarded as superior to the run-of-the-mill lawgivers who concerned themselves merely with the parochial affairs of a single *polis* (80–81).

His cosmopolitan viewpoint was a vital component of Isocrates' critical perspective and central to his attempt to elevate his own rhetoric above the public orations delivered and published by the Athenian rhetors. As a self-styled spokesman for Hellas, Isocrates was well aware that aristocratic Hellenic society found much to complain about in Athens' foreign policy, past and present, and he was sympathetic to many of their concerns. Much of his own critical voice, which emphasizes the close links between Athenian domestic politics and errors in foreign policy, is borrowed from these "Hellenic" concerns. The admixture of an extra-Attic perspective, focusing on foreign relations, to the traditional concern with *dēmokratia* per se helped Isocrates to distinguish himself from other Athenian writers of rhetorical *logoi*, while simultaneously linking him to a historical tradition that viewed Athens within a wider Greek context. Isocrates asserts the superiority of orators who focus on Hellenic issues to the writers of *(polis) nomoi* on the grounds that because laws are old and numerous, collecting them is simple, whereas oratorical originality is difficult (81–83). He castigates his fellow citizens in the *Antidosis* for their failure to accord appropriate praise and honors to the champions of the Hellenic cause (301–302). "You" [Athenians] are so mistaken about what is really to your advantage that "you are more pleased with those [orators] who cause you to be reviled [by the Hellenes] than those who cause you to be praised. You think that those who have made many [Hellenes] hate the *polis* are more loyal friends of the *dēmos* (*dēmotikōteroi*) than those who have inspired good will towards the *polis* among all they encounter" (303). Isocrates' implication is that the Athenian citizen masses regarded proponents of Athenocentric policies as inherently more democratic than advocates of policies that took into account the broader Hellenic frame. This underlines his establishment of a critically useful antithesis between a cosmopolitan aristocratic/panhellenic perspective and a parochial demotic/*polis*-oriented habit of thought.

The Fictive Frame of an Imagined Trial

The critics who confronted Isocrates were not limited to his fellow aristocrats. Isocrates may have lived his intellectual life in the Hellenic society of like-minded educated elites, but he lived his material life in and as a native-born citizen of Athens. As a prominent member of the Athenian elites of wealth and education, Isocrates could expect to encounter among his fellow citizens demotic voices willing and able to challenge his lifestyle on the grounds that it did not conform to egalitarian democratic norms. As he explains in the *Antidosis* (written in 354/353, when Isocrates was 82 years old), Isocrates became acutely aware of the potential seriousness of falling afoul of the Athenian *dēmos* when he was formally challenged to a property-exchange by a fellow rich man who felt that Isocrates' estate was more capable of bearing the burden of a trierarchy than was his own.[16]

Isocrates was willing neither to exchange properties nor to accept the liturgy voluntarily; his recalcitrance led to a trial. The venerable teacher of oratory expected that his rhetorical expertise would enable him to win the suit easily. After all it was his boast that those who had mastered the intricacies of epideictic would find it very easy to deploy forensic rhetoric to good effect (49). And so it came as a shock to Isocrates when he lost the suit. The outcome of the trial—at which his opponent painted a portrait of the rhetorician as hugely wealthy, the teacher of numerous students, and a diabolically clever speaker—convinced Isocrates that the Athenian *dēmos* had over the years formed a very inaccurate opinion of him (4–6). By the time of the trial this opinion had become so deeply ingrained that the jury was actually willing to accept his opponent's slanders at face value and unwilling to listen sympathetically to his own account of the matter. Isocrates concluded from this experience that the Athenian lower classes were driven to decide against him by jealousy that was, he now realized, both fanned and exploited by the low-rent courtroom orators, the sycophants who pandered to and willfully misled the Athenian people by attacking innocent victims in the people's courts.

No doubt the humiliating defeat in the *Antidosis* trial was painful for Isocrates. But the incident was also providential in that it provided the stimulus and background for the production of a unique oration. Isocrates' *Antidosis* features a self-consciously innovative structure (1) that allows the rhetorician the opportunity to identify and answer a wide range of "accusers." Better yet, it allowed Isocrates to present himself in the role of potential martyr for the cause of philosophical rhetoric.

The *Antidosis* trial itself was an inadequate platform for Isocrates' monumental *apologia*. The actual trial had ended in rhetorical defeat and only property, not life, was at stake. Isocrates therefore took the bold step of composing a new sort of speech, one which began by proclaiming its own uniqueness. This speech would be neither actual dicanic (*pros tous agōnas*) nor properly epideictic (*pros tas epideixeis*). Because of its novelty and distinctiveness it might even appear bizarre (*atopos*) if Isocrates did not explain what he was up to (1). He then proceeds to do so, describing the "actual" events associated with his trial and the liturgy, and underlining what a rude awakening the entire experience had been for him:[17] Whereas he had always known that "certain of the Sophists" (i.e., other Athenian rhetoricians and Plato's sort of philosophers) were wont to slander his profession (*diatribē*) by claiming it was nothing more than writing speeches for other litigants in the courts, he had supposed that their blatherings were without influence or effect (*dunamis:* 2–3).

He had imagined that, given his choice of grand topics for his earlier orations and the overall quietude (*apragmosunē*) of his life, he was regarded as a decent fellow by all private citizens (*idiōtai* [i.e., non-*rhētores*]: 3–4). After the trial, though, he realized that it was not only his fellow intellectuals, but many ordinary citizens who held him in deep and undue suspicion (4–6). He thus felt the need to vindicate himself in the present circumstances and for posterity with a lasting and worthy verbal monument to himself: "a *logos* . . . my own memorial (*mnēmeion mou*) . . . much fairer than any bronze statuary." This verbal monument would accurately characterize his life and thought and thereby refute the misapprehensions and slanderous insinuations that he now knew to be swirling about him on all sides (7).[18]

But what sort of *logos* should it be? The problem, as Isocrates perceived it, was jealousy (*phthonos*)—jealousy of Isocrates himself on the part of other intellectuals and jealousy of his class, the educated and rich, on the part of the *dēmos*. In an atmosphere of jealousy, self-eulogy was likely to be counterproductive; it would add fuel to the flames (8). Isocrates was quite happy to have his intellectual rivals consumed by envy of his skills and he intended that this oration should exacerbate their pain. But he did not want to inflame bad feelings among the many, feelings which were in any case based on ignorance of the "real" Isocrates (13).

Eventually the happy solution presented itself: Isocrates would explain himself and his profession in a defense speech offered in a fictional (*hupotheimēn*) trial brought by a notional sycophant named Lysimachus who employed calumnies similar to those brought out by his real opponent in the actual *antidosis* trial (8). But this fictional trial would be much grander than any mere squabble over property.[19] The charge brought by "Lysimachus" was that Isocrates corrupted the youth by teaching them to devise specious arguments capable of overthrowing the cause of justice (30). The penalty Isocrates faced if Lysimachus were to defeat him was death (75).

It is, perhaps, not surprising that Isocrates chose to write a fictional speech of self-defense on potentially capital charges. The pseudo-dicanic oration, written as if for but never delivered in the Athenian people's courts, was a familiar genre within the critical community by the mid-fourth century.[20] Isocrates' oration was, however, a hybrid rather than simple pseudo-dicanic. Smoothly merging dicanic and epideictic was no easy task, as Isocrates points out (10: "neither easy nor simple"; 11: "no small *ergon*") and it arguably leads to some clumsiness of exposition. Isocrates does not overestimate the difficulty, novelty, and distinctiveness of his undertaking: the *Antidosis* is unique in explicitly and repeatedly calling attention to its own hybrid and fictitious character.[21]

Why take such care to signpost as imaginary, to the point of irritating redundancy, a speech that is intended to be the lasting monument to a life and a career in rhetoric? A variety of explanations may be offered, but among the payoffs of Isocrates' metarhetorical explanatory proem is the establishment of the double, mass and elite, audience to which the speech purports to be directed. Even a slow-witted reader learns that this oration would directly confront (and refute) Isocrates' demotic critics by speaking of his merits with overwhelming persuasive force to an audience addressed as *andres Athēnaioi* and *dikastai*—the traditional terms used by litigants when addressing Athenian juries. Unlike Socrates of the *Apology*, Isocrates of the *Antidosis* radiates confidence in his ability to change the minds of his jurors (28, 169–170) even when making the standard claim to be unfamiliar with courtroom tactics (27, cf. 36–38) and despite having handicapped himself in this contest by his determination to speak only the truth (43–44). His presumptive victory in the mock trial will vindicate him and his profession before the Athenian *dēmos*. And yet because the speech was a self-proclaimed fiction, Isocrates could freely engage in digressions and asides overtly aimed at confronting and confounding his elite, intellectual critics. In the proem, Isocrates announces his intention to include not only things that might be said in a courtroom but also material inappropriate to a dicanic oration, "frank discussions about *philosophia* and expositions of its effective power" (*dunamis:* 10). And, as promised, at a number of points in the oration, Isocrates turns from the demotic jury to address an elite audience of cognoscenti (e.g., 55–56). That elite audience can variously encompass both his jealous rivals and his sympathetic supporters.[22]

Given Isocrates' goal of constructing, in a single speech, a lasting monument to his life and career, one that would be capable of speaking with equal eloquence to both his fellow citizens and his Hellenic peers, his overt fiction was an elegant solution: True dicanic rhetoric (or even seamless dicanic fiction) offered limited opportunities for engaging in extended "high culture" polemics, while epideictic was not aimed at a demotic audience. It was only by inventing a new, hybrid genre that Isocrates could depict himself as a brave, beleaguered citizen of both Athens and of Hellas, the hero-martyr who stood in the metaphorical middle of the battle and at the syntactic center of the antithesis—dealing out telling blows to the ignorant jealousies of *hoi polloi* on the one hand, while dispatching his pettifogging fellow intellectuals on the other.[23]

Isocrates' generically novel oration allowed him to distinguish between the mass and the elite: he apologizes to those who were intimately familiar with his earlier masterpieces (*ergo* students and admirers) for citing long sections of them, pleading the extremity of his danger (55–56).[24] But it also served to merge the two audiences: Mass and elite are imagined as serving together on the jury which would judge the political worth of Isocrates' *logoi* by deciding whether or not they harmed the *polis* and corrupted the youth. The imaginary context is in turn provided by the real and ordinary practices of the democracy: it was a real trial that stimulated the monument-speech. It is the danger presented by the *dēmos'* distrust to Isocrates as philosopher that is the justification for a key aspect of its monumentality: the presentation of long passages from the rhetorician's finest *logoi* to an audience that includes not only his fellow citizens, but also his students and his critics.

The requirement to defend himself presented the ideal "mixed" forum for a demonstration of Isocrates' true excellence as displayed in his *epidei-*

xeis, present and past, and of his special worth as Athenian and Hellene. And thus it is the democracy's "bad" attitudes and practices (especially its suspicion of the excellent man who stands out from the crowd) that provide the opportunity and occasion for Isocrates' grand monument of self-justification. The self-proclaimed excellent man requires this sort of expo-sure—at least in its fictive version—in order to advertise his own worth beyond the claustrophobic private circle of his (albeit numerous: 41, 86–88) students and admirers.[25] This need for (pseudo) public vindication before a double audience and the role played by the democracy in providing the op-portunity for such vindication, reminds us of a central question: By placing himself in the middle of the fray, even in this metaphorical sense, does Isoc-rates show himself capable of standing out as an original and independent critical voice? Or (as Plato would have it of all public orators) does he reveal himself as helplessly entangled in the web of democratic knowledge and practice?

Misperforming (Plato's) Socrates

Among the most striking aspects of Isocrates' *Antidosis* is its close rela-tionship to Plato's *Apology of Socrates*. The charges Isocrates pretends to face are very similar—although lacking the religious dimension—to those actually faced by Socrates; the potential penalty is the same. Isocrates makes numerous allusions that inevitably recall Plato's dialogue: He draws a dis-tinction between his old accusers and the current indictment (32: cf. *Apol-ogy:* 18a–b). As proof that he did not corrupt anyone, he notes that no one now comes forward claiming to have been corrupted by him (33–35: cf. 86–88: *Apology:* 33d). If, as his opponent claims, he actually did teach his stu-dents anything, their subsequent excellence suggests that Isocrates deserves greater gratitude than those feasted in the Prytaneion (95: *Apology:* 36d–e).

He requests that jurors restrain themselves from indulging in uproar (*thorubos:* 20; 272: *Apology:* 21a; 27b; 30c). His peroration centers on a principled refusal to parade friends and family before jury in a bid for sym-pathy (321: *Apology:* 34c–34d). Examples could be multiplied, but the ba-sic fact of the direct intertextual relationship is not in doubt.[26] Nor, in a speech that sets itself the task of explaining how rhetoric is *philosophia*, is there any doubt about whether Isocrates intended his audience to recognize the echoes. The question is not whether but why Isocrates chose to fore-ground Plato's *Apology of Socrates* as the model (in terms of form if not in prose style or primary content) for what he claims will be his own verbal monument to himself. After all, Plato was one of Isocrates' primary intellectual rivals. Isocrates claimed to be superior to mere lawmakers on the grounds of the difficult originality of his rhetoric. If the hierarchy of mimesis implies a subsidiary role for the imitation and the superiority of the original, then Isocrates seems to have put himself in a dubious position indeed.[27] What benefits did he perceive that might have outweighed the potential subordination of his own *apologia* to the Platonic model?

If we imagine Isocrates working within the "company of Athenian critics," at least part of the explanation for Isocrates' decision to mimic Plato's *Apology of Socrates* must lie in Socrates' distinctive status within a rapidly crystallizing critical tradition. By the mid-fourth century, Socrates was the one clear example of an intellectual martyr to popular rule.[28] His uniqueness is indirectly confirmed by Aeschines' (1.173) comment of 346/5 to an Athenian jury: If you let Demosthenes free now, your action would imply that your conviction of "Socrates the sophist" a half-century previously had been unjust. In addressing the demotic jury, Aeschines uses the conviction of Socrates as a convenient example of a problematic decision that might be proved unjust in retrospect: "you" jurors (he pointedly uses the second person plural) will be guilty of having wrongly condemned Socrates if you allow Demosthenes to get away with worse crimes. Aeschines' comment suggests that democrats and critics of democracy were united in their acknowledgment that Socrates' case was memorable and special.

For Isocrates, determined to address both democratic mass and critical elite audiences, eager to equate his own rhetorical *philosophia* with Plato's dialectical *philosophia,* and concerned to claim his rightful place in the critical community, there was little choice. Once he had determined that a hybrid oration that would merge dicanic and epideictic rhetoric was his best vehicle, the trial of Socrates inevitably became his model and Plato's version of it was the outstanding literary version.[29] In his introductory comments, Isocrates lets his audience know that the actual impetus for his speech was the "unfair" treatment he suffered in being assigned a trierarchic liturgy. Whining about how the greedy *dēmos* forced rich men to pay more than their fair share of liturgies was a constant refrain in the cacophonous symphony of elite complaints about popular rule. By transforming the subject of his trial from *antidosis* to the "corruption of the youth," by ensuring that his day in court would recall the trial of Socrates, Isocrates transubstantiates shopworn elite grumbles about democratic practice into a principled inquiry into the premises of the people's rule. By the magic of skillful and imaginative rhetoric, the standard and selfish squabble over liturgies familiar to every upper-class Athenian was elevated to the level of the martyrdom of Platonic philosophy's hero.

By slipping into the role of Plato's Socrates, Isocrates transformed himself from just another rich man forced to do his financial duty to the democratic state into a hero who bravely and defiantly proclaims his unwavering intention to adhere to a stern code of critical ethics. Isocrates thus laid his claim to a leading position within the critical community. Isocrates, like Socrates, presents himself as a persecuted intellectual, ill-understood by his fellow citizens who fail to grasp the great good that he in fact accomplishes for the *polis*. By assimilating himself to the model of Socrates, Isocrates situated himself at the cutting edge of the critical enterprise: the point at which the individual citizen pushed the prototypical Athenian political virtue of frank speech (*parrhēsia:* 10, 43–44, 179) to, and potentially beyond, the limit. This meant that he knowingly chose to risk death at the hands of the people rather than accept their authority to suppress his critical voice.

Privileges of Martyrdom

Isocrates' assumption of the Socratic martyr's mantle had many benefits. Most obviously, the man who faced capital punishment—and thus the possibility that his defense speech would be among his last words—might grant himself permission to speak in a manner that would appear over boastful and distastefully self-congratulatory in other contexts.[30] Plato's Socrates looked upon the trial as an opportunity to attempt provocative improvement of his fellow citizens, but his arrogant pride in his high principles and in his bravery under fire is clearly in evidence in Plato's *Apology*.[31] Isocrates, like Socrates, claims that his speech has an important pedagogical purpose: demonstrating to the public the content and worth of Isocratean *paideia/philosophia*. But, given that he had been charged "in regard to his *logoi*," the means of Isocrates' demonstration would justly be his *logoi* themselves: i.e., a recapitulation of lengthy passages from fine speeches he had written long before (52–54). These citations will allow the jurors to judge "not on appearances but from accurate knowledge" (*ou doxasantes alla saphōs eidotes:* 54, note echoes of both Thucydides and Plato). Yet they are obviously not meant as merely educational. They are collectively an *epideixis* of the speaker's persuasive power (*dunamis*, a key term in this oration, as it had been for Thucydides). The audience will appreciate, by hearing the extracts, Isocrates' *ēthos* and the *dunamis* of his *logoi* (54). Isocrates arrogantly claims that he will gladly pay the greatest penalty if the jury should find his *logoi* other than "incomparable" (75 cf. 80, 86–88; 144). Such an overt display of masterful power would normally be unsuitable, especially when one's opponents claimed that excessive persuasiveness in speech (the *dunamis* of his *logoi:* 5) constituted a threat to the public welfare. But the man who faced the greatest of dangers, and who felt himself to be superior to other men and believed that they could benefit by a clearer apprehension of his unique qualities, might reasonably choose to use the short time remaining to him in advertising his superiority in terms that were rather less guarded than the Athenian norm. "If I were to repeat my orations merely to make an *epideixis,* I would reasonably be liable to this sort of complaint, but now that I am on trial and I am in great jeopardy (*kinduneuōn*), I am forced to use my speeches in this fashion" (55).

At the beginning of the *Antidosis,* Isocrates expressed his unwillingness to eulogize himself in any sort of traditional way for fear of stimulating greater jealousy among his fellow citizens. But since he could soon be facing the hemlock, he might be allowed license to explain why it was that he held himself and his profession in such a high regard (178–179). And thus the setting in a capital trial allowed Isocrates to play the part of the central character in his own drama and the chance to make a demonstration of his own considerable powers as a rhetorician.

Isocrates confronted death only in the carefully transparent fiction of his speech. The very overtness of the fiction allowed him to ignore the restrictions imposed by the water clock and to write a super-*Apology,* several times the length of Plato's dialogue. The great size as well as the highly polished style of Isocrates' monument to himself compensated for any self-subordination that the mimesis might have entailed. With enough words, well enough arranged, Isocrates was confident that he could show himself and his *logos* to be more than worthy of his models: the man Socrates and the text of Plato's *Apology.*[32] The structure of the *Antidosis* allows Isocrates to have his cake and eat it too: he not only addresses a double audience, he equates himself with Socrates as a martyr to popular rule and claims the risk taker's special privilege of *parrhēsia* regarding his own self-worth. And he does all of this without incurring any actual danger and without the need to impose any restriction on the length or content of his oration.

Theory and Practice: Civic Education

Isocrates' audacious, mimetic, and highly rhetorical misperformance of the trial of Platonic philosophy's martyr-hero points us toward a central concern: the problematic unity of theory and practice, the question of what purchase philosophy broadly conceived might have on how we (as the subjects and objects of rhetorical practice) do and should act in the real world. It points, in brief, to "integrity" as a conjunction of *logos* with *bios*. Plato's Socrates willingly faced death because he regarded integrity as primary, and he conceived integrity as living one's life according to one's philosophical convictions.[33] And Isocrates himself proudly proclaimed his own performative achievement of that same felicitous conjunction.

Yet I have argued that Isocrates asserts his personal integrity from within the frame of an overtly fictional context, in a text in which the identity of "Isocrates" is merged with the identity of (Plato's) "Socrates." Here the unitary and performative self that is asserted to be the manifestation of a philosophical *logos* is very self-consciously doubled. That doubling, so I have argued, is a response to the social conditions into which Isocrates (as an Athenian) was "hailed" and to the matrix of critical debates within which his identity as a philosopher was constructed. Isocrates' assertion of personal integrity, in a text that is so obviously misperformative, must almost inevitably be read as subversive, as an act of resistance and provocation. Or at least it will tend to be read that way in our own age, in which "authenticity" is such a deeply desired and deeply contested state of being.

A "subversive" reading of Isocrates seems to me valid, and I have obviously encouraged it by prefacing my own discussion of the text with a nod to Judith Butler's reworking of Althusser's theory of interpellation. But we should, I think, guard against supposing that Isocratean subversion was nothing more than a local or personal act of resistance to otherwise dominant structures of (Athenian) social convention or (Platonic) philosophical doctrine. Isocrates, I believe, was quite serious in proposing that the complex form of doubled identity (rhetorical and philosophical, patriotic and cosmopolitan, democratic and aristocratic) he performs in the *Antidosis* was defensible as a sort of "integrity"—that is to say, it was an authentic union of theory and practice. Moreover, he supposed that the proper role of the teacher of rhetoric was to teach his students how to develop for themselves a complex and integral identity, and thereby how to perform as citizens of a particular state and of a wider world. This conjunction of "soul-craft" and "state-craft" is reminiscent, as I suggested above, of Plato's *Republic*. But Isocrates is convinced that his own form of teaching was eminently practical. Isocrates' fictionality in the *Antidosis* is of a different order from Plato's fictional Kallipolis. It is not an other-worldly *paradeigma* "laid up in heaven," but a practical *paradeigma* of civic education that could be carried out in the here and now of everyday social and political life.

Whether or not we accept the social and political ideals that inform Isocrates' audacious misperformance (for the record, I do not), we may honor Isocrates' conception of the goal of civic education as the development, through speech, of a complex yet integrated identity. He calls upon his students to become persons capable of intervening, through speech, in an equally complex social and political realm. This conception of civic education as union of theory and practice continues to serve as an elusive Grail for many of Isocrates' descendants in the modern academy. We continue to seek to explain to our own students and (at least in unguarded moments) to ourselves, why and how the texts we study and produce might help us to answer the authoritative "hail" of social convention in a "non-Pavlovian" manner. How may they help us to achieve an authentic and yet critical and complex sense of self? And how can they provide us, as citizens, with some purchase upon the realms (state and world) that lie outside the bounds of our academy? That two-fold goal of achieving personal complexity with integrity and of unifying critical theory with effective public practice remain, I suppose, the real and pressing challenge of civic education. And it is that challenge to which each of the essays in this collection responds.

Notes

1. Ober 1998.

2. Butler 1997.

3. Ober 1998: chap. 1.

4. The central sections of this essay (pp. 24–38) were originally published as Ober, *Political Dissent* 1998: 248–263. I thank Princeton University Press for their permission to reprint these sections.

5. The debate between Isocrates and Plato (explicit only at Plato, *Phaedrus* 278e–279e) is explored in detail by Eucken 1983: (esp. 270–283). See also Erbse 1971; Ford 1993; Nightingale 1995: 13–59. On Isocrates' debt to Thucydides, see Luschnat 1970: cols. 1276–1280; de Romilly 1963: 359–362.

6. An analogy is the verbose, ineffective cicada-like murmuring of the Trojan Elders in the Teichoskopia scene of *Iliad* 3.150–155, with the insightful analysis of Mackie 1996: 38–39. Theophrastus' (*Characters* 26) "Oligarchic Man" caricatures the type.

7. Innate ability, formal training, and practical knowledge in Isocrates' pedagogy: *Against the Sophists* 14–18; *Antidosis* 194, with Too 1995: 185. Whether Isocrates actually did influence men of affairs to undertake particular policies is another question; see, for example, Laistner 1930.

8. What Isocrates means by *paideia* and *philosophia* are elaborated in his early didactic essay, *Against the Sophists*, cited at *Antidosis* 195 in support of the claim that he used identical *logoi* to his students and the jurors. See further Eucken 1983: 5–35; Too 1995: 151–199.

9. Isocrates' speeches show that *philosophia* had become a highly marked term in intellectual circles by early- to mid-fourth century. The title *philosophos* was a valued prize well worth contending for; see Nightingale 1995: 10–11; 26–29; Wardy 1996: 94–96. The tradition that Isocrates had been a student of Gorgias (as well as Teisias and Theramenes) became very important in later attempts to write a sequential history of Greek rhetoric: e.g., Ps-Plutarch, *The Ten Attic Orators* 836f–837a, with Kennedy 1972: 174–185; Too 1995: 235–239.

10. For the Cynic and Stoic alternatives, see Long 1996.

11. Athenian rhetors punished by the *dēmos:* Cloché 1968; Hansen 1975; Roberts 1982; Knox 1985. Cf. Nightingale 1995: 5, noting that Plato typically attacks genres or individuals as synecdoche for genres.

12. Ober 1989: 318–324. The orators' criticisms of contemporary mores was one of the primary exhibits in the (now debunked) notion that the fourth century was an era of decline and decadence; see Ober 1996: 29–31.

13. On the history of circulation of symbouleutic speeches, Yunis (1996: 242–243) may place too much emphasis on Demosthenes' originality in this practice given the existence of Lysias 34 and Andocides 2 and 3, but he is certainly right to point out that there is a sudden floruit of publication of symbouleutic speeches in the mid-fourth century. Trevett (1996) argues that Aristotle's *Rhetoric* never cites written versions of symbouleutic or dicanic speeches, but he gathers considerable evidence for Aristotle's knowledge of speeches. For the chronological seriation of surviving speeches, see Ober 1989: 349 Table 1.

14. This elitist cosmopolitan tendency had a long ancestry. For the celebration of an ideal of aristocratic culture that emphasized extra-*polis* connections between elites at the expense of *polis* solidarity in archaic lyric poetry, see Kurke 1992; Morris 1996. In postwar literature, much of Xenophon's oeuvre (especially the *Cyropaedeia*) shares Isocrates' vision of a Greek cultural ideal that would include those not normally regarded as "truly" Greek, including some hellenized Asians; cf. Dillery 1995: 54. Walzer (1998: 126) generalizes the point: "old and established elites, aristocracies especially, are always more cosmopolitan than the men and women they rule." On panhellenism in Isocrates, see Mathieu 1926: 41–50; Bringmann 1965; Buchner 1958. Wardy (1996: 87–88) notes in particular Isocrates' use of the reality of growing Macedonian power to reorient rhetoric and its task, from the democratic *ochlos* to the great individual.

15. On the distinction between "similarity" (*homoiotēs*) and equality (*isotēs*) and the two kinds of equality, see Cartledge 1996.

16. On the *antidosis* procedure, see Christ 1990; Gabrielsen 1994: 91–95.

17. There is no way to prove that the *Antidosis* trial really took place, but it seems too elaborate to regard it merely as a conceit (and a highly unflattering one at that) to launch a greater conceit. I tend to think that the events really did happen and were quite well known—after all a trial featuring a rhetorician of Isocrates' stature was likely to make a mark in a city which loved a hot trial. For "onlookers" in Athenian trials, see Lanni 1997.

18. Isocrates here alludes to the long tradition of competition between verbal and representational art for the memorialization of persons and events. On the complex tradition of the poem or speech as a memorial, well known from archaic poetry, and the related tradition of the inscribed grave monument that "speaks" (usually in verse) to the passerby, urging him/her to pause to consider the life of the deceased, see Svenbro 1988: 13–52; Hedrick 1995; Steiner 1994: 139–142. Misch (1976) discusses Isocrates' self-description in this speech, with special reference to Plato's *Seventh Letter* and the tradition of the encomium.

19. Nightingale (1995: 26–40) offers an insightful reading of the speech, focusing on Isocrates' validation of his insider status and his claims to *charis* on the strength of his generosity with *intellectual* (as opposed to material) property. Cf. Too 1995: 109–111.

20. The "Apology of Socrates" seems to have become a subgenre of its own: Lesky 1966: 499. Other evidence for the genre of pseudo-dicanic depends on how many speeches in the oratorical corpus one supposes were not actually written for real trials, but rather as examples written by logographers seeking new clients. Dover, *Lysias*, remains seminal, although I believe he overstates the case.

21. E.g., 8, 10, and esp. 13: *tēn apologian tēn prospoioumenēn men peri kriseōs . . . boulomenēn de peri emou*.

22. Double audience: 55–56, 154, 170, 195. The double audience is not as bizarre as might appear, given that major political trials attracted considerable audiences in addition to jurors: Lanni 1997.

23. See esp. 13: Isocrates will exact just revenge (*dikēn labein*) upon his rivals by causing them to be consumed by the disease (*nosos*) of jealousy (*phthonos*). On the intertwined relationship between justice and disease, revenge and punishment, in Athenian thought, see Allen 2000.

24. Isocrates asks the clerk of the court to read the extended passages, pleading his own advanced age (59). By analogy with a real Athenian trial this would have the effect of stopping the water clock and introducing the passages of documentary "witnesses."

25. Isocrates' construction of a fictive audience that includes ordinary as well as elite citizens suggests the limits of such simulacra for self-presentation, given the enduring strength of cultural norms which allowed, even expected, a notable man to counter balance moderation and "quietism" with an overt display of excellence in the public spaces of the city. Relevant Athenian examples include Thucydides' Pericles and Demosthenes' self-portrait at 18.169–179. The depiction by Arendt (1959) of the *polis* as a human environment

uniquely suited to the public "appearance" and memorialization of great deeds by individuals, even if overstated, is relevant here.

26. Echoes of Plato's *Apology:* Too 1995: 192–193; Nightingale (1995: 28–29, with literature cited), arguing that the imitation is "part of Isocrates' attack on Plato's portrayal" of Socrates.

27. Inferiority of the copy: e.g., Plato *Rep.* 602b, *Statesman* 297c. Too (1995: 184–194) discusses *mimēsis* in Isocratean pedagogy with special reference to the imitation of Socrates in the *Antidosis.*

28. Wallace (1994) demonstrates that most other alleged persecutions of intellectuals by the Athenian democracy are literary fictions. He argues that the one exception, and so the only other possible candidate for an intellectual martyr, is the Athenian citizen and musical theorist, Damon, who was ostracized in the 440s, apparently because the Athenians sincerely believed that his musical experiments had potentially serious political ramifications. Damon is mentioned in *Antidosis* (235) as an excellent teacher of sophism and (along with Anaxagoras) a teacher of Pericles.

29. Whether Isocrates' choice of Plato's *Apology* tells us anything about the authenticity of Plato's account, per Brickhouse and Smith (1989: 7–9), is another question. Isocrates chose Plato's account because he needed to confront both Socrates (as martyr) and Plato (as intellectual rival). I doubt that it much mattered to him whether the account was "authentic"; the point is that it was (in the view of his key intellectual rivals) authoritative.

30. Athenian litigants did sometimes boast in their speeches, but they were usually careful to hedge their boasting by displays of demotic conformity: Ober 1989.

31. Socrates' pride and arrogance in the *Apology* has been the cause of some discomfort among modern scholars; see, for example, Brickhouse and Smith 1989: 210–234.

32. *Antidosis* runs to 77 pages in the Teubner edito minor *without* the extracts from other speeches; Plato's *Apology* is 33 pages. Misch (1976: 202) and Too (1995: 48) comment on the speech's prolixity. On monumentality as a desired attribute in earlier Greek literary culture, see Martin 1989: 221–231, 238.

33. See, for example, Kateb 1998.

Isocrates' Civic Education
and the Question of *Doxa*

PERICLES' funeral oration registers the keen sense of awareness the Athenians had of themselves as citizens, and affirms the immense significance that they attached to citizenship.[1] As the words of their leader make clear in this oration, Athenians saw citizenship not only as guaranteeing them equality before the law, but also as providing them with unique opportunities to participate in the political activities of the city, contribute to its ambitions, and perhaps attain public distinction for themselves—opportunities, in other words, that their individual position in society might otherwise never present them. As equal members of a community that valorized involvement in public affairs, Athenians knew that their citizenship was inextricably connected to the possibility of political excellence irrespective of social rank. They also knew that, as Pericles put it, "no man gets barred from a public career if he has it in him to do the state a service" (II. 37. 1). This awareness must have heightened one generation later, when speeches by political orators (Ober 1989) and public funeral speakers (Loraux 1986) presented a portrait of Athenian citizenry as an elite community whose members judged one another's merit on the basis of services, benefactions, and sacrifices made to the city.

Within a climate set by a proliferation of discourses celebrating citizenship and glorifying service to the state, it is hardly surprising to see Isocrates frame his rhetorical instruction as a program of civic education. As he remarked on a number of passages, his instruction of political discourse or *logos politikos* was meant to impart not a mastery over the art of *logos* but an ability to apply rhetorical principles to political situations (*Against the Sophists* 17–18; *Antidosis* 187). These are situations whose unknown outcome and unforeseen consequences called for sound judgments and intelligent decisions about the city's future courses of action. His program in rhetorical education was cast as equipment for civic life, a requisite learning for both orators-to-be and ambitious citizens.

This is the reason perhaps why he spoke about his prospective students without classifying them into any groups, choosing instead to refer to them in common as people "willing to work hard and to prepare themselves to be of service to the city" (*Antidosis* 305). In guiding students how to apply rhetorical principles to political situations, how to meet the demands of changing circumstances, and how to make choices about future courses of action, he was convinced that he empowered orators and citizens alike to play a leading role in the affairs of the state. Should they rise to the occasion, should they follow his guidance in addressing the city's problems by formulating sound judgments, they may very well expect—he leads them and us to believe—to become leaders of the city one day, at once successful orators and celebrated citizens.

To assess Isocrates' tacit claim that his rhetorical training amounted to preparation for civic life, we must attempt to discern how Isocrates conceived and taught the process of reaching intelligent decisions and making sound judgments, as well as what standards, if any, he considered to be guiding or shaping this process. In other words, we must undertake an inquiry into his notion of *doxa*. For his rhetorical training rested on an expressed confidence in his ability as educator to guide students to meet contingent occasions with good judgments and to resolve indeterminate situations through successful conjectures (*Antidosis* 183–184).

How he might have taught others to wrest reliable judgments out of ordinary opinions, or to elevate common beliefs to correct decisions, raises a question that lies at the very core of the type of education he claimed for himself. An examination of Isocrates' use of the term *doxa* (belief, opinion, conjecture, judgment) is necessary if we are to accept his claim that his instruction aimed at producing a genuinely educated person, one who would be "able by his powers of conjecture to arrive generally at the best course, ταῖς δόξαις ἐπιτυγχάνειν" (*Antidosis* 271), or a truly wise person, capable of "a judgment (δόξα) which is accurate in meeting occasions as they arise and rarely misses the expedient course of action" (*Panathenaicus* 30).

Discourses of *Doxa*

By the time of Isocrates, the term *doxa* had acquired a multiplicity of meanings and an impressive array of associations. Its various significations and
clusters of associations were organized according to Detienne (1996) by two
main traditions: the secular and the philosophical. Both traditions sought to
provide solutions to the crisis brought on by the disintegration of a social
system that had given speech its religious function. With the social structures that had sustained it gone, efficacious speech lost its power to dispense
truth. The archaic figures, the poet, seer, and king, likewise lost their privileged positions in relation to truth, while *alētheia*, at the heart of efficacious
speech, relinquished its supreme reign in the semantic field that had dominated mythical and religious thought. Formed in the aftermath of a bygone
era, these two traditions represented two different ways of coming to terms
with the devaluation of *alētheia*. With the advent of the classical city, Vidal-
Naquet remarks, truth "entered a world where things were relative" and, in
that world, "the orator's and the Sophist's universal *competence* in the domain of the relative [was contrasted] to the *knowledge* of the philosophical
and religious sects" (1996: 11).

The secular tradition replaced the religious and privileged knowledge
with a secularized and highly political mode of understanding. Detienne
traces the beginnings of this tradition to a time when poetry first turned
into a profession, the poet's memory became a technique, and the poem's
truth-value came to be located on artistic illusion, *apatē*. With poetry becoming a form of expression no longer guided by the religious function of
memory but by the positive side of deception, with *apatē* breaking loose
from its subservient relation to *alētheia*, the artificial nature of speech was
born. Political speech, the speech in and of the *polis*, coincided with the moment when *apatē* joined *doxa* to define a world of ambiguity that stood
in direct opposition to *alētheia*. In the words of Detienne, "[a]lētheia no
longer ruled; it had been usurped by *dokein*, or *doxa*" (1996: 109).

In the secular tradition, *doxa* came to signify an appropriate form of
knowledge for the imprecise world of politics, a world characterized by
change, ambiguity, and contingency. Its meaning revolved, as Detienne remarked, around the basic idea "to decide to do whatever one judges to best
suit the situation," an idea that conveyed the notion of choice as well as the
notion of choice varying according to the situation (114). In the secular tradition and within the domain of politics, *doxa* did not mean "opinion" in the

philosophical sense and had no connection whatsoever to the philosophical problem of being and seeming. This eventually gave *doxa* the derogatory sense of uncertainty leading to deception and falsehood. As André Rivier has shown with Xenophanes (1956), *doxa* at the time "does not mean an intellectual act a priori devalued in relation to the truth." Rather *doxa* and truth are distinguished "by the particular kind of reality that each aims to apprehend: the visible or the invisible." The difference between them is not "more or less objective value but rather of a greater or smaller degree of certainty for whoever employs them" (50–51).[2] In the sphere of politics, the noun *doxa* became a technical term in the emergent *polis* and the verb *dokein* came to connote a political decision (Detienne 1996: 115).

In contrast to the secular tradition, the philosophical or more precisely the philosophico-religious tradition assigned *doxa* a different set of associations and significations. Ever since the end of the sixth century, this tradition had concerned itself with maintaining archaic procedures and ancient modes of thought despite the new developments at hand. Amidst an increasingly politicized world, it had sought to maintain a focus on inwardness and to place a premium on individual salvation.[3] For the philosophico-religious sects upholding this tradition, truth (*alētheia*) was radically dissociated from deception (*apatē*), and the contrast between them presented human beings with two divergent paths and two contrasting ways of life: the bright path of *alētheia* and the dark path of *doxa*. Devoting themselves to exploring ways in which *alētheia* could detach human beings from the vacillating and unstable world of *doxa*, thereby bringing them closer to the immutable and stable world of Being, members of philosophico-religious sects understood themselves as knowledgeable in the ways of *alētheia*. In opposition to those lost in oblivion and swept away by the ceaseless flow of change, they thought of themselves as able to recognize *alētheia* in its various manifestations, however dim or subtle. For these sects, *alētheia* established a standard for judging other levels of reality, and the philosophers in search of Being took on the task of differentiating the stable and immutable from the unstable and changing. With Parmenides, the search to discover traces of *alētheia* in a world dominated by flux was extended to include *doxa* as well, since *doxa* was at the time considered to be sometimes false and sometimes true. This line of thought was followed by Plato, who described *doxa* in the *Theaetetus* as both true and false: "judgment (δόξα) turns and twists about and proves false (ψευδής) or true (ἀληθής)" (194b). Immersed in a world that included hidden aspects of the true in the deceptive and brief glimpses of the permanent in the fluctuating, philosophers from Pythagoras to Plato undertook the inquiry of distinguishing the real (i.e., the true) from the false.

These two traditions implicated *doxa* with two distinct worldviews that, after coming to a sharper focus under the Sophists and Plato, presented Isocrates with two contrasting alternatives. On the one side, *doxa* delineated a world of ambiguity and contingency that offered no possibility for grounding beliefs anywhere other than the ineffable and fleeting character of chance and circumstance. In this worldview, it was neither possible nor necessary to secure a context-invariant ground or reference point that would distinguish opinion from knowledge. For any ground posited and any reference point offered would itself be a construct created by human bias, and thus incapable of serving as an objective criterion. Furthermore, any "impartial" viewpoint posited in order to distinguish *doxa* from *epistēmē* would be a linguistic construct that, far from providing a window to "objective" reality, would in fact give meaning to the very reality it presumed to be representing. On the other side, *doxa's* inextricable connection with ambiguity created an urgent need to arrive at a starting point or ground that, independent of human contingency, would serve as a criterion against which claims to knowledge could be measured and assessed. In this worldview, human beings looked to anchor their lives on standards beyond the contingencies of everyday life, and to engage in the kind of reflection required to access these standards. According to this worldview, divine inspiration or dialectic procedure made it possible to secure a ground for human knowledge and for the apprehension of truth.

Isocrates practiced his own version of rhetorical training, then, within an intellectual scene already set by a debate over two drastically different ways of linking *doxa* to knowledge, truth, and language. The question whether political beliefs, opinions, and judgments could be secured by means of a stable foundation or ground, or else remain without foundation and utterly groundless—a question so frequently entering our own current debates between foundationalist and antifoundationalist positions—must have preoccupied Isocrates a great deal, even though he did not address it explicitly. Living at a time when the domain of human affairs had become a place in which, as Aristotle remarked, "the agents themselves must in each case consider what is appropriate to the occasion" (*NE* 1104a 8–9), Isocrates knew that any feasible conception of political speech would have to come to terms with the ambiguity of *doxa*. While the Sophists had associated *doxa* with a worldview Isocrates shared, Plato had provided a way to improve *doxa* through education, a premise Isocrates found most appealing to his own educational aspirations.

The Sophists provided Isocrates with one way of dealing with the problem that *doxa* posed for political deliberation. Taking the ever-shifting and unpredictable domain of politics for granted, they looked for ways to place a degree of control over ambiguity so as to make deliberative situations yield effective action. According to Gorgias, who saw *doxa* as volatile and unstable, an orator employing *doxa* to advance a given position was in fact advancing something most precarious: "on most subjects most men take opinion as counselor to their soul, but since opinion is slippery and insecure it casts those employing it into slippery and insecure successes" (*Helen* 11).[4]

To turn a proposal built on nothing other than the precarious character of *doxa* into a successful recommendation, an orator would have to rely on the kind of support mechanisms that only the workings of persuasion could provide. In other words, Gorgias saw the problem of containing the ambiguity inherent in deliberative situations as a task that required the making of a strong tie between opinion and persuasion, a link between *doxa* and *peithō*. For Gorgias, the strength of such a link depended on the orator's ability to tap into the linguistic conventions of the community in ways that would persuade others to perceive and think of the world in a similar manner. He looked at *doxa* as revealing not the way the world really is but the way language users speak about the world and the way they rely on conventions of language to give meaning to their discursive exchanges. For him, speech neither represents nor reflects external reality and the question of improving *doxa* by bringing it to a closer approximation of reality is a moot question. Gorgias accounted for the fact that one *doxa* dominates over another, not in terms of the correspondence between language and external reality, but in terms of rhetorically situated practices that give meaning to the ways we speak about external reality. This explains Gorgias' conviction that in order to understand the relationship between persuasion and opinion, one must focus on the rhetorical practices of a particular community of language users and study these practices—as, for example, "the words of astronomers who, substituting opinion for opinion, taking away one but creating another, make what is incredible and unclear seem true to the eyes of opinion" (*Helen* 13).

In a parallel vein, Protagoras had shown that ambiguity could be managed and contained if one imposed upon it the logic of contradiction. His notion of *dissoi logoi* had limited the infinite play of ambiguity to a dual set of propositions, thereby making it possible to regard the multiple signification of language as a problem of contradictory meanings. Once ambiguity was articulated in terms of duality, the multiplicity of possibilities available in a given case could be reduced to two principal alternatives, two opposing views on every issue or two contradictory theses on every question. In this way, the problem with deliberation in ambiguous situations could be reduced to a choice between two alternative *doxai*—a difficulty that an orator's skill with persuasion could readily resolve. In the words of John Poulakos, "[b]ecause every issue admits of at least two contrary *logoi,* and because the imperative to action generally permits only one of the two to prevail in a given instance, [Protagorean] rhetoric affords people a means through which they can persuade one another to favor, at a given moment, one logos over all others" (1995: 58). Redirected as a problem of oppositional duality, ambiguity could be confronted by an orator whose skill with persuasion sufficed to tip the balance in favor of one *doxa* over another.[5]

Unlike Gorgias, Protagoras had linked persuasion and opinion by insisting on a reference to the community's conventions, without positing conventional thought as a standard. For him individual experiences are made meaningful not only through individual speech but also through the *nomos* of a community, which acts as a receptacle for the disparate experiences of community members, and itself becomes shaped through a process of exchange and debate. Thus, to say that an orator can "make the good, instead of the evil, seem to be right to their states" (*Theaetetus* 167c) does not mean (as Kerferd suggests) that some judgments are for Protagoras "actually, objectively, beneficial" (1989: 130), but rather that individual speech can in fact affect the process of accumulating and ordering diverse experiences within the *nomos* of a community. Being both determined and challenged by the diversity of experience, the stability of *nomos* is for Protagoras situational and temporal: "whatever seems right and honorable to a state is really right and honorable to it, so long as it believes it to be so" (*Theaetetus* 167c). This is also evident with the norms of excellence in Protagoras' flute-playing city which, though set in place by the city, are nevertheless subject to challenge by any individual flute player who may surpass them.

However influential the Sophists' position on *doxa* might have been on Isocrates, it presented him with only one manner of dealing with ambiguity and only one side of the intellectual debate over *doxa* in his time. Plato furnished the other side of the debate when he placed *doxa* between knowledge and ignorance, between the guardians of the state who possessed "blind souls" and "those who have learned to know" (*Republic* 484c–d). The challenge for Plato was how to convert *doxa* into knowledge, a challenge he showed in the *Meno* could be met through the gradual process of recollection. Prior to the *Meno*, Plato had followed Parmenides in opposing *doxa* to knowledge on the basis of a difference in the object apprehended, the world of the senses or the world of Forms. Whereas the sensible world, which "becomes and perishes but never exists" is "judged by *doxa* with unreasoning sensation," that which "exists always and never becomes" is "apprehended by thought with a rational account" (*Timaeus* 28a).

In the *Meno*, Plato bridged these two modes of cognition and described *doxa* as a dim apprehension of the same objects that knowledge apprehends clearly and completely. The statesman's *doxa*, which can "hit" on reality even though unable to give a rational explanation, is the same true belief (ὀρθὴ δόξα) that appears in the *Symposium* as neither knowledge nor ignorance: "to have correct opinion (ὀρθὰ δοξάζειν), if you can give no reason for it, is neither full knowledge (ἐπίστασθαι)—how can an unreasoned thing be knowledge?—nor yet ignorance; for what hits on the truth cannot be ignorance. So correct opinion, I take it, is just in that position, between understanding and ignorance" (202a). Like the slave who "has had true opinions in him which have only to be awakened by questioning to become knowledge" (86a), *Meno's* good statesman possesses correct beliefs that guide him to make the right decisions for his city.

Yet even though true, his *doxa* is nothing more than a knack for hitting the right solutions to practical problems, a correct opinion without complete understanding. Thus, even as true opinion (ἀληθὴς δόξα) is shown to provide "as good a guide to rightness of action as knowledge" (97b), the difference between *doxa* and knowledge lies in this: "he who has knowledge (ἐπιστήμη) will always hit on the right way, whereas he who has right opinion (ὀρθὴ δόξα) will sometimes do so, but sometimes not" (97c). To turn correct opinion into knowledge and stop relying on empirical guesses, the statesman would have to complete the process of recollection and gradually come to know the essence of the unchanging Forms. By reference to the external standard of the immutable Forms, the statesman can seek through dialectic procedure an unchanging cause for his knowledge and, as a result, be able to give his practical policies uniformity and consistency.

Doxa as Conjecture

In attempting to discern how Isocrates might have positioned himself somewhere in between the Sophists and Plato, and how this positioning might be better clarified through his efforts to negotiate the tension between a groundless *doxa* and a *doxa* that could be improved through education, it is necessary to examine a strand traversing his writings—a discourse about stochastic arts (such as navigation, medicine, politics) that he deployed to speak about his art of *logos politikos*. Isocrates used this discourse in a way that acknowledged what a long tradition before him had already established as the common character of stochastic arts, namely, the problem of having to deal successfully with unpredictable situations, steering a ship through an unprecedented storm, administering drugs for an unknown disease, or guiding the city through a unique crisis (Detienne and Vernant 1991: 225–248). Best captured by the art of archery, the challenge encountered commonly by stochastic arts entailed the task of aiming at a mark and the skill required in hitting it. As Allen put it, the term *stochastic*, from the verb στοχάζεσθαι, indicated that the relation between an art and its end "was one of aiming, not always of hitting." But it also meant conjecture, he adds, "the kind of educated guesswork an artist employs in the absence of conclusive evidence" (1994: 86).

By deploying a conventional discourse about stochastic arts to present his own version of the art, Isocrates could cast political deliberation as a process of aiming at the right course of action in the face of uncertainty, and *doxa* as a conjecture aimed at making the right decision. Like the archer who bends the bow in the direction of the target, who aims at a mark in the hope of hitting it, a deliberating agent could similarly be regarded as addressing a problem that the city faced by utilizing *doxa* in the hope of hitting the right solution. This is exactly how Isocrates chose to speak about *doxa*, "a judgment which is sound and capable of hitting (στοχάζεσθαι) the right course of action" (*On the Peace* 28). By tapping on a traditional discourse associated with stochastic arts, Isocrates changed the terms of the discussion about the ambiguity of *doxa*.

Unlike the Sophists, who had addressed the question of how an orator might best defend or undermine a given *doxa*, Isocrates bracketed persuasion and focused instead on the issue of formulating the best *doxa* possible. As he remarked in *Peace* 8, "in dealing with matters about which they take counsel, [people] ought not to think that they have exact knowledge of what the result will be, but to be minded towards these contingencies as men who indeed exercise their best judgment (δόξα) but are not sure what the future may hold in store." So even as he shared with the Sophists a similar worldview and saw contingency and uncertainty as setting similar limits on *doxa*, he addressed these limits by looking not to persuasion but to the process of formulating sound judgments, a process he regarded, we will see, as conserving, clarifying, or even changing the established opinions of the community. For him, prior to persuading others about the legitimacy of one's judgment, one had to confront the task of formulating sound judgments.

Making a sound judgment in a stochastic art requires focusing one's attention securely on the target and, in Isocrates' political discourse, aligning one's *doxa* directly with the collective welfare of the city. It is the benefit of the *polis* that he regarded as supplying the sole criterion for distinguishing drifting from focused aims, directionless from purposeful *doxai*. Given this criterion, the task of formulating beneficial *doxai* positioned the Isocratean orator in the same predicament as Plato's statesman in the *Meno*, sometimes succeeding and sometimes failing to hit the mark. Like Plato, Isocrates similarly acknowledged the guesswork involved in making correct judgments and the role that pure luck played in it. Even with important deliberations, he remarked, the "wisest sometimes miss the expedient course of action, whereas now and then some chance person from the ranks of men who are deemed of no account and are regarded with contempt hits upon the right course and is thought to give the best advice" (*Panathenaicus* 248).

Unlike Plato, who sought to eliminate completely the grip of luck on decision-making, Isocrates attempted to lessen it. In fact, he considered his entire program of education as being oriented toward this single objective—the goal of removing *doxa* from the rule of *tuchē* and of bringing it as directly as possible under the control of *paideia*. It is a goal reflected in his characterization of the truly educated person as one who possesses "a judgment (δόξαν) which is accurate in meeting occasions as they arise and rarely misses (στοχάζεσθαι) the expedient course of action" (*Panathenaicus* 30). Even as he shared with Plato the assumption that *doxa* could be improved through education, Isocrates made his case for improving judgments not on the basis of some higher level of knowledge, but on the basis of an intelligence associated with stochastic skill and, as we will see, of his own belief that this type of intelligence could be improved by coming in contact with practical wisdom or *phronēsis* as he taught it.

Isocrates seized on the practical intelligence required of all stochastic arts as a way of distancing himself from Plato but also from the lesser Sophists of his generation, whom he accused in *Against the Sophists* of approaching political discourses with hard and fast rules, treating the art of *logos politikos* with the technical know-how of specialists, and relying on a mechanical application of the art's principles (10–12). According to tradition, practical intelligence was a gift belonging to persons who responded well to the challenges of a predicament they faced—having to cope in the absence of a visible path, and having to make a decision in the face of an oblique, stumbling knowledge with no other guide than the inventiveness of intelligence and the resourcefulness of experience.

By association with stochastic arts, *logos politikos* was also shown to require an intelligence that hinged on the ability to reach a conclusion about the future on the basis of a reflection on the present and a comparison with the past. It demanded fixing the mind securely on the project one had devised in advance, and waiting patiently for the calculated moment to arrive. Hence Isocrates' advice to students of his educational program: "you will take mental aim (στοχάσεσθε), as at a mark, at what is expedient for you, and you will be the more likely to hit it" (*Children of Jason* 10). It required most importantly a rich experience that would enable a better grip on the present by bringing onto a given situation the full weight of perceptiveness and insightfulness that had been accumulated over time. Experience with the past increased the awareness of possible outcomes in the future; it enabled one to look beyond the immediate situation, explore in advance all potential avenues, and anticipate how events might turn out.

Through experience, Isocrates pointed out, one can "conjecture the future by the past (*Panegyricus* 141), reach conclusions on the basis of past events (*Areopagiticus* 75), and "judge the future by the past" (*Archidamus* 59). Through intelligence and experience, it becomes possible to proceed by linking what is invisible to what is visible, thereby grasping the unknown in terms of the known. In Isocrates' thinking, this operation of practical intelligence was at the heart of political deliberation: "In your deliberations," he said to Demonicus, "let the past be an exemplar for the future; for the unknown may be soonest discerned by reference to the known" (*To Demonicus* 34).

Even though Isocrates provided no definitive standards that would control the ambiguity of *doxa,* he was nevertheless able to assert—by associating *logos politikos* with the culturally familiar operations of stochastic intelligence—a long experience with the past as a reliable guide for the future. Orators' conjectures concerning the proper course of action are to be guided by their resourcefulness and insightfulness accumulated over the years. To be sure, Isocrates' association of the art of political discourse with the practical intelligence of *stochazesthai* would have been vulnerable to Plato's critique of arts "concerned with opinions and pursu[ing] their energetic studies in the realm of opinion" (*Philebus* 59a). For any art that defined itself around what Plato regarded as oblique procedures and devious methods characterizing stochastic intelligence was for him nothing more than a skill, a mere "ability to make lucky shots which is commonly accorded the title of art or craft, when it has consolidated its position by dint of industrious practice" (*Philebus* 55e).

In addition, Plato had warned in the *Republic* against conflating the results obtained by an art's internal perfection with the results gained by a practitioner's application of the art. The true artist never misses the mark, since the demands of an art cannot be satisfied perfectly without hitting the mark every time. That an artist sometimes hits and sometimes misses the mark is evidence of an art's internal deficiency (342 ff). While Plato used this distinction to expose stochastic arts as deficient, Isocrates capitalized on this same distinction in order to mark the difference in the types of results produced by different agents of deliberation. On the one hand, there have been cases—by politicians in the assembly—in which political deliberation resulted in personal gain (*Peace* 127). On the other hand, there have been cases—by great statesmen and past leaders of Athens—in which political deliberation resulted in collective gain (*Antidosis* 231). By reference to such past practices of deliberation as those of Solon, Cleisthenes, and Pericles, Isocrates provided an additional criterion for guiding *doxai.* Conjectures about the future are not only to be guided by the orator's past experiences but also by precedent—examples of past practices that attest to the possibility that a *doxa* aimed at the benefit of the city can in fact hit the target successfully, and can do so most of the time.

Doxa as Wise Judgment

Isocrates' praise of past statesmen (231–236), still celebrated in his day for having advanced the cause of democracy and strengthened the city, marks an important point in *Antidosis*. For one, it sets the stage for presenting to his audience his own version of *philosophia* as he understood and practiced it (270ff.). As we will see, Isocrates' *philosophia*, defined explicitly as the study of practical wisdom or *phronēsis* (*Antidosis* 271), turns out to be closely related to and perhaps indistinguishable from the study of the deliberating practices of the great statesmen in the past. It also enables him to differentiate practical intelligence from practical wisdom, *stochasmos* from *phronēsis*. The discourse about past statesmen and their sound decisions allows Isocrates to make a distinction between the skillful guesses required of agents in stochastic situations and the prudence in decision-making required of great leaders, as well as between the cleverness associated with the domain of political oratory with the wisdom associated with excellent statesmanship. Still, even as the wisdom of Solon, Cleisthenes, and Pericles emerges as an activity higher than skill or cleverness, the exact relation of *phronēsis* to stochastic intelligence is left unspecified (in this section as well as in the entire Isocratean *oeuvre*), presenting us with two possible interpretations.

First, *phronēsis* can be read as the highest form of practical intelligence, the best version of *stochazesthai*. With this reading, Isocrates' discourse about *doxa* as a problem of skillfully aiming at the benefit of the city must be seen in the relation of continuity to his discourse about the great statesmen. In other words, we must see Solon, Cleisthenes, and Pericles as merely accomplished agents of stochastic intelligence and the wisdom they possessed as nothing more than a rare ability to guide conjectures to the betterment of the *polis* successfully and frequently. This reading, which distinguishes practical wisdom from conjectural intelligence only in terms of degree and frequency of success, is supported by Isocrates' definition of the wise person as someone "who is able by his powers of conjecture (δόξαις) to arrive generally at the best course" (*Antidosis* 271). In effect coinciding with the power of conjecture, *phronēsis* in this reading bears no similarity with Aristotle's notion of *phronēsis* and represents Isocrates' ultimate failure to reach the level of instruction he aimed at, where *doxa* as sound judgment becomes qualitatively different from *doxa* as pure conjecture.

Second, *phronēsis* can be read as a substantively different activity from *stochazesthai* and the decision makers' practical wisdom as fundamentally distinct from the deliberating agents' stochastic intelligence. In this reading, Isocrates' discourse about the great statesmen of the past must be seen in the relation of discontinuity to his discourse about stochastic arts. Organizing eloquence and political decision-making around the notion of practical wisdom, the discourse about past statesmen would have to be understood as operating at a level separate from and higher than the level at which the discourse about stochastic arts operates and organizes political oratory around the notion of practical intelligence. The gap between these two discourses, as between a person of practical wisdom and a person of practical or technical intelligence, is the distance between art and skill. According to this reading, the prudential activity of the great statesmen of the past is qualitatively different from the skillful activity of the technically intelligent persons. Conversely, the discourse about stochastic arts provides Isocrates with a preparatory step on the way toward establishing this qualitative difference, while those possessing the skilled or technical intelligence associated with *stochazesthai* may represent the kind of ability Isocrates looked for in his students.

The second reading of *phronēsis*, which clearly paves the way for Aristotle's theoretical notion of *phronēsis* (albeit with some important differences; see Depew this volume) is supported, I believe, by Isocrates' discourse about the great past statesmen. Isocrates characterizes them as wise statesmen and presents through them a portrait of *phronēsis* as a wise practice of decision-making rather than as a cognitive capacity, a practice that merged together wisdom, eloquence, and statesmanship, all in one. Because these statesmen gave "most study to the art of words," they became among the best ever to "come before you on the rostrum" and, consequently, they "brought to the city most of her blessings" (231).

In attributing their reputation as wise men to their conduct as excellent political orators, ἀρίστους ῥήτορας, Isocrates situated practical wisdom inside and not apart from the process of deliberation, thereby placing prudence and political oratory in interaction with and reciprocal influence of one another. Their wisdom engaged the highest form of rhetoric possible because they applied their minds to eloquence more than to other things (235). Clearly, he is using these famous statesmen to make the case for a decision-making process that saw the rare convergence of practical wisdom with an excellence in powerful eloquence. He described Solon as a person who paid so much attention to eloquence that he "was named one of the seven Sophists" (235). The convergence of a good statesman, a wise person, and a powerful orator obtains through Isocrates' deliberate change of the label assigned to Solon, from the usual "one of ἑπτὰ σοφῶν" to the untypical "one of ἑπτὰ σοφιστῶν." A similar convergence obtains through his characterization of Damon, who taught the power of eloquence to Pericles, as a Sophist "in his day reputed to be the wisest, φρονιμωτάτου δόξαντος, among the Athenians" (235).

Isocrates' articulation of Solon, Cleisthenes, and Pericles as wise statesmen able to realize a rare convergence of excellence in eloquence and political decision making would have been acceptable to his audience. For as Plutarch later reports, wisdom in the context of the Seven Wise Men did not indicate a distinction with speculative thought but an attribute of great statesmanship. Unlike Thales, "the only wise man of the time who carried his speculations beyond the realm of the practical," Plutarch notes, Solon and the rest of the wise men "got the name of wisdom from their excellence as statesmen" (Solon 3.5). Similarly, Isocrates' articulation of wise decision-making as a rare convergence of powerful eloquence, political intelligence, and practical wisdom would not have been received as idealistic. For the reputation of the earliest Sophists provided a precedent for such a convergence, since their eloquence was purported to be not merely a sign of accomplished oratory but an indication of political cleverness and a manifestation of practical wisdom.[6] Thus, also according to Plutarch, the earliest Sophists were thought to be wise advisers and to have possessed a wisdom akin to the Seven Wise Men, "cleverness in politics and practical sagacity, δεινότητα πολιτικὴν καὶ δραστήριον σύνεσιν" (Themistocles 2.4).

Yet if by phronēsis Isocrates indicated not a discernible cognitive capacity (as Aristotle did), but a context-bound convergence of wisdom with statesmanship and oratorical eloquence, how could Isocrates defend his notion of phronēsis as something more than cleverness without ever defining rhetoric as art rather than as skill? The remarks of Too (1995: 170), reminding us that definition is not Isocrates' strong suit and that the precision we expect of him is actually a demand on our part to have him conform to Plato's and Aristotle's scientific rigor, are instructive here. It is also fair to point out that Isocrates did make many distinctions based on usage, especially as concerns the political uses of oratory. These included petty and politically meaningful subject matter (Panathenaicus 11–13); politically astute users of the art and uncultured, technical experts (Panathenaicus 28–29); mechanical and imaginative application of the rules of the art (Against *the Sophists* 16–17); uses for private gain or for honorable reputation (*Antidosis* 276–278). Taken together, these distinctions pave the way for a *logos politikos* that, embodying the better uses of eloquence in political deliberation, would clearly emerge as an art rather than a skill. That *logos politikos* would, by coming in contact with *phronēsis*, exemplify the highest form of rhetoric has also been prepared for through many passages that link eloquence and wisdom together and show the reciprocal influence of the one on the other (*Antidosis* 48, 277; *Nicocles* 7; *Panegyricus* 9; see T. Poulakos 1997: 62–77). That Isocrates' notion of *phronēsis* is not predicated on a definition of rhetoric as an art means that, unlike Aristotle, Isocrates did not see this as his burden. His own burden was to discriminate among the various uses that rhetoric was made of by his contemporaries and predecessors—a task that he carried contextually and that he demonstrated, as we will see with *Panegyricus*, performatively. That Aristotle finally considered politics a higher art than rhetoric, and therefore closer to *phronēsis*, would have been immaterial to Isocrates who predicated his notion of *phronēsis* on the prediscliplinary assumption that *logos politikos* was an inextricably single practice.

Isocrates' notion of *phronēsis* is further clarified through the distinction he offered between wisdom and philosophy:

> For since it is not in the nature of man to attain a science by the possession of which we can know positively what we should do or what we should say, in the next resort I hold that man to be wise who is able by his powers of conjecture (ταῖς δόξαις ἐπιτυγχάνειν) to arrive generally at the best course, and I hold that man to be a philosopher who occupies himself with the studies from which he will most quickly gain that kind of insight (τοιαύτην φρόνησιν) (*Antidosis* 271).

The difference drawn here between the wise person and the philosopher is predicated on their common positioning. Both are ultimately situated within the world of opinions even as they seek to improve them. Wise people make the right decisions because they know how to align correctly their judgments with the benefit of the city. Part and parcel of their deliberations, their wisdom manifests itself in practice, and becomes evident when the consequences of the judgment reached and the action taken are made apparent. Only after their *doxai* end up, in other words, conferring benefits on the *polis*, can deliberating agents be said to have acted wisely.

Philosophers, on the other hand, study the ways wise people have acted in deliberative circumstances. The business of philosophy is to develop an insight, *phronēsis*, by reflecting on the manner in which other people's wisdom might have worked in past practices, and by determining the ways in which their wisdom might have come in contact with the arts of politics and rhetoric in such a manner so as to set in motion a process of wise deliberation. Even though *phronēsis* does not occur independently from the deliberations of the wise, philosophy sheds light on *phronēsis* in order to give it a concrete existence, make its presence visible, and cause its activity to be discernible. Philosophy develops this insight by turning its attention toward the past, the proper domain of *phronēsis*.

So situated in the past, Isocrates' notion of *phronēsis* anticipates Aristotle's.[7] To make a wise decision about a given case at present, according to Aristotle, one needs to take into account the closest precedent in the past —a case where *phronimoi* had exercised a wise decision—and to use this precedent as a guide for the present (Nussbaum 1986: 290–317). Isocrates conceived the dialectic exchange between a specific case of deliberation at present and a wise precedent in the past in much broader terms than Aristotle. Even as he similarly implicated *phronēsis* with the wise judgments of past statesmen, he was more interested in the excellence displayed by their judgments rather than in the specific content of their decisions. He looked at past cases to find not a source of guidance for dealing with particular situations at present but a source of inspiration for the degree of excellence that could be attained by political deliberation in the future. That he made *phronēsis* the object of study for his *philosophia* meant that he taught his students to reflect, above all else, on past cases so that they might better understand the concrete ways in which excellence in political deliberations had been realized in the past and could once again be realized in the future. A student of philosophy embarking on the task of political deliberation, he claimed, will select "those examples which are the most illustrious and the most edifying" and, after "habituating himself to contemplate and appraise such examples, he will feel their influence not only in the preparation of a given discourse but in all the actions of his life" (*Antidosis* 277). Teaching philosophy entailed for him the task of cultivating *phronēsis* on the basis of concrete cases of excellence in political deliberation, an excellence that students were expected to witness, marvel in, study, and learn from.

Unlike Aristotle, Isocrates judged excellence in political deliberation extrinsically on the basis of the amount of benefits conferred on the *polis* and the degree of reputation earned by the speaker. As Depew convincingly argues (this volume), Isocrates did not share with Aristotle an interest in *phronēsis* as an intrinsic good, an excellence for its own sake, nor did he regard the wise decision makers of the past as an occasion to conduct a theoretical or theological inquiry into what standards the *phronimoi* themselves might have followed. Wisdom for Isocrates was something to be assigned by the Athenian people, not something to be demonstrated rationally. Because past cases of *phronēsis* are only those which have been received as such by the Athenians, he regarded them as providing sufficient standards for others to follow—concrete ways of identifying how political deliberation in Athens had through competition and debate reached instances of excellence. It is these instantiations of excellence in political deliberation that constitute for Isocrates models for others to imitate, at once standards for and outcomes of political practices.

Like the Sophists, Isocrates positioned *doxai* in the community without imposing an external standard for discriminating among them—be it Plato's knowledge of the divine or Aristotle's glimpses of it. Unlike the Sophists, he did not address the epistemological tensions created by the gap between individual and common experience. Rather he saw knowledge as the common property of the community, the totality of collective experience, and the outcome of shared *logos*. Far more conservative than the Sophists, Isocrates placed his faith on the conventions of the community and took for granted the truth value of the language of the community's traditions. Yet this conservatism was tempered by his belief in the constitutive function of language, the power of *logos* to constitute human experience and thereby to redirect it. Through *logos*, the very conventions that propped up communal *doxai* as collective truths would eventually come under pressure, lose their stability, and become subject to refinement, redefinition, and change.

His pedagogy in the constitutive power of *logos* thus created the possibility for guiding the community rhetorically by reconstituting its conventional *doxai* and by redefining its traditional truths. In other words, he placed our humanity in the ambiguous and indeterminate character of the community and gambled on the humanizing potential of *logos* (*Nicocles* 5–9) as a sufficient guide to human progress. Making students wise, in the sense of enabling them to direct the *polis* to new possibilities of human progress, was the overriding purpose behind Isocrates' rhetorical training and civic education—the crux of his *philosophia*. Committed to a program which

grounded itself on concrete examples of past excellence and sought the convergence of *eu legein* and *eu phronein* in political deliberation, Isocrates
taught his students to engage conventional *doxai* rhetorically, to display
their finessing of tradition artistically, and to trust the community to determine the merit of their professed wisdom. In other words, his program in
philosophia entailed instruction in the process of enacting *phronēsis* rhetorically and performatively. The spirit of this instruction is made evident in
the *Panegyricus*, where Isocrates provides us with a specific case of the rhetorical performance of *phronēsis*.

Reconstituting Communal *Doxai*

Isocrates opens the *Panegyricus* by announcing his intent to counsel the
city: "I have come before you to give my counsels on the war against the
barbarians and on concord among ourselves." Convinced that the judgment
he is about to render will be beneficial to the city and, as a result, deserving
a degree of recognition from the community, he will be content, he claims,
to receive whatever measure of fame would be due to him. I am certain, he
remarks, "that I shall have a sufficient reward in the approbation (δόξαν)
which my discourse will itself command" (3). Through this dramatic opening, Isocrates assumes the role of a wise person speaking to the community.
What may appear to us as hubristic is a necessary practice for him, if he is
to perform his civic duty. For it was according to this practice, dating back
to the days of Solon, that governing officials devoting themselves to the
"care of the commonwealth" and acting "as servants of the people" felt "entitled to receive commendation if they proved faithful to their trust, and
content[ed] themselves with this honor" (*Areopagiticus* 26–27). In assuming this role, Isocrates sees himself as meeting his part of the contract that
bounded city and citizens together. Ever since the beginning of democracy,
giving wise counsel to the city was a way of fulfilling one's civic obligations
and of rendering the kind of service that a public servant was expected to.[8]
Acting in recognition of the service it received, the city was obliged, in turn,
to dispense to her public servants whatever reputation they might deserve
—which oftentimes resulted in great wealth as well. It is "owing to the exercise of good and wise judgment (φρονίμως βουλεύσασθαι), [that past
leaders] have attained great wealth and good reputation (δόξας) (*Panathenaicus* 196).

According to Isocrates, guiding the community's *doxa* necessitated a change from within. It required that one situate oneself before the community in accordance to its traditions, assume the position of a civic servant, and offer one's reputation up to the judgment of the *polis*. It also required engaging conventional wisdom, not merely proposing—as his predecessors had done—a course of action. Speakers in the past, he remarked, had similarly advised us to "compose our enmities against each other and turn against the barbarian, rehearsing the misfortunes which have come upon us from our mutual warfare and the advantages which will result from a campaign against our natural enemy" (15). The difference between their advice and his was a difference in the point of departure: "these men do speak the truth, but they do not start at the point from which they could best bring these things to pass" (15). With this remark, Isocrates points to the beginning of *Panegyricus*, the section in praise of Athens, as the place in which he actively engages communal *doxa*. While orators before him had advocated panhellenism solely in terms of a political proposal, he brings the notion of panhellenism in contact with the community's most celebrated traditions and advocates its significance through the city's most time-honored legacies. The proper site of his wise judgment in the *Panegyricus* is the display of Athens' greatness: it is in the process of displaying the city's glory that his wisdom becomes exhibited.

As Isocrates' portrayal of Athens indicates, the engagement of the community's *doxai* obtains through a dialectic exchange with the past. His glorification of the city revolves around Pericles' famous portrayal of Athens as a school of Hellas. Isocrates considered this portrayal as a sign of his predecessor's *phronēsis* and as a cause for his lasting reputation among the Athenians. He undoubtedly saw Pericles as capturing through this portrayal the essential difference between the Athenian and the Spartan ways of life, and as directing Athenians' perceptions of themselves as just defendants of a great empire. Instead of merely imitating a past case of *phronēsis*, Isocrates engages it creatively. He crafts onto his predecessor's analogy of Athens as a school of Hellas an enduring bond among the Hellenes and a great divide between them and the Persians: Athens' "pupils have become the teachers of the rest of the world" and "the title 'Hellenes' is applied rather to those who share our culture than to those who share a common blood" (50).

The cultural links Pericles had named as binding Athenians and their allies together are refigured here rhetorically, and in a way that forges a symbolic unification among all the cities of Hellas, including Sparta and its allied states. Relying on and at the same time changing Pericles' wise words, Isocrates creates the perception of Athens as having been unified with all Greek city-states from the very beginning, and thereby makes this perception part and parcel of Athens' glorious history. As a result of this rhetorical engagement of conventional wisdom, current concerns about panhellenism find their way into the city's timeless traditions. Capitalizing on the propensity of epideictic language to amplify and to augment, Isocrates finesses the stable *doxa* of the community and enlarges its boundaries so as to accommodate the less stable *doxa* of the present.

Pericles had spoken about the Athenian empire as an inheritance from the previous generation, and had presented the need to defend it as an inherent trait of Athenians of all generations from the very beginning— to leave their city better and stronger than the way they had inherited it (II: 36,1). Isocrates took this brief reference to the past and, following other funeral orators, built around it a lengthy narrative of Athens' glorious accomplishments, a laudatory recount of its legendary and actual exploits in the recent and mythical past. Far from an ineffective pastiche of received commonplaces, the laudatory account of Athens' history represented for him the combined outcome of an orator's linguistic craft and of a wise person's judgment: "For the deeds of the past are, indeed, an inheritance common to us all; but the ability to make proper use of them at the appropriate time, to conceive the right sentiments about them in each instance, and to set them forth in finished phrase, is the peculiar gift of the wise, εὖ φρονούντων" (9). Isocrates clearly saw himself as having the ability to set Athens' past glory in a narrative that reflected current concerns and acquired contemporary significance. In his retelling of the past, the few voices advocating panhellenism in his day blended together with conventional thought and became authoritative voices of tradition—ways of being in the future illuminated by history.

Combining a display of the city with a political proposal for the city, Isocrates presented the Athenians with what he regarded as the highest form of political discourse, one that "deals with the greatest affairs and, while best displaying the ability of those who speak, brings most profit to those who hear" (4). This is a new version of rhetoric, one that blends together the epideictic and the political genres and relies as a result for its success not only on the speaker's persuasive arguments but also on the auditors' identification with their past experiences as constituted by the speaker. In this version of rhetoric, where identification is as important as persuasion, epideictic oratory assumes an equal footing with political argumenta-tion, and *logos politikos* becomes inextricably linked with artistic perfor-mance. When the orator's performance with language takes as its subject matter the community's collective experiences with past values, traditions, and commitments, the excess of the orator's *epideixis* spills over to the space of politics and the domain of advocacy. Conversely, when political discourse grounds persuasion on a prior constitution of the community's past experi-ences, the tone of advocacy is already nuanced by rhetorical performance. Because in this version of *logos politikos* political judgment becomes indis-tinguishable from rhetorical performance, the orator's wise exercise of *doxa* (as judgment) can indeed coincide with the orator's *doxa* (as reputation). This at least is what Isocrates had hoped for, namely, that his reputation as a wise person and a great orator would converge in the Athenians' reception of his political judgment.

Notes

1. I wish to thank Pennsylvania State University Press for giving me permission to reproduce parts of my essay "Isocrates' Use of *doxa*," *Philosophy and Rhetoric* 34: 1, 2001: 61–78.

2. "δóκoς ne désigne pas un acte intellectuel dévalué a priori sous le rapport de la vérité . . . En vérité, nous avons affaire à deux modes de connaissance qui se distinguent en fonction de la réalité particulière que chacun vise à appréhender—le ⟨visible⟩ et l'⟨invisible⟩. Ils sont déterminés de telle sorte qu'il n'y a pas entre eux plus ou moins de valeur objective, mais une sécurité plus ou moins grande pour celui qui les met en oevre" (50–51).

3. For a discussion on the philosophical and religious sects in the sixth century, see Detienne (1996): 119ff.

4. For Gorgias' position on *doxa*, and its inability to maintain a stable position due to the workings of *kairos*, see White (1987), especially the first chapter.

5. A similar manner of handling ambiguity seems to be suggested by Protagoras' fragment "to make the weaker argument the stronger" which, as Schiappa (1991) argues, "is best un-derstood as companion to the two-*logoi* fragment" (107). Whether the weaker-stronger fragment is regarded as supporting Protagoras' relativistic views or, according to Schiappa, as indicating Protagoras' acknowledgment of a weaker and a stronger *logos* (109–110), ei-ther way, a triumph of one position over another is made possible by the intervention of persuasion.

6. Herodotus reported the myth according to which Mnesiphilus, the first Sophist, offered crucial advice to Themistocles on the eve before the battle at Salamis, who used it "as it were of his own devising" to persuade the other generals (*Persian Wars* 8.58).

7. For a comparison of Isocrates' practical notion of *phronēsis* with Aristotle's theoretical no-tion of *phronēsis*, see Schwarze.

8. See Clark on the Isocratean orator as public servant.

PART TWO

Isocrates and the Sophists

3

JOHN POULAKOS

Rhetoric and Civic Education:
From the Sophists to Isocrates

STARTING WITH the age of the Sophists, civic education in the Greek world assumed a distinctly rhetorical character.[1] What made it rhetorical was its focus as well as its scope and goal. Its focus was on *logos*, that instrumentality which influences human thought and directs human action. Its scope included primarily the affairs of the city-state and the ways in which they can be addressed, debated, and resolved. And its goal was the complete citizen, the citizen who can speak persuasively. For the most part, rhetorical education assumed that men are capable of persuasion and subject to it. It also posited that they can be taught to contribute to the vitality and character of their city-state by formulating and observing its norms, making and obeying its laws, serving and critiquing its institutions. Rhetorical education regarded the citizen as both a source and an effect of rhetorical discourse.

Despite these central understandings, early rhetorical education was far from uniform. Competing and conflicting claims about subject matter, methods, and results are evident in the fragmentary materials of the Sophists.[2] But these differences are not as important as those we encounter when we move from the Sophists to Isocrates. In this essay, I highlight one of the differences between them and him and attempt to explain it historically. Specifically, I show that whereas the Sophists held a *dynastic* conception of *logos*, Isocrates maintained a *hegemonic* one. This difference, I argue, can be explained by reference to three key moments in the period spanning the second half of the fifth century B.C. and the first half of the fourth. The initial moment concerns the emergence of the democratic city-state (and how it occasioned a dispersed pluralism followed by attempts to unify the Hellenic world). The second discusses the establishment of Isocrates' school (and how it changed rhetorical education from a tutorial enterprise to an institutional arrangement). And the third discusses the growth of writing (and how it afforded new possibilities for rhetorical discourse). These three moments furnish us with the background against which we can understand an important transformation in the early history of civic education.

The Sophists' dynastic conceptualization of logos finds expression partially in Protagoras' announced pedagogical goal: "the one who studies with me will learn to exercise sound judgment in political affairs, showing how he may be most powerful (δυνατώτατος) in conducting the business of the city both in speech and action" (*Protagoras* 318e–319a).[3] The same conception is also implicit in Thrasymachus' proposition that justice is nothing else than the advantage of the stronger (τὸ τοῦ κρείττονος συμφέρον) (*Republic* 338c).[4] But the most explicit articulation is to be found in Gorgias' view of *logos* as an overpowering force against which one cannot easily resist (*Encomium of Helen* 8–14).[5] In all cases, the point is twofold: first, *logos* itself is a powerful medium; second, those who know how to handle it effectively can themselves become powerful in their society.

The difference between this sophistical notion and its Isocratean counterpart becomes apparent when we juxtapose two well-known passages with explicit remarks about *logos:* Gorgias' *Encomium of Helen* 8–14 and Isocrates' *Nicocles* 5–9.[6] In the first passage, *logos* is portrayed as a δυνάστης (lord, master, ruler), in the *second* as an ἡγεμών (guide, authority, leader, commander, chief). Both of these anthropomorphic characterizations acknowledge the authority of *logos*. But while Gorgias stresses its power to exert influence over people, Isocrates emphasizes its ability to lead them to worthwhile ends. Both rhetoricians recognize people's susceptibility to and capacity for persuasion. But whereas Gorgias dwells on *logos'* psychological impact on the individual,[7] Isocrates underscores its civilizing influence on society. While the meanings of the two terms can be said to overlap, they nevertheless differ in tendency. As used by Gorgias, the term δυνάστης highlights the power of language to impose, to undermine, to violate, to deceive, and to distort. For his part, Isocrates uses the term ἡγεμών to underscore *logos'* capacity to collect, to unify, to lead, to shape, and to facilitate.

That the above two conceptualizations should be so is not surprising if we consider both their narrower and broader textual context. First, each conceptualization is consistent with the speech in and through which it is expressed. To prove Helen's innocence, Gorgias depicts *logos* as an overpowering force against which she could not resist: "What cause then prevents the conclusion that Helen . . . against her will, might have come under the influence of speech, just as if ravished by the force of the mighty?" (12). For his part, Isocrates makes the case for monarchy by asserting that *logos* constitutes the foundation of its existence and the promise of its welfare: "I regard those [discourses] as the best and most worthy of a king . . . which teach how men in power (δυναστεύοντας) should deal with the people, and how the rank and file should be disposed to their rulers. For I observe that it is through such discourses that states attain the highest prosperity and greatness" (10).

Second, each conceptualization is consistent with the tenor of its author's broader rhetoric. As a prominent member of the sophistic movement, Gorgias was one of those responsible for challenging the cultural domination of poetry via the dynasty of *logos*, a dynasty invested with seemingly unlimited powers. How these powers could be deployed is evident in his three preserved works (*Encomium of Helen, Defense of Palamedes*, and *On Non-Being* or *On Nature*). All three illustrate well the power of rhetoric to undo prevailing views or to make the weaker argument stronger: the *Helen* is an attempt to dispel the bad reputation of a woman, the *Palamedes* to dismiss the charges against a traitor, and the *On Non-Being* to disprove the self-evident "is-ness" of being. On the other hand, Isocrates seems to have accepted the dynastic notion of *logos* but to have been more interested in its potential for beneficial results and less in its awesome powers. Accordingly, his rhetoric consists of arguments for a panhellenic awareness, arguments to replace war with peace, social chaos with order, and political weakness with strength. His better known works (*Panegyricus, Antidosis, On the Peace, To Philip, Panathenaicus*) are designed to end the political turmoil and intellectual disorientation of the times, to harmonize individual and collective purposes, and to restore Hellas' sense of greatness.

From Pluralism to Pan-Hellenism

It is well known that the constitutional reforms of Cleisthenes in Athens were successful in replacing other forms of governance (i.e., aristocracy, tyranny) with democracy. But even after his reforms, tyrannical and aristocratic politics did not go away. Athens, for instance, managed to become the strongest power in the Hellenic world largely by virtue of her tyrannical policies toward her allies, violating their sovereignty, enslaving their population, and controlling their affairs. Inside Athens, reputedly the most democratic of the Hellenic city-states, there was no guarantee against tyranny. As the short-lived rule of the Thirty Tyrants in 404 B.C. attests, Athenians were not immune to tyrannical practices which included the closing of the rhetorical schools, the persecution of intellectuals, the confiscation of personal property, banishments, and executions.[8] Even those who had acquired power within the city-state by more "legitimate" means were not beyond the abuses of authority, a fact that gave rise to discourses praising aristocratic rule, most notably Plato's *Republic*.[9]

The above account suggests that from the exercise of tyrannical politics to the dynastic notion of logos was only a short distance. The distance becomes even shorter if we recall that the *"logos-dunastēs"* formulation was made by Gorgias, who, like most Leontinians, must have been quite familiar with the tyrannical rule of Gelon and Hieron at nearby Syracuse. Basically Gorgias argued that, like the typical tyrant, a specific form of *logos* rises to power by asserting itself and ousting its predecessor (*Helen* 13). Once in power, it employs its ways of deceiving (8, 10), constraining (12), frightening (9, 14), or even killing its subjects (14) until it is overturned by a more powerful *logos*. As the case of Helen illustrates, *logos* is a dynastic force that can determine the destiny of any one person in decisive ways.

Beyond this analogy, the dynastic notion of *logos* finds historical warrant and further explanation in the pattern of the politics of thought in the latter half of the fifth century. On that front, the sophistic movement exposed the arbitrariness and exploited the vulnerability of the traditional legacies of the culture. This movement amounted to a rhetorical revolt in which new and stronger *logoi* challenged established systems of belief while imposing new ones. Under the new logocracy, man was declared the measure of all things (*Protagoras*), the gods were portrayed as clever human fabrications designed to serve the purposes of social control (*Critias*), being was shown to be on an equal footing with non-being (*Gorgias*), and justice was defined not as obedience to laws but as the interest of the stronger (*Thrasymachus*). By virtue of the force of these new understandings, *logos* emerged as the new dynast by dethroning the traditionally "stronger" arguments and installing in their place "weaker" ones, which is to say, by undercutting itself. In one sense, logos deposed the tyranny of the tradition; in another, it imposed the tyranny of innovation. In both senses, it reflected and induced the aforementioned changes, thus prompting Gorgias' characterization "great *dunastēs*."

Naturally, these developments were not without consequences. As limited democracy replaced tyranny and as the sophistic movement shook the intellectual foundations of the culture, a plurality of forces came to the fore. Governing, no longer a one-man proposition, involved many people. In many states, propertied elites, merchants, workers, intellectuals, and aliens represented political interests to be reckoned with. The same trend toward pluralization obtained in interstate politics as Athens, having surrendered her claims to supremacy after the Peloponnesian War, was reduced to only one of several lesser powers. Likewise, in economics the once self-sufficient city-state yielded to the need for interstate and international commerce. As wealth, previously concentrated in one or two cities, became more evenly distributed, several states emerged as economic powers. Culture, too, once gathered primarily in Athens, was now being spread throughout Hellas by traveling Sophists, artists, and book merchants.

Not surprisingly, the consequences of pluralization included a spirit of competition and conflict. In the political sphere, several states attempted to assume the leadership of Hellas but all failed. Internally, they proved unable to unite the various factions within their borders. With each state and each faction looking after its own interests and disregarding the consequences, the result was prolonged strife within and war between the states. On the social level, the chasm between the rich and the poor widened while litigation increased considerably. Unable to meet the people's material and sociopolitical needs, the state could no longer command their unquestioned loyalty.

Interest in the state declined while interest in the individual grew. In thought, the deposition of the intellectual tradition led to the emergence of so many perspectives on and explanations about the world that soon nothing seemed universally valid. Excessive pluralization in all departments of life had precipitated a crisis of disunity and disaffection with traditional authority. Hence Isocrates' hegemonic notion of *logos* was presupposed by and inspired his project of panhellenic unification. Conceived hegemonically, *logos* could forge a new vision of cooperation and ὁμόνοια (likemindedness). The political adventures and intellectual experiments of the fifth century had unsettled the culture, sending it in search of new forms of consensus and stability. More than an epideictic address on *logos*, then, *Nicocles* (5–9) can be regarded as a promise of stability or a call to unification meant to reverse the results of excessive pluralization. Clearly, the changes in the political and intellectual domains of the times warranted the change from the dynastic to the hegemonic notion of logos.

Which of the two notions is superior is not at issue here. Both are historically grounded formulations describing ways in which rhetoric functions. In the case of the Sophists, the primary function of *logos* is critical. In this capacity, it often operates so as to create a crisis by casting doubt on and overthrowing the established realities. Whenever it does this successfully, *logos* stimulates the impulse to undermine what is actual and thus create new possibilities (*Helen:* 13). In the case of Isocrates, the principal function of *logos* is constructive (συγκατασκευάσας) (*Nicocles* 6). Insofar as it can shape social reality, logos works so as to build necessary institutions and create human communities held together by commonly shaped beliefs. When successful in doing so, *logos* articulates what eventually becomes accepted and stimulates the impulse to affirm and stabilize.

From Tutorial to Institutional Arrangements

At the level of the conceptualization of *logos*, then, Isocrates departed from the sophistical view. As I have shown, a plausible explanation for his departure can be had by considering the changes in the political and intellectual domains of the period. But if it be granted that politics and education are interrelated, a further explanation can be advanced, this time by exploring the differences between the sophistical and Isocratean educational practices. In this section, I submit that each notion of *logos* is supported by a different approach to and purpose of rhetorical education.

Like the older Sophists, Isocrates taught rhetoric. But while they had traveled from city to city to teach the new *technē*, he opened a school in Athens and had students travel there to attend (*Antidosis* 87–88; 224; 226). With this new arrangement rhetoric stopped being a nomadic show on the road and was given for the first time an institutional home. Athens had been familiar with the rhetorical education of the Sophists; but wherever they were going they were taking their lessons and performances along. Students interested in a sustained study of rhetoric but unable to follow the master's trail had to wait for his next visit. While itinerant teachers could only provide short-term, discontinuous instruction, the opening of Isocrates' school offered a stable setting in which the art of discourse could be studied at length and without prolonged interruptions. The new institutional setting meant more than uninterrupted study in a central location. It meant, first, that the art the Sophists had imported as a novelty had now entered the mainstream culture; as such, it needed to concern itself more with the enhancement of its status and less with the search for legitimacy. Rhetoric had to compete now with other forms of education, mainly philosophical, achieve high levels of excellence, and produce meaningful results. Second, it meant that a "prolonged and systematic course of instruction [could] be organized, instead of the cramming system to which itinerant teachers, however brilliant, necessarily tended."[10] Third, it meant that the student's relation to the school was more formal than the master-pupil relationship. There was less chance now that a clever student would turn the tables on an institution as Tisias had turned them on Corax. Fourth, and perhaps most important, it meant that rhetoric had to attend to the affairs of the state. Insofar as the new school purported to prepare students for the trials of public life, it had to keep the state's pulse in mind. In all four cases, Isocrates deviated from the sophistical enterprise by initiating a new challenge: how to institutionalize rhetorical education and how to specify its future direction.

Prior to this new challenge, the Sophists had promised to arm the interested citizen with the rhetorical equipment necessary "to become a real power in the city" (*Protagoras* 318e–319a). By contrast, Isocrates' own promise was to turn his students into insightful governors or responsible citizens. This difference is not to be traced to two different "philosophies" of education. Each program was mainly a response to the political conditions of its own epoch. The Sophists' program had grown out of the need to fill the seats of political institutions created by the political reforms (e.g., the Assembly, the courts). Theirs was a program driven by demand and designed to satisfy personal ambition. By contrast, the Isocratean program sought to compensate for the lack of enlightened statesmanship and mindful citizenship apparent throughout Hellas in the aftermath of the Peloponnesian War. Departing from the sophistical program, Isocrates linked rhetoric to the articulation of wise governance and civic conscience. Clearly, each program sought to fulfill a specific need: whereas the sophistical had construed rhetoric as the key to social survival and political prominence, the Isocratean turned it into an expression of and a guide to panhellenic welfare.

Although the Sophists did not have a common approach to rhetorical education, their differences can be understood as variations of a central theme: the command of *logos* is the means par excellence to personal and political power. This logocentric premise did not purport to spell out what one should do once in power; it only asserted the potency of *logos* to influence people's thoughts and direct their deeds. Accordingly, the sophists taught the properties of language, the rules of its operation, the possibilities of its structure, and the conditions of its impact. Their instruction specified neither purpose nor subject matter. For them, rhetoric was a formal, not a moral issue. Their chief task was to empower, not to enlighten. Once their students had mastered rhetoric, the road to personal effectiveness and political prominence was supposedly wide open.

Naturally, this practice and its implicit rationale left the question of the proper use of rhetoric unanswered. But unlike Plato's decidedly moralistic response, Isocrates' answer took a more practical turn. Committed to the proposition that the art of persuasion must be put to beneficial uses, he introduced two new requirements to rhetorical education: the thematic and the pragmatic. The thematic requirement asked that rhetoric concentrate on significant themes while the pragmatic demanded that it make a positive contribution to the life of the audience (*Panegyricus* 189; *Helen* 12; *Nicocles* 10). Both requirements were introduced to counter two questionable rhetorical practices (supposedly the result of sophistical education): disinterested verbal exhibitionism and the unscrupulous pursuit of personal advantage. Isocrates seems to have reasoned that rhetoric could not be fully justified or function meaningfully on aesthetic grounds alone. Eloquence for its own sake was for him a misplaced priority in a culture striving to come to terms with its political urgencies and civic irresolutions. Similarly, a self-serving rhetoric was often blind to the needs of a society searching for its center of gravity. For him, what was needed was a rhetoric that preserved the element of performative eloquence, without neglecting the major issues of the day or the audience's welfare. As he put it in *Panegyricus* 4, [t]he "highest kind of rhetoric [is] that which deals with the greatest affairs and, while best displaying the ability of those who speak, brings most benefit to those who hear."

As already suggested, Isocrates' rhetorical program was mainly an antidote designed to cure the Hellenic maladies of the early fourth century. In an age of intense individualism, the command of *logos* was often put in the service of reprehensible ends (*Nicocles* 2). The failings of the city-state were reinforcing the perception that the happiness of the individual was at odds with that of the state; it soon became apparent that being a good citizen did not amount to being a successful or happy person. Isocrates tried to reverse this perception by positing a fundamental interdependence between personal and public well-being. This reversal turned into a powerful argument for his school, which needed a raison d'être. Against the background of a lack of capable and loyal public servants, he could claim that his school was dedicated to educating men to see beyond their selfish ambition for power and to serve both Athens and Hellas with honor and distinction. To support this claim, he boasts that no other contemporary educator could produce as impressive a list of students who "had spent large sums of their private fortunes upon the city" (*Antidosis* 93–94).

The changes in the scope and purpose of rhetorical education went hand in hand with a change in the materials of rhetoric. The Sophists had derived much of their material from the treasures of mythology and poetry, a practice Isocrates did not altogether abandon. But whereas they had tended to stay within the mythopoetic tradition, he used its tales for analogical and illustrative purposes. With Isocrates, rhetoric began moving further from the poetical past and closer to the political present. Its focus began to shift from the adventures of the heroes to the affairs of the citizens. Similarly, its primary materials started coming not only from the storehouse of Hellas' poetic heritage but also from the commonly held notions of the Athenian public. This change was due less to personal preferences and more to situational differences. The Sophists emerged as a professional class at a time when poetry was still the chief means of inculcating cultural values.

Preserving parts of the very tradition they were attempting to change, they found in poetry ready-made, familiar stories from which they could extract useful themes and to which they could give new interpretative twists. Besides the mythological materials, there was precious little from which they could choose. As itinerants, they had neither intimate familiarity with nor deep loyalty to the politics of the host cities; and as alien residents they were disallowed from addressing the assembly on political issues. Insofar as they were limited to speaking at state-sponsored events and to giving private lessons, their public rhetoric had to be necessarily ceremonial while their private lessons had to be tailored to the personal interests of their students. By contrast, Isocrates came into prominence during a period of decline in poetry, growth in history, and instability in politics. After he abandoned the logographer's trade, he drew themes for his rhetorical compositions from current sociopolitical issues as well as from the glorious past of Athens and Hellas. He cultivated a new line of thought according to which rhetoric is at its finest when addressing common matters, not personal concerns.

Clearly, the Sophists' rhetorical education was dynastic in two senses: first, it undermined the existing foundations of belief by unleashing *logos'* formidable powers against the dominant institutions of the culture, and second, it empowered a new class of people by teaching them public eloquence. Although their curriculum was neither systematic nor comprehensive, they promoted successfully the close connection between well-crafted *logoi* and the acquisition of power. At the same time, they cultivated the skeptical attitude, an attitude informed by the principle of *dissoi logoi*. In contradistinction, Isocrates' rhetorical education was hegemonic in the sense that it attempted to harness the perilous powers of logos institutionally. His school became a place in which rhetoric could be housed and put in the service of his campaign for a panhellenic consciousness. Under his initiative, Hellas' sociopolitical problems were to be examined thoughtfully and solved so as to benefit all Hellenes. Unlike his predecessors who had shown how rhetorical prowess can help an individual citizen rise above the masses, he posited that rhetoric's fundamental mission is to unify divided political communities by articulating desirable visions and specifying common goals.

From Speaking to Writing

Thus far I have argued that if the dynastic and hegemonic notions of logos are seen as outcomes of the conditions in the fifth and fourth centuries respectively, the difference between the two can be explained by considering significant changes in politics and education. But since any notion of language is partly determined by the way in which discourse is produced and disseminated, the difference between the two notions cannot be fully explained without some reference to the technology of the word during that same period. In what follows, I propose that each notion was tied to a corresponding mode of the word: the dynastic was better accommodated by the spoken whereas the hegemonic was better suited to the written.

It is well known that the growth of writing constitutes a significant marker of the transition from the fifth century to the fourth. By mid-fourth century, writing had taken firm roots in the soil of an oral culture. Even so, it was still regarded as an innovation and, as such, with suspicion. The primacy of the spoken word was asserted again and again by such figures as Alcidamas, Plato, and Aristotle. Isocrates found himself at the center of this critical transition as he had to come to terms with his own vocal weakness on the one hand and the popular sentiment against written rhetoric on the other. In his *To Philip*, he acknowledges that there is much difference "in persuasiveness between discourses which are spoken and those which are to be read, and that all men have assumed that the former are delivered on subjects which are important and urgent, while the latter are composed for display and personal gain" (25). After this allusion to his dilemma as a writer, he asks the Macedonian king to put "aside the prejudices . . . against speeches which are composed to be read," and read his discourse with an open mind.

Despite the negative attitude against writing, rhetoric became increasingly written during Isocrates' lifetime. Even before him, the Sophists had done some writing in the form of handbooks of rhetoric, model speeches, and forensic orations for their clients' day in court. Still, the Sophists owed their notoriety to their oral performances before small gatherings of interested spectators, or larger audiences in state functions. By contrast, Isocrates became famous for his written works (*Antidosis* 87). Lacking the daring and the strong voice needed in the public arena, he turned into a writing orator whose very compositions functioned as arguments for producing, studying and practicing rhetoric in the written mode. Unlike its oral counterpart, written rhetoric could escape the eventfulness of public performance, transcend the demands of local audiences, and avoid the evanescence of orality. In and through these new possibilities, it could help the cause of Isocrates' panhellenic agenda.

Spoken rhetoric can be understood to have contributed to the dynastic notion of *logos* in several ways. First, it seemed to be omnipotent in manipulating and swaying crowds. An accomplished orator could turn out cleverly poeticized phrases and captivate his listeners, who were often caught into the collective kind of mindlessness known as "mob psychology." At least in theory, the Periclean democratic reforms had opened up public spaces in which the voice of the citizens could be heard. But judging from actual rhetorical events, it was the voice of the orators that benefited most from these reforms. Specifically, it was their voice that was most often heard and thought to be moving people to action, making them think guilty or innocent, telling them to vote for war or peace. For their part, the gathered masses seemed incapable of resisting the power and charm of the orators' words. Effectively, the orator became democracy's δυνάστης as his will was imposed on and made to appear identical with the will of the people. Second, because oral rhetoric had to adapt to the interests of local audiences, it helped perpetuate their provincial values by maintaining differences between one city-state and another. Any changes resulting from the orators' promptings were mostly confined within the borders of a single state without any chance of bringing several states together.

If this is so, oral rhetoric functioned so as to keep each city-state isolated from the rest. While it is unlikely that this is what the orators had in mind, their rhetoric nevertheless took the form of a force promoting division, a typical tactic of political tyranny. Seen in this light, the Sophists' declamations on the need for panhellenic unity could hardly have succeeded. Third, spoken rhetoric was bound to the possibilities and limitations of oral-aural communication; by virtue of its phonocentric character, it was evanescent and unreliable. Lacking materiality, it was fated to vanish as soon as it was uttered; and despite the mnemonic devices the orators had borrowed from the poets (meter, rhythm, and highly formalized tropes and figures), oral rhetoric could only serve the purposes of immediacy. What was said one day could not be trusted to hold the next. The same orator could say now one thing, now its exact opposite. Consistency and noncontradiction in speech were to be observed only to the degree that the memory of what was said dictated. Clearly, spoken rhetoric had a distinctly dynastic character. Like the proverbial tyrant, it was powerful, and not especially reliable.

In contrast to its oral counterpart, written rhetoric contributed to the hegemonic notion of *logos*. To begin with, writing brought about what Havelock calls the "silent revolution."[11] This revolution reversed the order of the experience of oral rhetoric by making the word visible and its impact invisible. The orator-writer could still turn out poeticized phrases, but these now amounted to phonic vestiges, inscribed signs of elegance unable to arouse and affect audiences directly and immediately. If we are to rely on and generalize from Isocrates' rhetorical compositions, writing invited readers to follow arguments, not cadences; it solicited their thoughtful responses, not their participation in ritualized public performances. In so doing, it asked them to put aside their localistic pride, read his texts, and ponder the possibility of a unified Hellas.

Spoken rhetoric could address only a small circle of people at a time, a circle defined by the radius of the orator's voice. But since texts can travel further than the human voice, Isocrates' written addresses can be said to have aimed simultaneously at a geographically broader audience, one that included distant readers throughout the Hellenic world. Even so, the low level of literacy in the fourth century suggests that the number of people addressed by his message must have been quite limited. Isocrates seems less concerned with this than with the fact that speaking to the masses is virtually useless when it comes to serious projects like panhellenism. As he puts it, "to burden our national assemblies with oratory and to address all the people there thronged together is, in reality, to address no one at all" (*To Philip* 12).

Although Isocrates had to take into account a greater diversity of opinion and sensibility than a local orator, his written rhetoric was directed primarily to those few who could make a difference (*To Philip* 13). Unlike a local audience of listeners, a national audience of readers required a rhetoric broad enough to encompass a wider range of political orientations. More importantly, it demanded a rhetoric focusing on matters of enduring rather than ephemeral character. To the extent that such a rhetoric could be produced, it could go beyond the boundaries of a single *polis* and turn many local assemblies into a single national audience. More precisely, it could change Athenians, Spartans, Thebans, and Argives into the Hellenes of Athens, Sparta, Thebes, and Argos. In other words, it could transcend provincial concerns and forge what was truly Hellenic. For Isocrates, this transformation could be accomplished through writing. Because writing did away with the requirement of presence, it could offer readers some detachment from local loyalties by addressing them privately, thus affording them time for contemplation and study (*Evagoras:* 76). In so doing, it could overcome the biggest obstacle against panhellenism, "the particularism and authority of the *polis*."[12]

Written rhetoric could last, finally, as long as the material on which it was inscribed lasted and as long as future readers found its message relevant. By virtue of its textual character, it acquired a high degree of permanence and reliability, carrying the written message intact and diminishing the need for a strong memory. Isocrates' *Antidosis*, a text citing large sections from five previous speeches, is a case in point. Once limited by the evanescence of speech, the demands of immediacy, and the unreliability of human memory, rhetoric could now secure a place in posterity and serve the needs of the future by putting its trust on the durability of textual materials and the human care to preserve the artifacts of the past.

Conclusion

Having examined briefly the ways in which rhetoric was conceptualized, taught, and produced during a period of approximately one hundred years, I have shown that the rhetoric of Isocrates differs appreciably from that of the Sophists. The major difference I have identified is one of direction in force: sophistical rhetoric was centrifugal, the rhetoric of Isocrates centripetal. The Sophists operated in a relatively more stable culture, a culture ready to receive and live out the implications of what was handed down. Sophistical rhetoric challenged the uncritical acceptance of the tradition, and became instrumental in demythologizing the legacies of the culture and in activating people's potential to question the way things are thought to be. With its center in doubt, the culture shifted its attention to the periphery, where the rhetorical revolution was taking place. Predicated on the dynastic notion of *logos*, and the tutorial enterprise of teaching eloquence, this revolution persuaded the culture to rethink its categories. But in a predominately phonocentric world, such rethinking could go only as far as the oral technology of the word allowed.

Unlike the Sophists, Isocrates found himself in a dispersed culture, one plagued with the ills inherent in excessive individuation — conflicting claims and competing interests. His reaction to this state of affairs manifested itself in a rhetoric pointing away from the periphery and towards a center. At this center, there lay arguments for the need of leaders, the importance of rhetorical education, the benefits of political stability, and the advantages of panhellenism. Supported by his hegemonic notion of *logos*, the opening of his school, and the growth of writing, these arguments provided the counterforce to the forces of dissociation and paved the way for the dawning of a new age: the age of empire.

Notes

1. I wish to thank the publishers of *Texte* for giving me permission to reproduce parts of my essay "Early Changes in Rhetorical Practice and Understanding: From the Sophists to Isocrates," 1989 (nos. 8–9): 307–324.

2. Consider, for example, Protagoras' claim that sets him apart from other Sophists: "Hippocrates, if he comes to me, will not be treated as he would have been if he had joined the classes of an ordinary Sophist. The generality of them maltreat the young; for when they have escaped from the arts they bring them back against their will and force them into arts, teaching them arithmetic and astronomy and geometry and music (and here he glanced at Hippia); whereas, if he applies to me, he will learn precisely and solely that for which he has come," (*Protagoras* 318d–318e).

3. See translation by Lamb 1977.

4. See translation by Shorey (Plato 1982).

5. See Sprague 1972. All subsequent references to Gorgias and other Sophists are to this edition.

6. See translations by Norlin and van Hook 1968–1982.

7. For a comprehensive discussion of Gorgias' view of rhetoric, see Segal 1962: 99–155.

8. For an elaboration on this claim, see Wilcox 1942.

9. For an insightful discussion of the three main forms of government (aristocracy, oligarchy, monarchy) and the cultural attitudes toward them in the fifth and fourth centuries, see David Konstan's essay in this volume.

10. Field 1930.

11. Havelock 1963: 41.

12. Heilbrunn 1975: 160.

4

EKATERINA HASKINS

Logos and Power in Sophistical
and Isocratean Rhetoric

JOHN POULAKOS has stressed the historical and situational discontinuity between sophistical and Isocratean visions of rhetoric. As he has
pointed out, the difference between Gorgias' and Isocrates' terms for *logos*
—*dunastēs* versus *hēgemōn*—indicates radically divergent perspectives on
the relationship between rhetoric and power. Gorgias exposes *logos* in its
untamed arbitrariness that is akin to a tyrant's lack of accountability and direction in dealing out favors and punishments (*Helen* 8). By construing *logos* as hegemonic, Isocrates, in contrast, creates an image of a civilized force,
at once a principle of social unification and a mechanism through which this
unification is achieved (*Antidosis* 253–257, *Nicocles* 5–9). According to
Professor Poulakos, Gorgias' metaphor of *dunastēs* designates a constant
agonistic struggle of discourses to topple each other—a situation Poulakos
ascribes to the Athenian democracy during the blossoming of the sophistic
movement. Isocrates' preoccupation with panhellenism and his distinct vision of hegemonic rhetoric are responses to the strife and cultural disintegration in the wake of the Peloponnesian War and the peace treaties of the
fourth century B.C.

Professor Poulakos declines, however, to choose between the Sophists[1]
and Isocrates. I take this strategic indecision as an invitation to join a debate
about the legacy of sophistical and Isocratean rhetorical education. In recent
years, an impressive group of scholars has attempted to reread the Sophists
in order to find a more pluralistic conception of discourse and power than
the one yielded by traditional histories of rhetoric.[2] By contrast, the bulk of
interpretations of the Isocratean corpus gives us a portrait of rhetoric that
is monologic and elitist at best, intolerant and reactionary at worst.[3] The
Sophists now appear as nomadic intellectuals, eternally playful and irrever-

ent towards any social order. Isocrates emerges as a pedantic political strate-gist, forever disdainful of social change. Sophistical *logos,* as now conceived, tends toward decentralization of cultural and political power, while Isoc-ratean *logos* tends towards its consolidation. As John Poulakos summarizes in his contribution to the symposium, "Sophistical rhetoric was centrifugal, the rhetoric of Isocrates centripetal."

In what follows, I hope to complicate this dialectic by demonstrating the ambivalent social potential of both sophistical and Isocratean rhetoric. I con-tend that Gorgias, as a representative of the first generation of Sophists, and Isocrates, as a self-proclaimed opponent of fourth-century Sophists, offer us two distinct—but not antithetical—ways of dealing with our own cultural and political situation: playful iconoclasm versus political responsibility. I show how these attitudes emerge not only in response to situational exi-gencies, as Professor Poulakos has described, but as strategic appropriations of the mythopoetic tradition: the common discursive fabric of the Greek culture. In the final section I speculate on how Isocrates' use of the past, both historical and mythical, might be reinterpreted in the context of today's problems of humanistic education and democratic politics.

Between *Alētheia* and *Doxa:*
Gorgias' Playful Criticism of Myth

Before I turn to Gorgias and Isocrates, let me clarify the terms "centrifugal" and "centripetal" with respect to their application to linguistic practices in the fifth- and fourth-century Greek culture. These terms were used origi-nally by Mikhail Bakhtin in reference to two forces—centralizing and de-centralizing—within any living language that has achieved a certain degree of national identity, such as European languages in the Middle Ages and the Renaissance. Centripetal and centrifugal forces produce linguistic stratifi-cation, or heteroglossia. Heteroglossia's "official" literary genres—poetry, epic, discourse of the church—occupy the top of the socioideological ladder, while the unofficial languages—street songs, folk sayings, anecdotes—swirl at the bottom and ridicule the "high" discourses of monks, poets, and scholars (Bakhtin 1981: 272–273). "High" discourses are practiced by liter-ate elites, while the "low" genres belong to the oral culture of the market-place with its "stages of local fairs and . . . buffoon spectacles" (273).

Given the nomadic character of sophistical education on the one hand and its ties to the oral culture and the literate and institutional nature of

Isocrates' practice on the other, it is tempting to apply the logic of Bakhtin's analysis of the cultures of medieval Europe to linguistic practices in classical Greece. Yet the same contrast between unofficial oral genres and established literary forms is not to be found in Greece of the archaic and classical periods. Thanks to studies of Greek orality and literacy of the past few decades, we can no longer assume the "literary" quality of ancient Greek lyric and epic poetry, the discourses that formed the backdrop of the emerging fifth-century rhetoric.

Much of the sanctioned transmission of cultural knowledge actually occurred through performance of Homeric epics and gnomic poets. According to Egbert Bakker, oral performance of an epic constituted an occasion during which the audience along with the singer partook in reactivating traditional truths of its culture. Bakker (1993), building on Gregory Nagy, argues that even the term for truth, *alētheia*, derives its form from the adjective *alēthēs*, that which is saved from *lēthē* (forgetting). "True" is what is "preserved by being *repeatedly and officially active* in the ongoing series of epic performances" (15). Despite the potentially large number of variations of Homeric "texts," oral performance afforded more avenues for preservation of tradition than for its critical questioning.

By contrast, writing and literacy, while still marginal, furnished an opportunity for reflection and scrutiny of taken-for-granted cultural verities. Yet the breaking down of the centripetal hold of the mythopoetic tradition and of the worldview it endorsed still relied on oral mechanisms of persuasion. As Havelock (1982) observed in his analysis of the pre-Socratics, criticism of the old world of myth, with its anthropomorphic deities and their deeds, does not try to break with the "thought world of the oral period"; instead, this type of discourse "seeks to alter the direction of a tradition" (236). The linguistic shape of much pre-Socratic writing is driven by what Kevin Robb (1983) terms an "oralistic" impulse.

In his analysis of the fragments of Heraclitus, Robb illustrates how the "philosopher's thought . . . was distilled into the form of the traditional saying or aphorism" (198). The philosopher also employed "persuasive euphony," for "he was forced to compete for an audience with street singers and rhapsodes, masters of aural appeal—no less than the poets of Greece in the persons of their reciters and performers, master artists—and to that competitive end he forged a rare verbal artistry" (199).

Against this discursive background, which weaves together criticism and use of the mythopoetic texture, we can appreciate the decentering gesture of Gorgias' *Helen*.[4] Positioned on the cusp between orality and literacy, Gorgias shares with his philosophical predecessors and the tragedians of the fifth century an ambivalent attitude towards myth and poetry. On the one hand, he displays critical distance with respect to the mythopoetic "past"; on the other, he strives to harness the sensual and social forcefulness of poetic performance. Gorgias definitely considered himself a critic of a legend and of the medium of its activation in the psyche of the hearers. Segal (1962) notes that Gorgias' "treatment of the Helen story . . . bears some resemblance to the later Euripidean techniques of treating mythological material in a 'modern' rationalistic and psychological manner, for the discussion of theoretical ethical and social problems" (101).[5]

In the *Encomium of Helen*, Gorgias at once acknowledges the efficacy of poetic performance of the myth and breaks its spell by revealing the chemistry of oral persuasion. He pronounces speech a "powerful lord (*dunastēs*) which by means of the finest and most invisible body effects the divinest works: it can stop fear and banish grief and create joy and nurture pity"(8). This personification of the *logos* as an arbitrary ruler echoes the mythical narrative casting used by several pre-Socratics as well as by the poets of the archaic age. The power of the *logos* is akin to *bia*, brute force (12) that moves the hearer in an almost physical way. In contrast with the pre-Socratics, however, Gorgias' narrative is not animated by a desire to judge the adequacy of *logos* to the cosmos; rather, he employs poetic technique to expose the psychosocial mechanism of *alētheia*. Comparing Gorgias' description of the *logos* with that of Heraclitus, Rosenmeyer (1955: 231) points out that in Gorgias the *logos* is emancipated from reality of the cosmos, it becomes "its own master." Speech in Gorgias also appears as a potent force that can be deployed to different ends by human agents. In addition to exposing the linguistic mechanism of enculturation, Gorgias sheds light on its new "rationalistic" uses aided by the onset of literate practices. Speech, as it is employed by the new "masters of truth," to use Marcel Detienne's expression, is now seen as a vehicle of social control. As exemplars of these new linguistic practices, Gorgias presents a motley crowd of experts:

To understand that persuasion, when added to speech, is wont also to impress the soul as it wishes, one must study: first, the words of astronomers who, substituting opinion for opinion, taking away one but creating another, make what is incredible and unclear seem true to the eyes of opinion; then, second, logically necessary debates in which a single speech, written with art but not spoken with truth, bends a great crowd and persuades; and third, the verbal disputes of philosophers in which the swiftness of thought is also shown making the belief in an opinion subject to easy change (13).

Opinion (*doxa*) is here juxtaposed with truth (*alētheia*), the latter having been interpreted, even by Charles Segal, as the truth of the phenomenal world (112–114). It is my contention that Gorgias is not contrasting *doxa*, the opinions crafted by speakers and received by the audience, with the truth of idealist philosophy of Plato's sort. He is pointing out instead a shift from orally reinforced, univocal cultural knowledge to the multiplicity of truths spawned by the emergence of literate practitioners of persuasion in the second half of the fifth century.

Gorgias' promise to remove blame from Helen by displaying the truth (*deixas talēthes*, 2) is a claim not of fact but of value, since he proposes to beat the inspired poets at their own game: "It is the duty of one and the same man both to speak the needful rightly and to refute those who rebuke Helen, a woman about whom the testimony of inspired poets has become univocal and unanimous" (2). Similarly, the expression "written with art but not spoken with truth" (*technē grapheis ouk alētheia lektheis*) applied to "logically necessary debates" (13) refers to a desire to take advantage of the audience, rather than to misrepresent reality.

The centrifugal thrust of the *Helen* relies not only on its subversive attitude towards the mythopoetic tradition, but on the criticism of doxastic cultural practices made possible by the powers of speech. Gorgias shows *alētheia* to be a product of *doxa*. Yet his truly decentering trick is to show how *doxa* can masquerade as *alētheia*. The myth of Helen is defamiliarized in order to display new possibilities of the *logos*. The dynastic power of the latter nonetheless contains a centripetal potential that can transform a discourse from a state of *doxa* to a state of *doxa* as *alētheia*.

In this context, we cannot discount the "mythologization" that took place alongside the new "rationalism" of the fifth century. We cannot presume, in other words, that the rationalizing tendency did away with the ongoing political influence of mythopoiesis. Athenian democracy produced its own myths. Such is the myth of Athens as the savior of Hellas that emerges in Aeschylus' *Persae* (472 B.C.), echoed throughout classical Athenian funeral orations as well as in the so-called "rational" historiography of Herodotus and Thucydides.

In her work on the Athenian funeral oration, Nicole Loraux (1986: 263) referred to the transcendence of Athens as the "spell of an ideality." These discourses were public performances that furthered cultural reproduction just as much as Homeric epic recitations. The new political mythology did not displace the old world of epic but coopted it by weaving it into the existing cultural texture. Witness, for instance, Herodotus' intermingling of historical and mythical details in the narrative about the origin of the feud between the Greeks and the barbarians. In a similar fashion, American democracy created its own civic religion without displacing traditional religious practices. One can recall Frank Capra's famous "documentary" series *Why We Fight* where the ideal of Liberty and of the United States as the land of Liberty crystallize as a divinely sanctioned social order and a bastion against the dark forces of fascism around the globe. In the classical Greek usage, *eleutheria* ("freedom") also became one of the terms that distinguished not only a particular social organization but also public and private conduct. It is precisely this centripetal spell, with its assertion of Athens' cultural uniqueness, that Isocrates had to contend against in his effort to redirect the commitment of the Athenian audience towards a panhellenic ideal.

The Sophists self-consciously functioned within the ambiguous domain of *doxa,* in a way that was ruled by the "principle of contradiction" (Detienne 1996: 117). Yet the educational and political practice founded on such ambiguity admits of both social permanence and social change. Takis Poulakos (1994: 75) sees *Helen* as a text symptomatic of the crisis of aristocratic power and suggests that Gorgias introduces a socially decentering possibility of "opposition to aristocracy." At the same time, the rule of *logos,* which supplanted the rule of aristocratic blood, made it possible for the elites to get their way by "voicing" the culturally embedded attitudes of the *dēmos.*

According to Josiah Ober's (1989: 315) description of the relationship between elite rhetors and their democratic audiences, "Athenian politicians were well aware of the climate of public opinion in which they operated, and no public speaker could afford to contradict central principles of the Athenian belief structure very often." Though in principle these *doxa* were easy to uproot, the "Athenian belief structure"—a continually reinforced ideology of the Athenian democracy/empire—constituted a centripetal force which a rhetorician could exploit but not easily challenge.

Playfully unveiling the illusory tactics of poets, philosophers, and rhetoricians, Gorgias performs the very rhetorical and political ambiguity that is the object of his discourse. His ambivalence, communicated by the use of the word *paignion* (*Helen* 21) precludes a definitive answer about the political trajectory of his performance. Gorgias' verbal artistry, however fascinating its self-reflective potential, is art for art's sake: he brackets the question of the social function of discourse, leaving us in awe of magical powers of *logos*. Not so with Isocrates, who implicates himself, a citizen and an educator, in the act of negotiating the political and rhetorical legacy of the Athenian democracy.

Logos Politikos, Hegemony, and the Ambivalence of Political Performance

Isocrates' vision of the *logos* as *hēgemōn*, coupled with his repetitive assertions of his role in the *polis* and his call for war of the Greeks against the barbarians, to some appears authoritarian and even imperialistic. I don't wish to explain away such an impression to "exculpate" Isocrates. Instead, I want to interpret his "Hymn to *Logos*" in the context of the rhetorician's relationship with the oral rhetorical culture of his contemporaries. This relationship, I argue, produces a new type of rhetoric which is linked to Isocrates' political identity. I speculate that Isocrates' rhetoric is not locked into a predetermined political path, but constitutes the condition of possibility for an ongoing pluralistic democracy.

Unlike Gorgias and the other Sophists, Isocrates is a literary rhetorician, seemingly removed from concerns that must have occupied Gorgias as he was grappling with the mythopoetic heritage of rhetoric. Isocrates explicitly shuns and even attacks the oral culture of his contemporaries, as does Plato. On the other hand, he promotes the type of rhetoric that coopts, thematically and stylistically, oral elements of composition and address for its political impact. What, then, shall we make out of Isocrates' "quietist" literary strategy and how do we assess the oral resources of his *logos politikos*, which he proposes as an alternative to rhetorical practices of fourth-century Athens?

Despite what ancient biographers and some contemporary critics say about his choice of the literary medium, Isocrates' preference for writing did not stem from his physical weakness as an orator. As Too (1995) convincingly argues, Isocrates' *ipsissima verba*, on which many traditional accounts are based, constitute a deliberate strategy of self-depiction, a part of a carefully constructed public image. Isocrates engaged in writing not to compensate for his bodily weakness or lack of resolve. Rather, he pursued writing with the dual goal of shifting the focus of contemporary political practices from their traditional sites to a broader rhetorical forum and crafting his own distinct civic identity. By the same token, his shunning of the courts and the assembly—the places where citizens could influence the affairs of the *polis* through the power of their oral performance—marks Isocrates as one of the "quietists," or *apragmones.*

According to Steiner (1994), these individuals' choice of reading and writing as well as their conspicuous absence from public spaces of the *polis* signal "disenchantment with democracy and the desire for different social and political discourse" (187). Gunter Heilbrunn (1975) buttresses this interpretation when he interprets Isocrates' quasi-biographical statement about the lack of "voice and daring" in *To Philip* as an "accusation of the Athenian democracy" (175). Yet, unlike other literary *apragmones* of his generation—especially Plato and other Socratics—Isocrates adopts the quietist stance in order to reinvent democratic rhetoric, not to disavow its legitimacy altogether. As Ober (1998: 249) puts it, "unlike Plato, Isocrates did not abandon hope for democratic amelioration; the question, Isocrates suggests, is how to improve *dēmokratia*, not how to replace it with *oligarchia.*"

To be sure, as an elite "outsider" Isocrates finds much to object to in Athenian speech practices. His criticisms of contemporary rhetoricians are well known: he rarely misses the opportunity to castigate demagogues in the assembly, sycophants in the law courts, logographers, and teachers of eristic disputation. Demagogic orators, who have undermined the civic potential of Periclean democracy, exemplify the excesses of oral powers of *logos.* In the pamphlet *On the Peace,* Isocrates expresses his disapproval of the abuse of public performance through the persona of a pacifist speaker who confronts a hostile crowd:

> I observe that you do not hear with equal favor the speakers who address you, but that, while you give your attention to some, in the case of others you do not even suffer their voice to be heard. And it is not surprising that you do this; for in the past you have formed the habit of driving all the orators from the platform except those who support your desires. . . . Indeed, you have caused the orators to practice and study, not what will be advantageous to the state, but how they may discourse in a manner pleasing to you (*On the Peace* 3–5).

One may conclude from this passage that Isocrates objects to aesthetically pleasing oral performance, just as Plato does in the *Gorgias* when he chastises loudmouthed politicians who pander to their audiences in order to achieve selfish ends or when he banishes poets from the city in the *Republic*. Plato's animosity, however, targets rhetorical instruction and poetic performance because they fail to measure up to the philosophical ideals of justice and truth. Unlike Plato, Isocrates does not condemn the aesthetic dimension of rhetoric. It is not the power of the spoken word he questions, but the unrestrained pursuit of individual gain to the detriment of the collective good of the *dēmos*, which has become the dominant type of rhetoric in the courts and the assembly. Isocrates' concern is echoed by other prominent Athenian orators of the fourth century, Demosthenes and Aeschines, who castigate their audiences for becoming "prisoners" (*cheiroētheis*) of the crowd-pleasers and thereby weakening the democracy (cf. Ober 1989: 321–322).

Earlier I proposed that sophistical education, despite its commitment to the centrifugal "principle of contradiction," may have in practice given rise to a procedure whereby a rhetor was more likely to gain adherence if he most eloquently expressed the established collective *doxa*. Given the relatively short time allowed for deliberation, the audience was prone to follow the *logoi* of such a rhetor, even to its own collective detriment. The role of a critic, which Isocrates adopts in *On the Peace*, helps the audience to question the terms of a democratic political engagement and its *locus* of power.

Criticism of contemporary rhetorical culture does not exhaust Isocrates' textual performance. By leaving the traditional venues of public performance for writing, Isocrates pursues a different type of democratic rhetoric which he terms *logos politikos*. Such a rhetoric, remarks Takis Poulakos (1997: 68), "was an indistinguishably ethical and political art," for it combined both *eu legein* (the art of speaking well) and *phronein* (prudential thinking) for the benefit of the *polis*. The difficulty in articulating the difference and value of this educational project, in comparison with teachers of oral persuasion, had to do not only with the lack of immediacy and power of oral address, but also with the suspect status of writing in the fourth century B.C. Despite the use of writing by historians Herodotus and Thucydides, as well as by dramatists of the late fifth century, Athens was still mainly an oral culture, where writing functioned either as a supplement to oral communication, or, among the elites, as a diversion, *paignion* (Harris 1989: 65–92).

To disassociate his craft from both of these functions of writing, Isocrates goes after logography (ghost writing) and the intellectual exercises of the literate elites. To Isocrates, the former is contemptible because it is an instrument of the new politician and the litigious sycophant. The latter, though it does not promote an unscrupulous quest for political power or material gain at the expense of others, is self-indulgent and often inconsequential. It is precisely the novelty and elite nature of such writing that may cast doubt upon Isocrates' own compositions. That is why, in a famous passage in *Antidosis*, Isocrates explicitly contrasts his version of rhetoric (*logous Hellenikous kai politikous*) with other types of prose writing: "genealogies of the demigods," "studies in the poets," "histories of war," "dialogues," and "private disputes" (45–46). In short, Isocrates defends his written discourse against potential accusations of technical amorality, on the one hand, and on the other, elitist esotericism.

In crafting *logos politikos*—the discourse that is at once aesthetically pleasurable and politically beneficial—Isocrates looks to the mythopoetic tradition as his resource. In *To Nicocles*, he instructs a rhetorician seeking the approval of the audience to follow Homer's lead: "Those who aim to write anything in verse or prose that will make a popular appeal should seek out," he writes, "not the most profitable discourses, but those that most abound in fictions; for the ear delights in these just as the eye delights in games and contests. Wherefore we may well admire the poet Homer and the first inventors of tragedy, seeing that they, with true insight into human nature, have embodied both kinds of pleasure in their poetry" (48).

As I have suggested, the appeal of mythopoetic discourse is not purely thematic in the sense of the audience's recognition of familiar characters and stories. It relies on the reactivation of shared cultural knowledge (the Greek expedition against the Trojans) through a rhapsodic performance. The effect of such a performance depended not only on the skill of a rhapsode, but on the audience's direct involvement in the "performance event" (Bakker 1993: 2). But Isocrates is not a rhapsode who captivates the hearers by his mimesis of Homeric verses. He is a prose writer who adapts mythopoetic discourse for his educational and political project. Isocrates appreciates the potential of oral performance even as he disdains the uses to which it is put by demagogic orators.

As Too (1995) points out, Isocrates repeatedly draws attention to the lack of his bodily presence in his writings; on several occasions he describes his prose as "bereft."[6] Too also suggests, however, that repeated references to the apparent weakness of discourse stripped of the speaker's voice and the immediacy of the occasion "anticipate and defuse the criticisms that may be brought against the written text, above all the *logos politikos* which he produces" (120).

While Isocrates loses the advantages of the oral performative situation, he gains something that only literacy can grant—*time*. According to Takis Poulakos (1997: 70), "with time on its side, eloquence would have a chance to develop its intrinsic qualities even as it continued to cater to an external situation, and to become a self-sufficient art even as it continued to be shaped by a purpose outside its form." The question arises, however, how would the writer's discourse, which is "more closely tied now to the cultural and the thematic" (70), exercise its influence on the audience? In the absence of the author's body and voice, what features of the written text would secure the delight and wisdom embedded in common cultural references?

The main distinction between rhapsodic and Isocratean performance resides in the identity of the performer. Whereas the fabric of Homeric epics is held together by recurring performances of the *Iliad* and *Odyssey* at the Feast of the Panathenaia in Athens (Nagy 1996: 69), textual integrity and political influence of Isocratean writing is secured by the author's constructed identity. Rhapsodic *mimēsis* brought to life the characters of an Achilles or an Agamemnon or even Homer himself, while the rhapsode's persona remained in the shadow despite considerable inventiveness and variation that he could bring to the performance. Nagy argues that when the "rhapsode is re-enacting Homer by performing Homer, . . . he *is* Homer so long as the mimesis stays in effect and so long as the performance lasts" (61). In Isocrates, on the other hand, the author's "I" refers most of the time to himself, and mythopoetic material is often employed to highlight his own constructed identity as a citizen-rhetor and educator. To exemplify this point, I turn to the *Antidosis* and *Panathenaicus*, Isocrates' two intensely self-reflective compositions.

In *Antidosis*, a piece dramatized as a courtroom defense speech, "Isocrates" asks the clerk to read from previously published speeches—*Panegyricus, On the Peace, To Nicocles*, and quotes his "Hymn to Logos" from the *Nicocles* to display "what sort of eloquence it is which has occupied me and given me so great a reputation" (43). It is certainly possible to conceive of the *Antidosis* as a panoply of examples of eloquence intended primarily as instructional showpieces. A reading attuned to the performative aspect of this lengthy "court speech" shows Isocrates' writing as a response to challenges against his character and his educational agenda. It would not be too large a leap, I think, to compare Isocratean defense in *Antidosis* and other writings to the *muthoi* of epic heroes.

As Richard Martin's (1989) study of language taxonomy in the *Iliad* explains, "*muthos* in Homer is a speech-act indicating authority, performed at length, usually in public, with a focus on full attention to every detail" (12). *Muthos* tends to be the "speech of one in power, or of someone, for example, of the boasting warrior who is laying claim to power over his opponents" (22). In *Antidosis*, too, the reputation (*doxa*) of the speaker is contested and speech performs an authoritative function, as Isocrates compels the reader to consider the deeds done in writing as his witnesses. In order to enhance the image of a performative setting, the author draws a parallel between his discourse and "works composed in rhythm and set in music" (47).

He urges the audience "to fix their attention even more on what is about to be said than on what has been said before" and "not to seek to run through the whole of it at the first sitting" (12). Significantly, written discourse is presented as an answer to previously uttered speech, and as a composition to be heard (or read aloud) by "those present" rather than by a solitary reader. Despite the written mode of composition, Isocrates emphasizes the act performed by the speech rather than presenting it as a mere expression of his thoughts. His *logos*, in other words, is not an autonomous medium that guarantees transmission of the message; the author portrays himself in a constant agonistic dialogue with the audience (cf. Too 1995: 113–150).

Panathenaicus, a speech composed to celebrate Athenian leadership among the Hellenes, vividly illustrates the construction of the author's political identity by its association with mythical personae. By invoking the memory of Agamemnon and his deeds, Isocrates not only underscores the common heritage of the Greeks but also draws an analogy between the Homeric hero's reputation (*doxa*) and his own lifelong literary labors of promoting *homonoia*, or unity, among the Greek states. As the following passage suggests, leadership is a reputation that must be earned by a political agent:

> Although he took command of the Hellenes when they were in a state of mutual warfare and confusion and many troubles, [Agamemnon] delivered them from these. Having established concord (*homonoian*) among them and despising deeds which were superfluous, prodigious and without benefit to others, he assembled the army and led it against the barbarians. None of

those with a good reputation at that time or coming later will be found to have engaged in an expedition finer or more useful to the Greeks than this individual (*Panathenaicus* 77–78).

Although not a military leader, Isocrates sees his *doxa* resting on his being a leader of words, *tōn logōn hēgemōn* (*Panathenaicus* 13), who through his *logos* has worked to foster concord and goodwill between the Athenians and other Greeks. Thanks to the literary medium, he can appeal to the textual record of his statements as a proof of his stable identity as a citizen-rhetor and a prudent deliberator.

Over the period of his long career, Isocrates sought to craft through prose an oppositional political identity that was nonetheless presented to the reader as a role vital to the welfare of the polis. Both sides of this public persona, its critical and its hegemonic aspects, are well within the range of the possible subject positions occupied by rhetoricians in democratic Athens. According to Ober, the roles of "leader, critic, opposer of people's will" were salutary for the democratic balance of power: "The good orator not only praised the people, he also criticized and opposed them. Orator and audience alike recognized that criticism and opposition to the will of the masses were central to the orator's political function" (323).

Having observed Isocrates' decentering and centralizing moves, we can now return to *Nicocles*. Isocrates impersonates a tyrant offering kingly advice to his subjects. Isocrates' advisory role to the kings (*Evagoras, To Nicocles, To Philip*) generates some doubt about the rhetorician's political motives. But this particular defense of monarchy seems to jeopardize his civic identity as an Athenian and as a self-proclaimed supporter of democratic balance of power. Does, then, the "hymn to *logos*," by virtue of its utterance by a "tyrant," become a case for monarchy and so overturn the agonistic principle that is the core of a democratic rhetoric? I suggest that it does not, unless we read *Nicocles* too literally.

We know that Isocrates was able to assume different identities in his compositions, as the case of *On the Peace* leads us to believe. The persona in whose language Isocrates happens to speak in a particular piece is also, if partially, his own. As distinct from epic performance and public speaking, writing allows Isocrates to be at once distinct from and identical with the "I" of the speaker. He can simultaneously inhabit the "voice" of another and retain a critical distance from it. To be sure, we cannot overlook Isocrates' sympathy towards monarchy, and the "tyrant" identity of the speaker may be a vehicle for attacking the "slackness and irresponsibility of contemporary democracy," as Norlin implies (Isocrates I: 75). Conversely, *Nicocles* may be interpreted as imposing a democratic role upon a tyrant; for a supposedly sovereign subject is forced to *defend* his rule in an argument.

The arrangement of *Nicocles* is noteworthy in this regard. The praise of logos as *hēgemōn* (5–9) precedes the king's arguments for monarchy against democracy and oligarchy (14–27), which, in turn, take precedence over the tyrant's claim to ancestral right and defense of his kingly conduct (27–48). Speech is described as *hēgemōn*, and the tyrant obeys the hegemony of speech just as any democratic subject. The speaker's role as a leader (*hēgemōn*) is far from guaranteed. It rests upon the force of the argument and hence makes even the king subject to the audience's approval. Additionally, the fact that the praise of *logos* is incorporated verbatim into the *Antidosis* further supports the latter interpretation since this composition is intended as the author's display of loyalty to the democratic *polis* and, as such, asks the audience to consider previously composed "speeches" in light of his democratic commitment.

The arbitrariness of *logos*, conveyed in Gorgias by the term *dunastēs*, is replaced in *Nicocles* with an image of a leader, *hēgemōn*, whose dynastic powers are neither sovereign nor inscrutable. Isocrates poses a new vision of *logos* and power, in which power depends upon rhetorical performance for its legitimacy and political impact. Isocrates' own performance over time indicates that *logos* is productive of both dissent and unification. Centrifugal and centripetal tendencies are therefore present in each utterance, and are most strikingly invoked in the author's dual identity of a critic and a leader.

Towards the "Usable Past"

Both Gorgias and Isocrates address the "grand narrative" of the Greek culture. In Gorgias' playful decrowning of traditional knowledge in the *Helen*, many see a welcome example of a playfully aesthetic attitude towards rhetoric and politics. One can understand why Gorgias' articulation of the *logos* would be congenial to a postmodern intellectual-political project. By deconstructing the myth, Gorgias shows that the past is not fixed but depends on continuous reenactment by human agents. Gorgias denies that there is a single center of power; thus, when a certain discourse does achieve domination in the form of *doxa*, its rule is temporary and precarious. In short, the recognition of the fluidity of power and of its link to linguistic performance makes Gorgias and the sophistical movement he represents attractive to a variety of scholars who wish to see humanistic education as an ongoing critique of the homogenizing regimes of their political, economic, and social institutions and, no less importantly, their academic disciplines.

The continuing interest in the sophistic movement is animated not only by a desire to set straight the historical record by reversing the harsh judgments rendered about the so-called sophists by their contemporaries and intellectual rivals, as well as by commentators of later epochs. At stake is also an enduring cultural dispute about our commitment to a particular classical model of education and a theory of discourse. This double focus—on the historical rereading and on the contemporary appropriation of ancient discourse—keeps our scholarly polemic alive, with strong advocates lining behind a Gorgias or an Aristotle. Isocrates, however, remains a highly ambiguous character.

One of the major reasons, I believe, is Isocrates' palpable presence in most of his compositions. Isocrates does not produce a disembodied theory of *logos politikos* and hence does not lend himself easily to the status of a model. Whereas we know that the words of Gorgias and Aristotle have been reported and possibly altered by others and through this dissemination have achieved immortality apart from the efforts of their supposed creators, we cannot fail to hold Isocrates accountable for what he had written. If we intend to bring Isocrates to bear on our educational and political controversies, how should we proceed? Can we separate the "democratic strand," to use Takis Poulakos' phrase, in Isocratean articulation of *logos* and power from the historical baggage of Isocrates' engagement in the political affairs of the Greek world of his time? And, if we can, why should we?

Like Gorgias and other Sophists, Isocrates does not ground his vision of logos in a metaphysical absolute. As I have argued, he presents his compositions as performances rather than as expressions of a set of immutable philosophical or, for that matter, political principles. Unlike the Sophists, Isocrates insists on the necessity of a defensible and contestable—not sovereign—identity, a subject position from which one could intervene into the political. Isocrates' use of the mythopoetic tradition to craft his public identity and to promote cultural unification against the backdrop of the agonistic Athenian democracy appears problematic to contemporary rhetorical historians. In what follows, I address charges of "elitism" and "cultural imperialism" leveled at Isocrates.[7] These charges come most forcefully from

Victor Vitanza's (1997) recent book *Negation, Subjectivity, and the History of Rhetoric.* Vitanza singles out Gorgias as a premodern inspiration for a poststructuralist "Third Sophistic." He argues that Isocratean *paideia* and his vision of the *logos* lead to the class bias of the modern European educational system and, in retrospect, justify the ideology of the Third Reich. These claims cannot be dismissed simply by calling attention to the critic's anachronistic, or "metaleptic" as he prefers to call it, "reading protocol" (140). After all, by invoking the past—archaic, classical, or medieval—we illumine our present condition in order to better articulate terms that constitute our pedagogical and political "equipment for living" (Burke 1973: 293). We need carefully to distinguish between reactionary appropriations of Isocrates' corpus and the potential of his vision of civic performance in a contemporary democracy.

First, let us examine the claim of "elitism" associated with Isocrates' appeal to the past. This claim is based on M. I. Finley's 1972 lecture, later reprinted under the title "The Heritage of Isocrates," in which the author critiques modern historians' nostalgia for "traditional" education, of the sort often connected to institutions like Oxford and Cambridge (quoted in Vitanza 153). Finley links Isocratean literary *paideia* to socioeconomic bias of educational institutions "designed for members of the ruling elite, a socially and culturally homogeneous group, whose common values were formed and repeatedly reinforced by their continuous association and shared experience" (208). For Finley, such paideia, if it serves merely as a "common code," a mark of social status, inevitably degenerates into a "cult of the past" (210). As an example of such cult-like elitism, Finley quotes Dean Gaisford of Christ Church, who is "supposed to have said early in the nineteenth century that a classical education 'enables us to look down with contempt on those who have not shared its advantages'" (203).

What Finley wants to teach to modern students—and I wholeheartedly support him—is "a relevant past" (213). I disagree, however, that Isocrates' critique of Athenian rhetorical practices and his use of the mythopoetic tradition have nothing to teach modern Americans. Ironically, the original title of Finley's lecture is "Knowledge for What?"—a resoundingly Isocratean concern. Isocrates, as I have shown earlier, also questioned the purpose of contemporary rhetorical education and literary exercises, faulting the former for its service to political and material self-advancement and the latter for furthering politically disinterested knowledge.

The problem with today's university training, even within the humanities, is its increasing stress on technical skills, "a general cultural drift which may reduce Anglo-American democracy to an oligarchy of expertise" (McGee 1985: 9). In the sphere of language education the "drift" has been away from civic rhetoric toward the business-friendly "plain style" celebrated by Carnegie and codified by Strunk and White's *Elements of Style*. In spite of its ostensible virtues of clarity and humble simplicity, this style has naturalized some of the most pernicious constructs of the technocratic culture. As Kenneth Cmiel (1990) astutely summarizes:

> The plain style also creates the illusion that language can be like glass, a medium without the infusion of a self. It pretends the facts can speak for themselves in ways that the old rhetoric never did. The very style has helped perpetuate the belief that there are technical, apolitical solutions to political problems. It is perhaps the most deceptive style of them all (260).

The intimate connection between poetic style and political performance in Isocrates no doubt goes against the grain of the current Anglo-American linguistic norms. I am even willing to hazard a guess that the resurrection of Aristotle's *Rhetoric* as a paradigm for public discourse in the second half of the twentieth century stems from a particularly felicitous match between the great philosopher's demand for clarity (*saphēneia*) and our own cultivated preference for a middling political style unmarked by class, race, or gender. Isocrates' prose makes us suspicious and uneasy precisely because it violates this expectation of homogeneity. Yet this incongruity can also illuminate both the historical conditions of Isocrates' rhetorical practice and our understanding of contemporary democratic discourse. We should not seek the perfect fit between ancient models and today's theories. Instead, we should cultivate a "perspective by incongruity" so that we can maintain a healthy self-reflexive stance while scrutinizing historically remote cultures.

In this light, Finley's remark about the "literary" emphasis, and hence, elitism, of Isocratean *paideia* is only partially justifiable. Despite their literary medium, his compositions and training were oriented towards what can be called "popular culture" of the Hellenic world. Epic poetry and drama in antiquity were popular genres. It is modern philological tradition that has severed them from their performative context, rendered their civic character into timeless expression of the Greek genius, and transformed them into a corpus of texts to be perused by the elites. Isocrates' legacy did not escape this process of formalization or, if you will, mummification, with the resulting attitudes of protective nostalgia on the part of the "traditionalists," and resentment toward the "dead white males" on the part of the younger generation of academics.

There is yet another, more disconcerting feature in Isocrates' record. Having adopted Finley's "elitism" claim as a point of departure, Vitanza goes on to find a more politically malevolent ramification of Isocratean panhellenism—its cultural imperialism. In Vitanza's words, "it becomes a forerunner of 'manifest destiny' and the Third Reich" (1997: 140). The basis for Vitanza's causal argument is the identification of reactionary German philosophical historiography and philology with the Greco-Roman ideal. I will bracket the validity of Vitanza's "reading protocol" which, he claims, is a "language game" like any other "canonized protocol of reading" (140). Nevertheless, I would like to object to the lack of differentiation between the discourses that have appropriated Isocrates to their reactionary political agenda and the ambivalent political potential of his rhetorical practice.

The association of Isocrates with proto-Nazism emerges from Vitanza's reading of Jaeger's *Paideia,* which epitomizes a rhetorical historiography predicated on "an *abstract timeless* conception of the mind as a realm of eternal truth and beauty high above the troubled destinies of any one nation" (Jaeger, quoted in Vitanza 146). Vitanza shows how Jaeger constructs two links—the "Greece-Rome-Germany continuum," and a parallel between Isocrates and himself (147). Vitanza explains the Isocrates-Jaeger construction as follows: "The hero of the *Paideia* story is not Plato, though he is commonly considered to be of a greater intellectual weight; instead, the hero is Isocrates—either the pragmatic or xenophobic political strategist—in his constant attempt to argue for panhellenism and war against the barbarians" (147).

It is easy to see how Jaeger's idealistic abstraction, or extraction of Isocrates from his historico-political context could implicitly justify the logic of cultural chauvinism culminating with Nazi ideology which equated culture with race. If read as programmatic philosophical or moral positions, Isocrates' references to the war of the Hellenes against the barbarians might sound unequivocally xenophobic. But so would Aeschylus, Herodotus, and Aristotle. Within the Athenian democratic imaginary of the fifth and fourth centuries B.C., the terms "Hellene" and "barbarian" function as rhetorical place holders, ready to be filled with insignia of Greekness and its ideological (rather than ethnic or racial) opposite. The barbarian, in fact, is "invented" in order to delineate the Greek identity.[8] In Aeschylus' *Persae* (472 B.C.), the "barbarian" servitude to King Xerxes is depicted to highlight the freedom (*eleutheria*) of the Athenian democratic polity. Herodotus goes even further by framing the Trojan War as the conflict between the Greeks and the barbarians (3–5). In Aristotle, the opposition between the Greek and the barbarian achieves theoretical status: in the *Politics* "barbarians" are presented as "natural slaves" (1252a34).

If Isocrates resembles Jaeger, it is only because his appeal to the cultural capital of the Greeks is treated as a transcendental principle and not as a series of statements crafted in response to a concrete historical situation. As McGee (1985) points out, in Isocrates the past works not as a model to be reproduced in the present, as it does in the rhetoric of fascist nationalism. Rather, "the past is related to the present through analogy, as memory to action. The analogy does not prove; it illustrates and clarifies" (11). Distancing himself from rhetorical practices that have led to oligarchy in Athens and war among the Greek city states, Isocrates adopts the old theme of panhellenism in order to criticize the contemporary historical situation by comparing it with mythologized historical past and to remind the audience of its collective identity. As distinct from the Homeric rhapsodes of the oral tradition, Isocrates promotes the rhetoric of political responsibility by assuming, in his writing, the identity of the "leader of words."

The democratic tenor of Isocratean political aesthetics may seem suspect, for it is complicated—if not tarnished—by the nationalism of Athenian democracy and misappropriation of Isocrates' heritage by modern nationalistic historians. Yet by acknowledging both of these tendencies—one past, the other still present—we can move beyond labeling Isocrates' rhetoric as progressive or reactionary. Taking into consideration the gray areas between the oral word and the written, between myth and rationality, between democracy and nationalism, we can begin to ponder what we can accomplish through the rhetoric that is culturally sensitive, pragmatically oriented, and aesthetically influential.

Notes

1. The term "Sophist," of course, is polysemous both in the fifth century B.C. and during the times of Isocrates and Plato. Here, I am using it not as a historical marker but as a contemporary term to designate teachers of speechmaking with whose legacy Gorgias is associated.

2. See especially Farrar 1998; Jarratt 1991; J. Poulakos 1995; T. Poulakos 1994; Vitanza 1997.

3. See, for instance, Too 1995 and Vitanza 1997. T. Poulakos (1997), by comparison, steers clear of judging Isocrates' specific political proposals while considering his statements in their sociohistorical context.

4. *Helen* is one of the most studied texts in the classical tradition. It will be impossible to acknowledge all the different readings of the text here. For a summary of these various readings, see Schiappa 1996.

5. See also Buxton 1982.

6. See, for instance, *To Philip* 25–28.

7. An earlier version of this argument appears in Haskins 1999: 88–91.

8. Hall 1989.

PART THREE

Isocrates and Plato

DAVID KONSTAN

Isocrates' "Republic"

WERNER JAEGER began the first of the chapters dedicated to Isocrates in his magisterial book, *Paideia* (1957: 830), with the observation that "Isocrates, as the most prominent representative of rhetoric, personifies the classic antithesis of what Plato and his school stood for." Jaeger's view, and the contrast between philosophy and rhetoric which it presupposes, have had an enormous influence on classical scholarship, and especially on the modern image of Isocrates, although there has been significant dissent, especially in recent years.[1] In what follows, I shall put the emphasis rather on what Isocrates and Plato had in common as thinkers about the nature of society and, more particularly, in their response to the democratic experiment in Athens that was unleashed by the reforms of Cleisthenes in 508 B.C.[2] I shall conclude with a consideration of how their views of civic education were shaped by this shared political attitude.[3]

The Greeks of the fifth and fourth centuries B.C. typically identified three kinds of political regime: democracy, aristocracy, and monarchy, under these or similar labels. In approaching Isocrates' and Plato's conceptions of civic society, it is instructive to examine what innovations they brought to this traditional classification. The subject has a special interest in the case of Isocrates, insofar as he was a political philosopher and public figure who professed himself to be committed to democracy and, at the same time, both eulogized and served as tutor and counselor to reigning kings. We may begin by taking a backward look at how the *topos* was treated in the previous century, during the heyday of the Athenian empire.

Although there are hints of the threefold classification as early as Pindar's second Pythian ode (ca. 475),[4] as Jacqueline de Romilly (1959) has noted, the *locus classicus* is the famous debate that Herodotus (3.80–83) stages between three members of the Persian aristocracy, after the death of Cambyses and the thwarted plot of a pretended magus to seize power. In this discussion, Otanes defends democracy as the best form of rule, emphasizing the value of equality before the law (*isonomia*), Megabyzus makes the case for aristocracy, and Darius, who wins the day, argues in favor of monarchy, citing among other reasons that this is the traditional form of government in Persia, and it has brought the empire to its present grandeur. The alternatives imagined by all the speakers are precisely three in number, a point that Darius states explicitly (cf. de Romilly 1959: 82).

In fifth-century texts this ternary pattern may be reduced to a polar contrast between two forms, one of which is always democracy, while democracy's opposite may be figured as aristocracy or as kingship.[5] An early example is the contrast between democracy and tyranny or absolute monarchy drawn in Aeschylus' *Suppliant Women:* when Pelasgus, king of Argos, insists on the need to consult the *astoi* or citizens before making a decision about protecting the Danaids who have fled Egypt (365), they reply: *su toi polis,* "But you are the city" (370; see 370–375). The importance of the *dēmos* or people in the political process is a leitmotif throughout the tragedy (cf. 397–401, 417, 600–624, 739–740, 942–949). But Pelasgus is acutely conscious of the difference between Greeks and barbarians in this regard: he notices Danaus' outlandish attire, which prompts Danaus to recount his Greek origins, and later insults the Egyptian herald as being a barbarian and offending the Greeks (914). In this respect, Aeschylus reproduces the Hellenic ideology implicit in Herodotus' account: barbarians are characterized by tyrannical behavior and a preference for monarchy.

In Euripides' *Suppliant Women,* produced around 420, there is a formal debate or *agōn* (403–466) between Theseus, king of Athens, who affirms the value of democracy, and a Theban herald, who defends monarchy. The irony is that a king is assigned the role of vindicating popular government (at 404–405, Theseus declares: "this city is not ruled by one man, but is free"), while a common herald insists on the superiority of kingship. That there is a relationship between this passage and the debate recorded by Herodotus is commonly assumed,[6] even though Euripides reduces Herodotus' three variants to two: democracy vs. tyranny.[7] Of particular significance is that Euripides locates the contrast between monarchy and democracy within Greece itself, rather than between Greeks and barbarians, as both Aeschylus and Herodotus had done. To be sure, Thebes, a traditional enemy of Athens, had sided with the Persians in their invasion of Greece. But the more salient factor at the time the *Suppliant Women* was produced was Thebes' alliance with Sparta against Athens. For the Peloponnesian War was imagined as a conflict between a combination of democratic regimes, led by Athens, and an oligarchic system under the hegemony of Sparta.

On the eve of the great Athenian expedition to Sicily in 415, dispatched with the mission of overthrowing the pro-Spartan regime in Syracuse, there occurred, according to Thucydides, a debate in the Syracusan assembly in which a certain Athenagoras drew a sharp contrast between democracy and aristocracy.[8] Nothing else is known of this Athenagoras, although his name (if he was a real person) suggests a connection with Athens: perhaps his family were *proxenoi* or representatives of Athenian interests in Syracuse. Athenagoras points a finger at oligarchic conspiracies allegedly afoot in Syracuse, and extols the virtues of democracy. On the one hand, his speech brings home the contrast between Athens' democratic regime and that of its enemies, thus recalling the situation in Euripides' *Suppliant Women*. But the fact that the discussion is internal to ostensibly democratic Syracuse, rather than between representatives of two different regimes, allows it to serve as a surrogate for class conflict within Athens itself. The antithesis that had earlier distinguished Greeks from barbarians, and was later appropriated, at least in Athenian discourse, to discriminate between democracies under Athenian hegemony and their oligarchic enemies within Greece, also defined the parameters within which civil dissension or *stasis* was conceived.

In the *Phoenician Women*, produced after the oligarchic revolution in Athens that took place in the year 411, Euripides stages a debate between Eteocles, who brazenly proclaims his preference for tyranny, and his mother Jocasta, who defends *isotēs*, that is, democratic equality among all citizens (503–567).[9] Eteocles seeks to justify, or at least explain, his determination to retain sole power in the state, rather than grant his brother, Polyneices, the annual turn at rulership to which he is entitled as twin heir of Oedipus. The play is set in Thebes, which had sided with Persia and was now allied with Sparta, and it is natural to see the representation of Eteocles as one more instance of Athens' projection onto its opponents of an inveterate disposition to tyranny. But the debate between Eteocles and Jocasta is internal to the city, like the controversy in Syracuse reported by Thucydides, and it is attractive to suppose that the debate alludes also to the danger of an oligarchical regime in Athens. Already in Aristophanes' *Wasps*, produced in 422, Bdelycleon complains that every shop-keeper in the marketplace cries "tyrant" if you buy at a different stall, though until recently the word was scarcely heard in Athens (486–492). The charge had clearly become popular among radical democrats during the Peloponnesian War as a way of disparaging perceived enemies within the state.[10]

The absolute power of the people or *dēmos* might also be described as tyrannical.[11] Few citizens were bold enough to accuse the democracy openly of exercising tyrannical rule over the rich. Yet Plato's *Gorgias*, possibly among Plato's earliest dialogues (Kahn 1996), puts in the mouth of Callicles, apparently a democratic leader in the time of Socrates, an open defense of the advantages of tyranny. Nothing further is known of Callicles, and he may be an invention of Plato's. Be that as it may, the dialogue perhaps captures something of the political atmosphere prevailing in Athens in the late fifth century, when aristocratic partisans cast the charge of tyranny back at democratic partisans, and some of them, in turn—if Plato is to be trusted—frankly acknowledged its attractions.

As is well known, Plato, having inherited the distinction between three forms of government, produced a more elaborate scheme. Early in the *Republic*, Plato is content to describe the three forms as being universally accepted (338d7–e6). When he comes to his account of the degeneration of human character, however, which he imagines on the model of successively worse political regimes (449a, 543c–d), Plato expands the conventional triad. In addition to his ideal state, to which he applies the name of aristocracy, Plato says that there are four inferior kinds of government: one that he denominates the Cretan or Laconian (later called timocratic), followed by oligarchy, democracy and, last and worst of all, tyranny (544c). The timocratic form degenerates into oligarchy in the strict sense (550c), in which the ruling class is motivated more by the pursuit of riches than by honor. When, as a result of exploitation by the rich, the poor rebel, they install democracy (557a), and tyranny arises from the crises to which this last constitution is prone (563e).

This fivefold system is rather messy, and de Romilly (1959: 90–95) remarks that the new, complex pattern of constitutions only assumed a stable form with the symmetrical, sixfold division proposed by Aristotle. On this scheme, each of the three fundamental constitutions potentially takes two forms, a better and a worse. In the case of monarchy, there was ample historical precedent for a division between kingship, which might be construed positively, and tyranny, in which the ruler had regard only for his own pleasure and profit (de Romilly 1959: 84–85). From there, it was a small move to the distinction between two types of regime in which only a few people controlled the state: a good form, dubbed aristocracy and now understood as the rule of the best, versus the corrupt type, which retained the simple label of oligarchy. So too, democracy might be doubled, according to whether the people ruled fairly or not. In this last case, Aristotle prefers to call the good form *politeia*, employing the word for constitution in general as the name of that system in which the entire *dēmos* or people participates and reserving the term *dēmokratia* for the negative type or deviation (*parekbasis*).

The threefold division was, as we have seen, a commonplace both in the fifth and in the fourth centuries, and many other instances can be cited (e.g., Aeschines *Against Timarchus* 4, *Against Ctesiphon* 6). Given the widespread occurrence of the tripartite model, moreover, it is no surprise to encounter it as well in the writings of Isocrates. A paradigmatic case is in the *Panathenaicus* (132), where Isocrates affirms: "I say that there are only three forms of government: oligarchy, democracy, and monarchy." Isocrates, however, gives evidence that he has in mind the more evolved system that we associate with Plato and Aristotle, which presupposes that each of the basic types comes in both good and bad versions. Thus he writes that those early Athenians who inherited the city after the reforms instituted by Theseus are beyond praise because, although they were ignorant of the various kinds of constitutions, they nevertheless selected that which is universally agreed to be the most just, advantageous and pleasant, namely democracy—but not democracy of the sort in which intemperance is thought of as freedom, and the ability to do what one likes as happiness (cf. the similar language in *Areopagiticus* 20), but rather that which makes use of aristocracy, that is, rule by the best. Then, after defining the three basic types of regime, Isocrates goes on to say that in each form, life is excellent when those who live under it put the best men in charge, while it is racked by difficulties when the worst and most selfish are in power (*Panathenaicus* 130–133).

I have dwelled at length on the basic constitutional forms because I believe they offer an important clue to the nature of Isocrates' political project, as well as helping to clarify the conundrum raised at the beginning of this paper concerning Isocrates' ambidextrous relationship with both democracies and monarchies. What I have called the fifth-century Athenian model (though of course it also endures into the next century and beyond) takes as the fundamental criterion for classifying regimes the scope of popular access to or exclusion from political power. Democracy is judged to be superior because the many contribute their wisdom to collective decisions in which they have a stake. Opposed to this form is any regime in which people are subordinate to the authority of another (or others), and cannot legislate on what they perceive to be their own interests. Seen this way, the difference between a legitimate monarch and an autocrat or tyrant is in principle immaterial; so too, it is easy to assimilate kingship with aristocracy or oligarchy. The basic issue is always whether the Athenian public, assembled in the theater, the courtroom, or the assembly, is included as full participant in all political decisions that concern them, or whether this power resides in the hands of others.

The fourth-century model, as developed by Plato, Aristotle, and doubtless many others as well, is different. Here, the mere fact of popular involvement does nothing to assure that the resulting regime is a good one. It is not just a matter of making mistakes, which any government can of course commit. Rather, a bad democracy differs not at all from a bad oligarchy or a tyranny, nor does a well-run democracy have more in its favor than an aristocratic government or an enlightened monarchy.[12] The essential principle that distinguishes good regimes from bad is no longer, on this model, the question of access to power, but rather virtue or the lack of it among the ruling element in each of the three basic forms of polity. How civic virtue is defined is a question to which I shall return shortly. The point I wish to emphasize here is that, on Isocrates'—or Plato's or Aristotle's— description of the multiple kinds of *politeiai*, it is perfectly possible to be in favor of an individual king or aristocratic regime, or any mixture of the basic types, and at the same time represent oneself as a supporter of democracy, at least a democracy of the correct sort. Democracy is not, in this scheme of things, a value in and of itself, as had been presupposed by the ternary model that prevailed during the previous century.[13]

How this change of perspective on the nature of governments came about is a matter more for speculation than for detailed demonstration, but I think one can tell a plausible story about it based on Athenian history in the fifth and fourth centuries B.C. The fifth century began with the consolidation and expansion of the democracy, to the point that all property distinctions were abolished as a basis for full participation in civic institutions and a radically egalitarian regime was established, at least insofar as free adult males of Athenian birth were concerned. This process came to a head with the reforms instigated by Ephialtes in 461, which were to remain in ef-

fect throughout the century, apart from the two counter-democratic revolutions in 411 and 404. During this epoch, moreover, the Athenian drive to
consolidate its empire was projected as a defense of Greek liberty against
Persian overlordship; thus, the opposite of democratic rule was doubly determined not just as tyranny, but as a barbarian form of subjection, in which
all but the Great King were imagined to be slaves rather than free.

The second half of the century was marked less by the struggle to maintain democratic institutions at home, and more by the ideological constraints
of the looming and then open conflict with Sparta and her allies, in which
Athens represented itself as the champion of democracy in Greece generally. Under these conditions, to which the two oligarchic interludes contributed a particular sense of urgency, popular rule was not taken for granted
but remained a theme of ideological and sometimes armed struggle. One
was for democracy or against it; allegiances were radically polarized and in
addition thematized around the issue of class.[14]

After the defeat of Athens in the Peloponnesian War, and in the course
of the fourth century generally, the ideological landscape changed considerably. At home, the threat that an oligarchy might seize power receded. As
P. J. Rhodes observes: "In the fourth century the Athenian democracy was
stable."[15] On the international front, Athens found itself allied now with
one, now with another of its ancient enemies, from which it had previously
distanced itself by painting them as by nature hospitable to oligarchy and
tyranny—places such as Thebes, which had served throughout the fifth
century as Athens' political and cultural "other,"[16] Sparta, which had been
the mainstay of oligarchic regimes in the previous century, Macedonia,
which was dubiously Greek, even if Isocrates professed to believe that its
royal line was Hellenic, and Persia itself. Thanks to these labile and shifting
alliances, the opposition between democratic and non-democratic regimes
began to lose some of its political salience.[17]

This is not to say that attachment to popular institutions waned simply
because of complacency or a shift in the complexion of international relations. There were various ways of adapting the civic ideology of Athens to
meet the new conditions. One was by insisting on the direct connection between autochthony, which the Athenians saw as their special birthright, and
egalitarianism, and thereby stigmatizing all foreigners, Greek or otherwise,
with alien blood and a propensity to tyranny; this is the kind of propaganda,
for example, that is satirized in the funeral oration that Plato, in his *Menexenus*, attributes to Aspasia, the concubine of Pericles.

There were other, less racist defenses of democracy as well. But those who harbored suspicions of the radical democracy of the 400's could, under the changed circumstances of Greek inter-city politics in the 300's, exploit the off-and-on friendly relations with oligarchic and monarchical states as a way of disarming the automatic polarity between such regimes and Athenian institutions, thereby enabling a more tolerant point of view, according to which some non-democratic *poleis* might be approved as being good of their kind as opposed to their deviant forms, just as democracies too exhibited a negative variety. One sees how the enhanced paradigm of *politeiai* developed by Plato, Aristotle, and others neatly served such a political program.

This is at best a likely story, and I do not want to press the historical determination of the new classification of state types any further on this occasion. Rather, I wish to explore what the shift from a taxonomy based essentially on whether or not the populace had direct access to power to one predicated on differentiating good from bad regimes of whatever kind might have meant for the question of civic values and education. For in order to sustain the distinction between ideal types and their deviant forms, it was necessary to posit certain principles of good government over and above universal participation in the organs of the state. And this task was as imperative for Isocrates as it was for Plato, even if the effort carried Plato rather farther along the road to a transcendental metaphysics of virtue.

Before proceeding to inquire into the nature of Isocrates' view of civic virtue, which underlay the separation of good from bad regimes, I should like to note in passing that any such principle had to be grounded in some conception of stable values. Extreme forms of relativism, such as those associated with Protagoras and especially with Gorgias, who denied that anything was knowable, would not serve, since they would render it impossible to distinguish securely between better and worse rulers.[18] The antimetaphysical notion of an irreducibly rhetorical terrain, in which truth is a matter of persuasion rather than absolute verities,[19] might be at home in the fifth-century atmosphere of democratic optimism, but it was foreign to Isocrates' political ideals. Whatever Isocrates' ostensible relations with Gorgias, which the ancient biographical tradition conjectured and which Jaeger (1957), committed to seeing in Isocrates the antithesis of Platonic idealism, took for certain (833–835), it is wiser, in my view, to take Isocrates at his own word as being inimical to the sophists (cf. esp. the fragmentary oration, *Against the Sophists*). His affinities were more with Plato in this regard.[20]

If Isocrates, like Plato, was committed to seeking fixed principles of political virtue, how did he go about establishing them? One approach, to which Plato himself was not entirely averse, was to insist on respect for tradition. In the fourth century, one of the touchstones of political discourse was a defense of the ancestral constitution associated with Solon. Because the reforms of Solon were remote, they could be invoked as well by innovators as by conservatives. We have already seen how Isocrates could appeal, in the *Panathenaicus*, to the generation immediately after Theseus as the authors of a model constitution. In the *Areopagiticus* he treats Solon's constitution as the ideal which contemporary Athenians must recover. Isocrates affirms that, in the matter of government, nothing can be achieved by mere luck or the virtue of a single individual. Everything depends on proper deliberation concerning the management of public affairs (11). What matters is not walls or the size of the population, but that people govern wisely and rightly (13). In a famous analogy, he proclaims that the *politeia* is the soul of the city, as wisdom (*phronēsis*) is of the body, and that laws, political leaders, and the population at large must be assimilated or adapted (ὁμοιοῦσθαι) to it (14). The problem with contemporary Athenian rule is that the Athenians have abandoned the constitution bequeathed them by their forebears (*progonoi*, 15). It is the Solonian order, reconfirmed by Cleisthenes after the expulsion of the tyrants, to which Athens must return (16).

The proof of this, Isocrates asserts (17), is the extraordinary success of Athens in achieving hegemony over the Greeks. Arguments from success rest on historical narratives, and Isocrates cheerfully manipulates the record, whether of Athens or of Evagoras' Cyprus, in order to corroborate his claims concerning the virtues of one or another political regime. But what was it in the Solonian constitution that distinguished it from the Athens of the fourth century? Isocrates responds to this question by discriminating between two kinds of equality, one of which grants the same thing to everyone, while the other involves a distribution according to merit (21–22). In Solon's time, leaders were selected according to ability rather than by lot, which depends on simple luck (23–24). In a word, says Isocrates, the populace may be capable of judging the achievement of those in office, but the officials themselves should be those who have the leisure and the means to devote themselves to government as faithful servants (26). In the idyllic times of yore, when power was thought of as service rather than as a means to aggrandizement, the young respected their elders, and there was no conflict between rich and poor; class conflict was overridden by social conscience, which was inculcated in the citizen body as a whole under the tuition of the best.

It was not so much Solon's legislation, then, that made his constitution pre-eminent and guaranteed peace both at home and abroad, as the character of the people. Laws reflect to some degree the nature of a community, but Isocrates has already indicated that laws are to be adapted to the *politeia;* they do not define or constitute it. A city is judged, Isocrates continues, not by the quantity of its *nomoi,* which is rather an index of its corruption, but by the daily practices (*epitēdeumata*) of its people (40). No need to plaster the stoas with new decrees: it is thanks to its character, not its edicts, that a city is well run or the reverse (41). Martin Ostwald (1986) has argued that in the course of the fifth century B.C. there had been a shift in the Athenian conception of sovereignty: whereas at the beginning of the century "the popular will had been sovereign" (523), after Athens' defeat in the Peloponnesian War and the experience of the Thirty Tyrants, the "Athenians insisted that the new order be based on written laws" (511).[21] Isocrates, though he was no exponent of popular sovereignty, nevertheless saw in the proliferation of written laws a mark of democracy run wild.

Isocrates' criterion for good government was not the rule of law as such, any more than it was popular control of the organs of the state. His view is a far cry from the modern conception of the constitutional state or, in the Spanish phrase, *el estado de derecho,* in which "the totality of the management of public power is subject to law [*ley*] and to justice [*derecho*]" (Navarro 1992: 211). The modern view does indeed provide a basis for a positive evaluation of monarchies and aristocracies, in the measure that they respect civil rights. But this was not Isocrates' position. In place of law or rights, Isocrates offers as the criterion of political excellence the moral character of the government.

Isocrates expresses the fear in the *Areopagiticus* (57) that he may appear to favor oligarchy and be hostile to the people (*misodēmos*). He defends himself against this charge by claiming that he is recommending nothing new; the appeal to the ancestral constitution thus serves as a cover for what might be taken to be an antidemocratic stance. Toward the end of the speech, Isocrates goes so far as to affirm that even when they are badly managed, democracies are responsible for fewer disasters than are other forms of government (70). But none of this disguises, or is intended to disguise, Isocrates' frank elitism: he believes that some people are more capable of ruling than others, and that just they should be entrusted with public office.[22] It is not difficult to see how such a doctrine might dispose Isocrates to admire aristocracies and monarchies, provided that they are ruled well. The clearest statement of this disposition is to be found in the oration that Isocrates puts in the mouth of the young Cypriot king, Nicocles.

Nicocles affirms that the reason why the people should give approval to the monarchical *politeia* under which they live is not compulsion, nor the fact that they have endured it for a long time, but rather that it is the best of constitutions (12). Everyone agrees that it is an awful thing, Nicocles asserts, for good and bad people to be rewarded alike, and that it is more just to discriminate and bestow honor according to worth (14). This is the very idea that Isocrates puts forward in his own voice in his *Areopagiticus*, where he identifies this principle with the Solonic constitution of Athens. According to Nicocles, democracies and oligarchies tend naturally to seek equality among those who have a share in the *politeia*, which is to the advantage of those who are wicked. Monarchies, on the contrary, award highest honors to the best, less to the second-best, and so forth in proportion to excellence, and even if this is not always the case, it is at least the intent of such regimes (15).

Nicocles offers various arguments to show that monarchy is superior to oligarchy and democracy. His speech culminates in the appeal to experience, which was Isocrates' touchstone also in demonstrating the virtues of the ancestral Athenian constitution. In particular, Nicocles points to the rise of the Persian empire, which he, like Darius in the debate reported by Herodotus, attributes to the Persian's high regard for monarchy, and to the achievements of Dionysius, the tyrant of Syracuse (*Nicocles* 23).[23] Nicocles concludes his discourse with a series of commandments addressed to the populace (48–62), ending with the admonishment: "consider my words [or arguments] to be laws, and attempt to abide by them, in the knowledge that those of you who most do what I wish will soonest have the power to live as they themselves wish" (62). These words, in which it would probably be wrong to detect Isocratean irony, confirm the orator's indifference to the independent authority of law in a constitutional state.

As for the monarch himself, his first duty is to be kind to those under his charge. As Isocrates puts it in his essay on kingship addressed to Nicocles, "it is impossible to govern horses or dogs or anything else well unless one pleases those one is supposed to take care of" (*Ad Nicoclem* 15). In addition, a wise ruler will establish laws that are just, advantageous, consistent with one another, and least subject to equivocation (17)—although the source for their authority resides, as we have seen, entirely with the monarch himself. Above all, a good prince must rule himself no less than others: "deem it most royal if you are slave to none of the pleasures, but govern your desires more than you do your citizens" (29). None of this is so profound as to make one wish passionately that one had been a classmate of Nicocles while he was attending Isocrates' school in Athens, in the way one would give a fortune to have sat in on Plato's lectures in the Academy. But the insistence on controlling the appetites and serving the interests of the governed is not un-Platonic.

I shall close this paper with a brief consideration of the implications of Isocrates' notion of civic virtue for his panhellenic ideals and his fixation on the idea of a Greek military campaign against Persia. Before doing so, I should like to look at a passage in the *Nicocles* (6–9), repeated almost verbatim in the *Antidosis* (253–257), that Jaeger (1957: 876, 938 n. 105) described as a veritable hymn to *logos* (cf. T. Poulakos 1997: 9–19), and which Takis Poulakos has singled out as the closest Isocrates comes "to theorizing rhetoric" (9). Isocrates asserts that *logos*, as the capacity to persuade others and clarify matters to ourselves, is specific to human beings, and the basis of civic life, law, and the crafts. By means of *logos*, we discriminate the just from the unjust and educate the ignorant. Speech (*to legein*) is the surest sign of intelligence, and the guide of all action and thought. It is a powerful statement. What did Isocrates mean by it, and why did he put it in the mouth of a Cypriot tyrant?

A well-run polity, whether it is democratic, oligarchic, or monarchical in nature, may be recognized not only by its military triumphs but also by its domestic harmony, and this latter depends upon the approbation of the governed. If the people are not to be constrained by mere force, then they must be persuaded of the advantages of a regime in which they are not equal in power to those who rule them, as will be the case in any state other than the extreme democracy of fifth- and fourth-century Athens. Reasonable persuasion, which is perhaps the best way of rendering *logos* here, is thus an indispensable instrument of politics. Isocrates believes that a properly educated people will recognize that it is better off being ruled by wiser folk.

No doubt kings did not always perceive the need to convince their subjects of the superiority of monarchy by means of general arguments. In this respect, the mere device of having Nicocles defend his reign before the *dēmos* is radical, because it implicates monarchy in the civic process of public discussion. To this extent, I agree with Takis Poulakos (1997: 27) that the speech evokes "Nicocles' status as a citizen," although I am not convinced that this status "exceeds in authority his status as king."

Poulakos goes on to suggest that the speech might have been "an invaluable lesson to Isocrates' students and an important part of their training in political deliberation" (ibid.); if so, it would have taught young Athenians (and others) that an enlightened monarchy is not far different from a democracy that chooses as its leaders those whom Isocrates himself denominates an "aristocracy." If Isocrates casts his kings as orators, he also conceives of democratic leaders as an elite entitled to govern. Both will be able to demonstrate the benefits that derive from their authority, provided that the people are suitably educated, but their title to rule does not derive from popular consent. Nicocles makes this entirely obvious in respect to his claim to sovereignty; if he is the model citizen, then the implications for leadership in a democracy are clear.

That Isocrates could assume the voice both of a conservative Athenian democrat and of a Cypriot prince explains his confidence in the possibility of panhellenic unity. Greek cities need not alter their inherited constitutions for the sake of an alliance. In Isocrates' view, the divergence in their systems of government was negligible, provided that they were ruled wisely and virtuously.[24] In spite of the traditional rivalry between Athens and Sparta, which in the fifth century was cast as a conflict between democracy and oligarchy, the affinities between them could be seen as being in principle more profound than their differences, since each was potentially a government of and by the best. Isocrates was prepared to compare Sparta favorably with Athens, even though it might arouse in an Athenian audience the suspicion that he was sympathetic to oligarchy.

In the *Panathenaicus*, he adopted the extraordinary strategy of praising Athens and then going on to describe how, upon rereading his own discourse, he experienced the misgiving that he had been unfair to the Spartans. To relieve his doubt, he assembled his disciples so that they might hear the speech and offer criticism. Isocrates reports that one of them was bold enough to speak up and address the issue that had worried Isocrates. Although a sophisticated reader would realize, the student concedes, that Isocrates had subtly given Sparta due praise, it would have been better to speak more candidly (239–240). Isocrates then records at length (241–263) the disciple's eulogy of Sparta, and concludes by observing that his argument found favor with the rest of the group (264).

Isocrates achieves several purposes at once by this device of incorporating in his oration the ostensible comments of a critic in his own school. For one thing, he distances himself from a too vigorous defense of Sparta, which might offend the Athenian public. He had used a similar device in the paired discourses, *To Nicocles* and *Nicocles*. In the first oration he expounded to Nicocles the duties of a good king. In the second, he put in the mouth of Nicocles himself the corresponding advice addressed to the Cypriot *dēmos* concerning their obligations to the monarch. In addition, Isocrates points up the oppressive political climate in Athens, where it is dangerous to offer honest and just praise to adversaries who do not share the Athenian commitment to radical democracy. In the earlier *Panegyricus*, Isocrates had adapted his discourse to this prejudice, and then felt obliged to explain that his intention was not to contribute to the negative image of Sparta, but rather to summon that city back to a correct policy (129). Most interestingly, Isocrates' stratagem in the *Panathenaicus* affords a special glimpse into the way in which his own school served to promote political solidarity among Greeks by creating a forum for frank and honest criticism and the free expression of ideas. More philosophical and scientific (*technikos*) speeches might find favor over rhetorical appeals to prejudice.[25] The conversation among Isocrates' pupils, far from the clamor that accompanied public speaking in Athens, is the living proof of his doctrine that the best of the Greeks, properly educated in the nature of political virtue, could achieve a common purpose through dialogue, and that all three kinds of constitution—democracy, oligarchy, and monarchy—were in principle compatible, provided that they were managed by a naturally gifted and enlightened elite.[26]

Plato's Academy too drew students from various parts of the Greek world, but Plato's political reflections seem, on the basis of his *Republic* and *Laws*, to have centered on reforming the individual *polis*, with only secondary regard, at best, for the possibility of panhellenic unity. Isocrates' vision was more pragmatic: proper leadership was achievable in the Greek cities, whatever the nature of their regimes, and agreement among the ruling strata created the conditions for allied action against the Persian empire, which Isocrates saw throughout his career as the natural enemy of the Greeks. Isocrates' militant endorsement of a war against the barbarian east is the other side of the coin to his optimism concerning good government in the Greek city-states.

For Isocrates, it was not the institution of monarchy that distinguished the Persian system of rule from that of the Greeks, as had been the case in the democratic discourse of the fifth century; Isocrates' antagonism derived rather from his contempt for barbarians.[27] Evagoras' great achievement as king was to restore the political morale of the Cypriots after the decline caused by years of Persian suzerainty. Philip's credentials as leader of a panhellenic expedition against Persia were guaranteed by the myth of his Greek descent, although the people he ruled were of foreign stock. It was of no consequence to Isocrates, needless to say, that Philip was an absolute monarch.[28] Not that Isocrates was incapable of seeing merit in non-Greek rulers: a case in point is his praise for the legendary Egyptian king Busiris, who is described as having instituted in Egypt a caste system remarkably similar to that which Plato prescribed for his ideal republic (*Busiris* 15–16).[29]

In a letter to Philip (*Epistulae* 2), Isocrates gently scolds the Macedonian king for risking his precious life in battle, and holds up as a salutary model for royal caution the Persian king himself (7). But barbarians were fit only for monarchy, among the several possible regimes, and Isocrates' hopes for political solidarity based on the rule of the best and wisest in whatever form did not extend beyond the realm that he regarded as Greek.

Like Plato, Isocrates had an ideal of political virtue that could be excogitated through systematic contemplation, albeit without the underpinning of metaphysics and mathematics that gives Plato's philosophy its special character.[30] Like Plato, again, he believed that understanding is advanced by dialogue, when this is carried on in a proper spirit and away from the narrow interests and prejudices that are typical of public debate.[31] Isocrates agreed with Plato finally that good government depends essentially on rule by a philosophically sophisticated elite, which he sought to encourage and train in his role as political educator.[32]

Where he differed from Plato was in his confidence that even a democracy like that of Athens might be reformed, provided that the system of election by lot was replaced by election of the best and brightest, which Isocrates saw as the cornerstone of the Solonic constitution. He continued to address his fellow citizens, albeit discreetly and from the margins. In turn, he believed that a well-run democracy, in which a natural aristocracy controlled political offices, was not fundamentally different in character from a good monarchy or oligarchy. (Such a democratic regime was possible only among Greeks, in Isocrates' view.) Isocrates was heir to the traditionally pro-Spartan sentiment of the fifth-century Athenian aristocracy, but he

gave it a new twist through his emphasis on philosophy or *logos* as the criterion of excellence.[33] Isocrates' view of *politeiai* followed upon his conception of government by an elite, and it served as the basis for his panhellenic
ideal and his abiding ambition to promote a united Greek campaign against
the barbarians.

Notes

1. See esp. J. Poulakos 1995: 113–116.

2. For the process, see Fornara and Samons 1991.

3. For a detailed examination of the evolution of Isocrates' and Plato's thought as a product of
their reciprocal influence on one another, see Eucken 1983. Eucken's arguments are speculative and not always convincing, but he makes plausible the likelihood of mutual interaction between the two thinkers.

4. See Pindar *Pyth.* 2.86–87, which refers to tyranny, alongside cities governed by an impetu-
ous army, which presumably corresponds to democracy, and by the wise, i.e., aristocracy.

5. Cf. de Romilly 1959: 83. The binary model was facilitated by memories of the Pisistratean
tyranny in Athens, which was seen as the opposite pole of the democracy installed by Cleisthenes. For discussion, see Raaflaub (2003). Parker (1998) argues cogently that a sharp distinction between the ideas of king and tyrant in the modern sense of the terms is Athenian
in origin, and is first securely attested in Thucydides. Cf. esp. pp. 164–165. For the radical
opposition between king and tyrant in the fourth century, see Eder 1995a: 163–166.

6. Cf. Collard 1975: 212; Schrader 1979: 163n.

7. On the reduction, cf. de Romilly 1961: 179.

8. Thucydides 6.39; cf. also 1.70.1, and 2.37.1 (Pericles' funeral oration).

9. For Jocasta's impassioned defense of equality, see esp. vv. 531–550.

10. Cf. also ps.-Xenophon *Constitution of Athens* 1.14, 2.18, and Critias' speech against
Theramenes in Xenophon *Hellenica* 2.3.24–26. In a paper entitled "Polities, Politics and
Polite Letters? Some Athenian Oligarchic Pamphleteers," presented at the conference,
"Law and Literature in Athens and Rome," held on 16–18 April 1999 at Brown University,
Paul Cartledge identified in Pericles' funeral oration, as reported by Thucydides (2.34–46),
a model defense of the Athenian democratic constitution, and suggested that the Old Oligarch was responding, in his pamphlet, to Pericles' "politeia" (as originally delivered) or to
comparable political tracts in the form of "constitutions." Nor was the Old Oligarch alone
in his riposte: Cartledge suggests that Critias, who was active in the oligarchic revolutions
both of 411 and of 404, may have been the source (possibly along with Antiphon) of the
two antidemocratic "constitutions" recorded (in however garbled a fashion) in Aristotle's
Constitution of the Athenians (ch. 30–31). Cartledge's brilliant reconstruction of this debate grounds the argument over constitutions in the factional politics of Athens during the
Peloponnesian War.

11. Cf. Aristophanes' *Knights* 1111–1114; Thucydides 1.122.3, 1.124.3, 2.63.1–2, 3.37.2,
6.85.1; Connor 1977; Tuplin 1985; Raaflaub 2003.

12. On the fourth-century image of the king as the embodiment of aristocratic virtues, see Eder 1995: 166–171.

13. After the oligarchic regime of 411 was overthrown, there was a brief phase of limited democracy (or limited oligarchy)—the regime of the five thousand—before full citizen equality was restored. Thucydides regarded this regime as the best constitution he had known (8.97). As Paul Cartledge (see n. 10 above) points out, Thucydides "could think in terms of only the two mutually exclusive and antagonistic groups of citizens, the few and the many/majority. Later, more sophisticated versions theorised rather in terms of a mixture or a balance of types of rule."

14. See Konstan 1994.

15. Rhodes 1995: 318.

16. Cf. Zeitlin 1990.

17. For a detailed analysis of the politics of the fourth century in relation to Isocrates' political program, see Bringmann 1965. There seems to be a similar disposition to criticize the shortcomings of democracy in the United States, since the end of the Cold War. Marc F. Plattner, who is coeditor of the *Journal of Democracy* and a codirector of the International Forum for Democratic Studies, writes in a review of Robert Dahl's book, *Democracy* (Plattner 1999): "While equality is a fundamental principle of liberal democracy, this does not mean that maximizing equality should be the paramount political goal. (I would say the same with regard to freedom.) Indeed, in the spirit of Tocqueville, one might argue that liberal democratic societies tend to have certain characteristic deficiencies—of community or civility, for example—and that shoring up such weaknesses is more important than maximizing democratic strengths. In short, the problems of democracy cannot always be solved by more democracy." Isocrates would have nodded his approval, I expect.

18. See Halliwell 1997: 117–121.

19. Cf. J. Poulakos 1995: 26–29.

20. As Halliwell (1997: 117–121) shows, it is wrong to associate Isocrates with the view of rhetoric that Gorgias is made to entertain in Plato's *Gorgias*. Isocrates did not regard persuasion as nonrational, nor was he a relativist in the Protagorean sense.

21. Cf. Collard (1975: 226) on Euripides *Suppliant Women* 429–432: "Tyranny's arrogation of the law was a prejudice native in every Athenian."

22. Alexiou (1995) shows, by a review of terminology relating to honor, ambition, and reputation, that Isocrates cast Evagoras of Cyprus and Philip of Macedon in the role of Theseus or Heracles (97, 131); what is more, he saw his own achievement as parallel to that of these ideal monarchs (143–144; also Heilbrunn 1975: 165).

23. Parker (1998: 165) notes that Isocrates, alone among fourth-century Athenian writers, tends to use "τύραννος and its derivatives in a positive or at the very least neutral sense as a synonym for βασιλεύς with reference to the kings of Salamis" and other contexts.

24. As Bringmann (1965: 103) notes, in the fourth century most Athenian intellectuals had active relations with kings and tyrants; in this, Isocrates was no exception.

25. See *Panathenaicus* 271, and cf. 263–264; on the role of *technē* in Isocrates' thought, see Wilms 1995.

26. On the importance of talent, see *Antidosis* 187–188 and T. Poulakos 1997: 94–95; on the futility of mass oratory, *To Philip* 12 and J. Poulakos 1995: 138.

27. Cf. Masaracchia 1995: ch. 2.

28. This is not to say that Isocrates wished Philip to rule as tyrant over all of Greece; see Heilbrunn 1975: 162.

29. Eucken (1983: 176–132) argues that Isocrates' *Busiris* was a response to Plato's utopian views, which were circulating prior to the publication of his *Republic;* as a result, Plato was obliged to locate his ideal state in Greece rather than Egypt (194–195).

30. Bringmann (1965: 66) affirms that Isocrates, in contrast to Plato (or Socrates), regarded virtue merely as a means to external success, but so pragmatic a view of Isocrates' moral vision seems to me to be unnecessarily reductive.

31. Usener (1994) argues that Plato and Isocrates both occupied a kind of in-between or "Janus-headed" (9) position between oral and written culture.

32. For a crisp comparison between Plato and Isocrates, see J. Poulakos (1995): 114–115.

33. On Isocratean *logos*, see Kathryn Morgan in this volume.

6

KATHRYN MORGAN

The Education of Athens:
Politics and Rhetoric in Isocrates and Plato

Introduction

As THE new millennium opens, Isocrates seems primed to become an intellectual hero and promoter of a specifically democratic rhetoric and education.[1] A recent commentator notes that "It is quite possible to see Isocrates' mild skepticism as an important humanist voice, a persistence of that liberal, nondogmatic strain of sophistry that conceived of study as being directed 'not at art but at education.'" The same critic writes of Isocrates' "resistance to theory" and his attempt to distance himself from dialectic and "overly regulated speech."[2] A model educator indeed. It seems that we are asked to place Isocrates and democracy on one end of a pendulum swing and Plato and the idealists on the other. The first goal of the present paper is to assert that this is an oversimplification. Rather than trapping ourselves into binary oppositions, I suggest a more nuanced approach wherein Isocrates occupies a middle ground between Athenian populist education and the rigors and exclusions of Plato. He attempts to construct a practice of education and politics that valorizes democratic deliberative practice (although democracy is conceived in a particularly Isocratean way) while remaining intellectually "respectable."

Isocrates uses a panhellenic perspective as a tool for imposing his own version of educational culture. In order to understand Isocrates' vision we have to understand the culture out of which it arises and the rivals it seeks to dethrone. Only by examining the tense play between competing educational models will we fathom the peculiarities, incoherencies, and achievements of the Isocratean model. Isocrates' civic/political education is a rhetorical education. Isocrates constructs his model by identifying political and rhetorical excellence. He wants to elevate his Athenian audience to the level of *philosophoi* by making them apply, in particular, a principle of intellectual consistency to their lives. Although Isocrates resists strict rhetorical theory, then, his works do not lack a guiding intellectual principle.

Consistency begins within the soul, where it monitors individual behavior. In the civic arena, the same principle must ensure a coherent polity, and ultimately, at the panhellenic level, it should govern the entire Greek community. Isocratean *philosophia* therefore rejects the Platonic model wherein a democracy is incapable of rationality and orderly deliberation. Yet his intellectual model also turns its back on current Athenian political practice, which he considers inconsistent and self-centered. Athens' neglect of broader panhellenic issues threatens to undermine Athenian achievements and preeminence in the larger Greek community. Isocrates thus sees himself and his civic education as mediating between empty intellectualism and hedonistic ochlocracy, mob rule.

Since Isocrates implies that there should be a seamless continuum between psychic, civic, and panhellenic behavior, his model for civic and rhetorical education is also a model for life. It is a totalizing educational approach to the life of the citizen within the *polis* and is therefore a powerful intellectual tool. One might well elevate such an approach as a model for democratic deliberation. Nevertheless, this Isocratean project ultimately runs aground on its own intellectual standards. Isocrates' works exhibit rhetorical and intellectual diffusion and inconsistency. In what follows, I shall argue that to make this assertion is not to take part in a long tradition of Isocrates-bashing (since I think that Isocrates' sophistication is often underestimated) but to uncover an endemic tension in democratic education and rhetoric.

Isocrates' orations are both individual arguments set in a historical context and rhetorical models meant to be emulated by his students. Pedagogy demands that a variety of approaches and possibilities be canvassed in a paradigmatic text. Argument requires focus and consistency. Also crucial is the very nature of Athenian rhetorical culture, which emphasizes and rewards opportunism. Isocrates desires to reform the democracy and attempts to do so by using all the refinements of Athenian rhetoric, but he underestimates the extent to which his tools influence his content. The genius and strength of the democracy and of democratic rhetoric are their opportunism and consequent possibility for inconsistency. Like any system, this one has the defects of its virtues.[3] If Isocrates wants the democracy to be less capricious and opportunistic, his means for achieving this end are unfortunate.

The body of this paper has three parts. In the first, I examine the competing traditions of civic *paideia* in fourth-century Athens. We shall see that Isocrates constructs for the city an idyllic intellectual past that has its roots in the genre of the funeral oration. He contrasts this happy past with current Athenian mistrust of *logos* and rhetorical skills. A comparison with the Platonic approach to the same problem will show that Isocrates and Plato, for all their differences, conceive a common paideutic enemy: the "education" offered by current *polis* culture.

The second part surveys relevant passages in the Isocratean corpus in order to identify the Isocratean plan for democratic intellectual reform. The identification of rhetorical with political excellence and the elevation of the Isocratean audience to the status of *philosophoi* make Isocratean *paideia* crucial to the survival of the *polis*. A fundamental aspect of this *paideia* is the achievement of consistency on the individual, the civic, and the panhellenic level. Like Plato, Isocrates brings the city and the soul into a close analogy, although he uses the comparison to different effect. Although both reject current *polis*-education, Isocrates pitches his reform as a purification of excess and a return to traditional values.

In the final part, I shall consider whether Isocrates adheres to his own intellectual ideal in his orations. First I shall examine inconsistency internal to individual speeches (such as "loss" of control) as representative of Athenian rhetorical culture: the characteristic Athenian vices of insatiability and opportunism are emblematic of the liberty of the orator. Second, I shall revisit the old problem of inconsistency of approach between the various orations. The political importance of kairotic skills and the use of indeterminacy as a sign of moderation exist in tension with a focused endorsement of the rule of the best in panhellenic interests. In order to demonstrate his rhetorical expertise and enthrall his audience, Isocrates must diffuse the focus and methodology of his program. He is caught inescapably between the need to appeal (and make his appeal effective), the self-imposed necessity of being a rhetorical paradigm, and the desire to change the framework within which the Athenians think and speak. For this he deserves our sympathy. Which of us can cut away the ladder on which we stand?

Competing *Paideiai*

Isocrates is sometimes taken to be a fairly straightforward supporter of Athenian political and cultural practice. In particular, he glories in Athenian leadership in matters oratorical. Thus in the *Antidosis*, he remarks that, as a result of its *paideia* in wisdom and speech, Athens has become the leader (*hēgemōn*) of Greece. It is the teacher (*didaskalos*) of orators and of those who teach oratory: the prizes for oratorical excellence are greatest there, as is mental flexibility and love of *logos* (294–295). This formulation looks back to Pericles' funeral oration as reported by Thucydides, where the speaker, after enumerating the virtues of the Athenian way of life, sums up by saying the "city as a whole is an education to Greece" (2.41). Indeed, as Loraux has shown, Isocrates' comments on Athens are often deeply implicated in the laudatory *topoi* and strategies found in the Athenian funeral oration.[4] Athens' paradigmatic role in educating the rest of Greece is matched on an internal level. As Ober has pointed out, education for the Athenian citizen was not "limited to literary culture and its popular by-products. A major part of a citizen's education came through performance of his political role." Even more telling, he suggests "in both popular ideology and elite political theory, was the normative role of the ethos of the polis, expressed through the organization and actions of governmental institutions."[5] This position is related to the one taken by Protagoras in the Platonic dialogue that bears his name. The Sophist argues that a citizen is trained by his parents, his teachers, and by the state through its laws (324d–326e). The similar suggestion made by the conservative Anytus at *Meno* 92d–93a (any respectable Athenian gentleman should be able to teach virtue—and in particular the virtue of running a city) indicates that the idea of a normative education provided by the *polis* itself was not uncommon. The accumulation of laws would be an expression of group consensus and these would provide, en masse, a consistent civic code.

So much for the communal ideal. There is a problem, however. A state committed to rational discussion should welcome the contribution of those who have made a special study of argument. Yet in spite of Athens' reputation for rhetorical culture Isocrates repeatedly complains throughout the *Antidosis* and elsewhere that there is a disjunction between Athens' external reputation and its internal practice (297 f.). Athenians, particularly the sycophants, disparage those who study oratory, although they seem to admire those who are eloquent by nature (291). This disjunction is part of a much wider phenomenon: the profound mistrust felt by many Athenians towards professional teachers or Sophists, among whom even Socrates was numbered.[6]

The dilemma faced by intellectual professionals in Athens is encapsulated in the situation faced by Protagoras: Athenian democracy does not seem to recognize political experts, but attributes the virtue of a citizen (*politikē aretē*) to all men. How can Protagoras teach it without running afoul of Athenian ideology? Protagoras' answer is that all do indeed possess this virtue (or more precisely, as I have argued elsewhere, that it is a societal imperative that they be perceived to possess it).[7] There is always room for expert tutelage.

This is an uncomfortable compromise, and indeed, some have felt that Protagoras' professions hide a subtle agenda of political and rhetorical manipulation. But the tensions that Protagoras, as well as Plato and Isocrates, deal with are at the heart of the problem of civic education. What is the place of educators like Isocrates or Plato in Athenian educational culture? In spite of their vastly different metaphysical allegiances, Plato and Isocrates share the feeling that they are marginalized in and maligned by the culture in which they operate. Pericles' paradigm of devotion to intellectual culture and respect for preeminently gifted individuals is transformed in Isocrates and Plato into a picture of widespread suspicion of intellectual training and rhetorical expertise.

Plato thinks that such marginalization is the unavoidable fate of the philosopher, while Isocrates implies that it is an aberrant phenomenon. We might say that Pericles' claims for Athenian society are overdrawn and idealizing, as they surely are (especially given the genre of his speech). Or that, as Isocrates himself would have us believe, everything went downhill after Pericles (and even before him), as the necessities of war and empire encouraged the proliferation of evil demagogues. Yet something more profound is at work than rhetorics of idealization and convenient degeneration. The answer lies in understanding how the city of Athens itself is conceived as a school or teacher of a certain kind of political and rhetorical behavior. Once we see that the political culture of the city as a whole is conceived as a primary educator, it is easier to understand how the Academy, or Isocrates' school, can be viewed as a threat to the political order—especially given that the two schools attracted foreign pupils from different political traditions.

Let us take a closer look at the disrepute of "philosophy" and intellectual culture in Plato and Isocrates. This disrepute is intimately connected with alternate models of civic education. I deal first with Plato's *Republic*, and then with Isocrates' treatment of the same themes in the *Antidosis* and elsewhere. In the *Republic*, after making his startling proposal that philosophers should be kings, Socrates must deal with the objection that most people who do philosophy in contemporary Athens are either vicious or useless (487d). He admits the seeming truth of this, but counters that they are useless because no one makes use of them. As for the wicked, it is an unfortunate truth that the most intellectually gifted are most likely to be corrupted by the *polis*. The problem of intellectual corruption is crucial, since it was a widespread perception among the Athenians that this was what sophists and other shady intellectuals did to the young of the city.[8]

What defense can be offered? Socrates' solution is, typically, to turn the tables on popular perceptions. He declares that although the general opinion is that it is the private (*idiōtikous*) Sophists who corrupt, those who make that argument are the *real* Sophists, who "educate (*paideuein*) most perfectly and make young and old, men and women into the kind of people they want them to be" (492a–492b). This education takes place in the assemblies, the courts, the camps, the theaters, and other public gatherings. The censure or approval of the crowd overwhelms any private education (*paideian idiōtikēn*), and the young man will say what the crowd wants, follow the same pursuits and be the same kind of man. These "educators" and "Sophists" (*paideutai, sophistai*) punish the recalcitrant with disenfranchisement, fines and death; thus no private exhortations (*idiōtikous logous*) can prevail against them. In fact, the private teachers (Sophists) teach only the beliefs of the many (493a6–493a8): a very strange kind of education (493c8). The crowd is cast as the most important educator of the young. Since it is the teacher, it is also the corrupter. The crowd, however, cannot be a philosopher and will always disapprove of philosophy. Anybody who gives the many mastery over himself "beyond what is necessary" will have to do only what the many approves (493d). Those who remain true to philosophy must withdraw from politics (496). In order for the many to change their opinion of philosophers, one must explain what philosophy really is and expose the pretenders.[9]

Several elements in this splendid piece of invective are worth noting. Most important is the contrast between two systems of education, ironically reinforced by calling the populist anti-intellectuals "educators." There is a private system, labeled as *idiōtikos*, controlled by hired private personages—or occasionally, we might add, by philosophers in the Platonic sense, like Socrates. None of their teaching can prevail against the system of public education administered in gatherings of the many. For the most part, says Socrates, private education inculcates only mob values. We note too that, as in the *Protagoras*, punishment is assigned educational value. But whereas in Protagoras' Great Speech, punishment is conceived as part of universal instruction in civic virtue, this idealizing conception is inverted in the *Republic* into a system of disciplinary coercion.

The second thing to note is the strategy whereby Plato turns the tables on those he conceives to be anti-intellectuals. They are the real sophists, the real corrupters of the young. So far, then, private education is either ineffective or mere reinforcement of popular standards. The harm attributed to sophists and philosophers is more accurately laid at the door of their accusers. Public education is conducted through praise, blame, and punishment, and trains the speaker to say what will please the many. The only antidote is gently to explain to the many the true nature of philosophy.

A vast gulf separates the Isocratean and Platonic visions of education. Isocrates associates the rhetoric he teaches with the benefits that have accrued to Athens from a long tradition of orators starting with Solon and ending with Pericles (*Antidosis* 231–236). His teaching is useful to the city because the kind of excellence and wisdom he espouses is agreed on by all (*Antidosis* 84). Unlike Socrates/Plato, Isocrates dismisses the possibility that we might obtain scientific knowledge about what we should say and do. Instead, we should use our powers of conjecture (*doxa*) to arrive at what is best (*Antidosis* 271). It is important that one's learning be given a practical application (*Panathenaicus* 28). This approach clearly repudiates the Platonic withdrawal from democratic politics as practiced. Isocrates aligns himself with iconic Athenian political figures (contrast Plato *Gorgias* 515c–517a) and stresses the importance of benefiting the city (*Antidosis* 85). Yet for all Isocrates' protestations of engagement and conformity with tradition, elements of Socrates' critique recur in some of his orations. We cannot escape the impression that Isocrates feels that he and his philosophy are under siege.[10]

Let us proceed to passages in the *Antidosis* where Isocrates feels compelled to defend himself from slanderers. The slander is double. Some charge that education cannot improve a pupil, and that Isocrates' teaching is a sham (this argument he will disprove on grounds of internal inconsistency). He must then defend against the accusation that education makes people depraved (197), the very charge with which Socrates deals in the *Republic* passage discussed above. Isocrates' response reduces to a rhetorical question: why would any teacher want to have a reputation for corrupting the young, and how could he then be successful? Most interesting for pres-

ent purposes is his assertion that people attribute to Isocratean philosophy
the villainy of those who profess to be Sophists (the term is used here in the
positive sense), but are really nothing of the kind (215).

We should compare here the very similar sentiments expressed by
Socrates when he stresses the necessity of exposing the depraved pretenders
to philosophy (*Republic* 495c–496a). As in Plato, the real malefactors are
the accusers. At *Antidosis* 237, Isocrates states that he can show the places
where the names of the officious and those who are truly liable to the
charges leveled at the Sophists are published: in the lists of public offenders,
where one finds the names of his accusers, but no Sophists. In fact, it is the
disrepute attached to Isocratean philosophy that is responsible for the de-
plorable state of contemporary youth (286).

We should not ignore the fact that Plato and Isocrates are engaging in
some mutual sniping. Socrates' defense on the charge of the uselessness of
his philosophy clearly takes aim at Isocrates, among others; and Isocrates'
contempt for impractical intellectual gymnastics attempts to undermine the
Academy. It must have been a great annoyance to both of them, given that
the bases of their respective philosophies were so different, and given their
respective desires to distinguish their teaching from the sophistic mainstream, that they could both be lumped together under the general heading
"Sophist" (in its negative sense) and suffer the prejudice that term brought
with it. Nevertheless, they are to a great extent troubled by a common enemy, a *polis* "education" that distrusts those who set themselves apart as
experts.

Even a cursory reading of the Isocratean corpus reveals that Isocrates
feels that good advice and valuable admonition is wasted in the face of his
contemporary rhetorical culture. Thus in *To Nicocles* (an oration not aimed,
in the first instance, at a democratic audience), Isocrates states that popular
success is enjoyed not by those who give good advice, but by those who say
things that please the crowd. So too, and most fully, in *On the Peace*. There,
Isocrates analyses Athenian rhetorical culture in terms very similar to those
of Plato. The Athenians are accustomed to drive away those who do not follow along with their desires. "Indeed, you have made speakers study and
philosophize (*philosophein*) not what things are going to be advantageous
to the city, but how they may speak words which are pleasing to you." (5).
"You are only willing to hear those who speak with a view to your pleasure"
(*hēdonēn*, 9) (cf. *Panathenaicus* 140).[11] Mankind in general, and politically
vocal Athenian citizens in particular, are by nature jealous of those who

possess superior talent and/or training. Both Plato and Isocrates, then, characterize Athenian democracy as encouraging those who speak with a view to pleasure rather than long term benefit. It *educates* them to do so. Many of Isocrates' orations to an Athenian audience are defensive in tone, and before we congratulate Isocrates too much on coming up with a paradigm of specifically democratic rhetorical deliberation, we should remember that he positions himself as a member of a beleaguered minority that seems to be institutionally unsuccessful. Might he not be just as idealizing as Plato (although to different ends)?

The trouble is not a lack of *paideia* on the part of Athenians, but competing *paideiai*. Although it would have been easy for Plato and Isocrates to assert that their perceived unpopularity was a simple matter of unschooled ignorance, they do not exercise this option. Instead they magnify their problem by suggesting that people have been *educated* into ignorance and prejudice against them. They are, moreover, at a disadvantage because the competing school pretends not to be one, and this means that the average citizen cannot get the issues straight. Pericles' view of Athens as an education to the rest of Greece, and the epideictic *topos* of the superiority of Athenian *paideia* have been transformed from positive to negative aspects of Athenian culture.[12]

Isocrates expresses this reversal most trenchantly in the passage cited above, where he says that the Athenians have made speakers study and philosophize (*philosophein*) not what is advantageous to the city, but how they may speak words which are pleasing (*On the Peace* 5). The importance of the vocabulary choice here cannot be overstressed: the Athenians make speakers practice a debased form of *philosophy*. Whereas in the *Protagoras*, Protagoras can propose that the city educates its citizens as a way of downplaying the novelty and threat of his profession, the *Republic* and *Antidosis* use the same proposition as an explanation of why their authors are considered a threat. They do not conform to the civic practice of speaking with a view to pleasure alone.

Plato's response is to withdraw entirely from the contemporary practice of politics. The mob is not educable in the current situation, although his Socrates clearly hopes that, if one were to explain philosophy to them slowly enough, they might be brought not to philosophize themselves, but to entrust themselves to philosophers. Isocrates, on the other hand, is committed to the life of the city and to being effective in politics. Given that there are competing models for educated civic speech, how is he to justify his model? Even in Plato there is a hint of another possibility. When Socrates discusses the corruption of the political speaker, he speaks of one who gives the many authority over him "more than is necessary" (*Republic* 493d5). But what if one gave the many *only* what was necessary?

This seems to be the Isocratean plan, as is clear from the *Antidosis*.[13] When Isocrates advises the hapless Timotheus on public relations, he states: "Those who are active as citizens and who wish to please must choose the most beneficial and noblest deeds, the truest and most just discourses, but they must also watch out for and consider this: how they shall be seen in all things to act and speak with grace and friendliness" (132). He sets a similar standard for rhetorical education in *Against the Sophists* (18), where the ideal teacher brings it about that the pupils who imitate him clearly speak more gracefully than others. The Isocratean politician, then, must charm and please the audience while giving good advice. His speeches cause pleasure on the stylistic level while fearlessly advocating what is best. Whereas Plato thinks that corrupt oratory is endemic to democracy, Isocrates considers it an aberration of the recent past. This leaves open the possibility of recuperation.

One then asks: are charismatic presence and elevated style, balanced clauses and lack of hiatus, going to solve the political problems of Athens? Of course not. In the end, for Isocrates as for Plato, one has to have a certain kind of audience. Isocratean education is not merely a matter of teaching rhetoric to aspiring orators, but teaching the audience how to receive his oratory. His speeches are paradigms for his pupils, but are also published for, and sometimes addressed to, a wider Athenian audience, as well as having panhellenic aspirations.[14] They are also written documents, and this adds a further level of complexity. As Usener has pointed out, all references to a hearing public in the orations are fictions: the reader of the text is the real recipient.[15]

Does this mean that Isocrates directs his speeches only at the educated elite? In fact, the double audience (the implied and the actual) allows for multiple reception. Isocrates does hope primarily to influence the educated reader who will take a leadership role in the state and put his theories to practice, and he expects these future leaders to take an active role in reforming the desires of the audience. But, if we can trust the testimony of *Antidosis* 55, he also expected that his speeches would be "commonly reported" among the representative group of citizens who form the fictive jury there. Although the majority of Athenians would not have been reading Isocrates at bedtime, it is not unreasonable to suppose that there would have been a substantial "trickle down" of his comments and suggestions.[16]

The Isocratean speaker rails at, reasons with, and cajoles his audience. When he addresses the Athenians, he attempts to teach them to be an idealized version of themselves.[17] But what is the content of this teaching? One might reply that Isocrates uses the considerable charms of his style to persuade his audience to follow specific advice on specific occasions. Or even that his overall program is panhellenic unity. This reply seems weak, however, because it is hard to see how individual policies make people a better audience. What we need is a principle by which the audience can guide its conduct. Yet would not Isocrates' resistance to theory, commitment to individual educational interaction, and flexibility block appeals to and inculcation of principles?[18] Not necessarily. In the next section I shall argue that Isocrates does indeed appeal to a guiding intellectual principle, that of consistency.[19] Application of this principle will make the audience *philosophoi* and enable them to create beneficial policy in the private, civic, and panhellenic arena.

The Principle of Consistency

I propose now to outline the contours of Isocrates' idealized audience and expose some of its intellectual underpinnings. Isocrates' plan for political goodwill and truth is based upon an identification of rhetorical with political excellence. A good speaker will be a good person and a good citizen. A good citizen will be a good audience. But all of this depends on consistency and a lack of mental confusion, and a willingness to extend this consistency from the interior of the self up to the *polis* level, and beyond it into the panhellenic world. Whereas Plato thinks that the many can never participate in philosophy, Isocrates' ideal would be to elevate the Athenian public into members of his school.

We can see this most easily from the vocabulary he uses in *On the Peace* 116.[20] When he invites the fictive audience in the Athenian assembly to "reason and examine" what causes the downfall of states, the Greek he uses is noteworthy: *philosophēsete kai skepsesthe*. "Philosophize" is the name Isocrates gives the intellectual activity of himself and his students, and is programmatically opposed both to the sterile teachings of Plato and other eristics on the one hand, and to the tawdry training in rhetoric purveyed by sophistic pretenders. It was also the name ironically applied by Isocrates in

On the Peace 5 to the educative activity of the city, one which forced speakers to *philosophein* what is pleasing to the audience. As Nightingale has shown, there were several claimants to the mantle of "philosophy" in the early fourth century.[21]

Isocrates' *philosophia* must be imagined to stand in the tradition of Periclean funeral oration (as reported in Thucydides) that told the Athenians they were "lovers of wisdom" (*philosophoumen* 2.40). Isocratean *paideia* relies upon reasoned deliberation as the key to political success. By following Isocratean reasoning both the student who takes the text as a paradigm and the wider audience can engage in philosophy. Other things being equal, Isocratean rhetorical education will make its recipient a better person (*Antidosis* 274–275).[22] Sound reasoning is the key to both rhetorical and political success; rhetorical excellence is identified with its political and moral counterparts (*Antidosis* 255). In this ideal world, there will be no disjunction between rhetorical expertise and political success.

The key to sound reasoning for Isocrates is the principle of consistency. This means that the same principles must operate inside the self, within Athenian civic discourse, and in the discursive relationship of Athens with other Greek states. Inconsistency (caused by pleasure and greed) is a rhetorical, a political, and in the end a moral flaw, whereas rhetorical consistency is taken to be a guarantor of moral and political consistency. Isocrates is not alone in advocating a type of consistency in intellectual and political practice. We may think of Thucydides' speech where Pericles complains that the Athenians change (*metaballete*) while he remains the same (2.61).

Similarly, Thucydides' Cleon echoes this sentiment when he reproaches the Athenians for changing their minds over the fate of the Mytileneans (3.38). These pleas to stand by a policy already voted upon in the assembly do not, however, amount to a principle of consistency, although they do allude to one of the most famous complaints about the Athenian *dēmos*, its changeableness.[23] We do find the avoidance of contradiction and the pursuit of consistency valued as a principle in the work of Plato. The Socratic *elenchus* functions (at a minimum) by exposing inconsistencies in the theses put forward by Socrates' interlocutors.[24] This kind of logical consistency is not, however, what Isocrates has in mind. He finds its scope too limited.

Let us examine some passages where the Isocratean ideal is expressed. In his *Letter to the Children of Jason*, Isocrates lays out the approved intellectual procedure. He tells his students of rhetoric that they must consider first what is the object of the discourse, in whole and in part. This purpose is then elaborated and fulfilled by rhetorical elements (8). The procedure applies not just to oratory, but to other matters too. First one should deliberate one's aim in life and then conceive one's actions such that they are in conformity with one's ethical goal. The rhetorical, the ethical, and the political merge together (8–10). In his advice to the young ruler Nicocles, Isocrates exhorts him to make judgments unindebted to *charis* (favor or gratitude—as we have seen, speaking for the sake of *charis* characterizes corrupt Athenian orators). He also deprecates judgments that contradict each other (*enantias allēlais*). Rather, Nicocles should always make the same judgments about the same things (*To Nicocles* 18).

The principle is cited again in general terms at *Antidosis* 203 in connection with a defense against the critique of Isocratean *paideia*. Against the claim that his rhetorical education is useless and fails to improve students, Isocrates retorts "people who have sense should not make unequal judgments about similar matters" (*ouk anomalōs poieisthai tas kriseis peri tōn homoiōn pragmatōn*). They must not demand from Isocratean *paideia* what they do not demand from other recognized arts. He repeats this thought at 253 ff., this time in connection with the charge that rhetoric corrupts. He finds this view full of many contradictions (*enantiōseis*, 251). We do not blame the authors of wealth when their descendants use it to bad ends. Why then should we blame rhetoric if it is used to evil ends? We should have the same opinion about the art of speech as we have about the other arts, and not form contrary opinions about similar things (*peri tōn homoiōn tanantia gignōskein*), especially when speech is so foundational. And because it is so foundational, the principle that should be applied to the evaluation of speech is applicable in other areas also (*Antidosis* 253–257). Successful thought and civic and panhellenic activity all depend on its correct application. Isocrates' advice to the people of Athens and to all his intended audiences at home and abroad thus matches that which he gives to his pupils: consider the end and act in conformity with it. The decision as to ends is an ethical one. The Athenians are to become his pupils and reverence *philosophia* and the intellectual practices it brings with it. Isocrates has subtly brought it about that ethical and civic consistency entails approving of him and his *paideia*. His audience is meant to approve of him because his *paideia* is characterized by the same principles he recommends.

In Isocrates' polity there is a coherent continuum between the personal and public/political spheres.[25] There is no qualitative difference between what goes on inside the soul and what goes on when we speak to others:

"We use the same arguments when we deliberate as we do when we persuade others in speech; we call rhetoricians those who are able to speak before a crowd and we consider well-advised (*euboulous*) those who within
themselves (*pros hautous*) best discourse (*dialechthōsin*) about matters"
(*Antidosis* 256).[26] Note that the general principle is held to operate in the
internal cognitive realm and in the civic realm. We should not take for
granted the claim that we use the same arguments in internal and external
deliberation. This is not obviously true in any public rhetoric with which we
or Isocrates are familiar. The claim is prescriptive, rather than descriptive,
of civic rhetoric.

The demand for continuity between the public and private spheres is,
again, not original with Isocrates. It was a well-known feature of Athenian
public life that an active politician had to be prepared for minute scrutiny
about the details of his life, whereas a private citizen could engage in a variety of unusual and/or unsanctioned behaviors. One thinks of Alcibiades,
whose excesses eventually caused such mistrust among the Athenian public that they indirectly led to his fall from influence (*Thucydides* 6.15). In
the case of sexual and sometimes intellectual behavior, private thought and
action were thought to impact on the public.[27] There was a perceived continuum between public and private life. As Wallace has argued, "Individual
behavior that directly harmed the *polis* was subject to legal control. Individual behavior that affected only the individual was not."[28] In the passage
quoted above, however, Isocrates widens the scope of the principle to apply
it to types of deliberation as well as behavior. Furthermore, in *Against the
Sophists* 7, he castigates the eristics who are on guard for verbal contradictions (*enantiōseis epi . . . tōn logōn*), but ignore contradictions in deeds
(*epi . . . tōn ergōn*). The worlds of speaker and audience are connected, since,
ideally, both internal and external speech and word and deed will be consistent with each other. In this universe thought maps nonproblematically
onto persuasion.

This model of coherence is reflected in a particular vision of the relationship between soul, body, citizen, and *polis*. Isocrates' plan for civic
education necessitates grasping *polis* culture as a whole in order to establish
the correct relationships between its constituent parts. Athens, he implies,
needs to design a coherent polity.[29] But the very diversity of the Athenian
experience renders coherence problematic. Athens, he says, "because of its
size and the number of its inhabitants is not easy to conceive as a whole with
any precision, but just like a swollen torrent carries along whatever it hap-

pens to pick up, whether men or things, and it bestows on some a reputation opposite to the one it ought (*doxan . . . tēn enantian tēs prosēkousēs*). This is precisely the thing that has happened to my system of education (*paideia*)" (*Antidosis* 172). This difficulty affects both the popular estimation of Isocrates' school, and "many other matters without number"(171). What kind of a model could one possibly use to compass Athens mentally? Unless we can grasp it, how can we educate it or legislate for it?

The answer is surprising, for Isocrates chooses precisely the *topos* that Plato used in the *Republic*, that is, the analogy between the city and the soul.[30] By personalizing the city, he makes it easier to apply to it personal principles, to treat it as a single entity with which he can enter into an educational relationship. The model enables him to sidestep a potential problem in applying his ideal of consistency, that one cannot educate the mass of citizens the way one can a private pupil. Isocrates uses the analogy to present a vision of the Athenian constitution that is true to his conception of Athenian culture as a seamless rational continuum between the soul and the larger Greek world. The analogy presents the ideal, while current practice is portrayed as a falling away from a "natural" rational condition, as a state of confusion that is expressed on an intellectual level as inconsistency.

Since I have explored the use of the city-soul analogy in detail elsewhere, I shall concentrate here on the most obvious instance, the famous passage at *Areopagiticus* 9 ff.[31] "The soul of the city is nothing other than its *politeia* and has as much power as the judgment has in the body. This it is that deliberates on all matters, preserving what is good and warding off misfortunes. Both laws and orators and private citizens must assimilate themselves to it" (14). The state is the person, the constitution its soul and direction. Confusion in the latter leads to problems in the former. This analogy is significantly related to the city-soul analogy of Plato's *Republic* (368–369). There the comparison is between the entire city and the entire soul, and is directed towards an examination of the proper nature of the relationship between the constituent parts of city and soul respectively. The point is that both cities and men fare better when the rational and best part is in control.

In Isocrates, the soul is not divided into parts, and the explicit point is that a good constitution makes the citizens like itself. What does this mean? The *politeia* directs the city as the mind directs the body. This implies that the *politeia* must be an intellectually consistent entity, a guiding intellectual force. This seems a little abstract. We have no doubt when we read the *Re-*

public about the nature of the guiding force. It is the philosopher/kings and guardians. In Isocrates, as David Konstan points out in this volume, the Platonic and Isocratean good city both run on fixed principles; for Isocrates, this principle is Athenian tradition. Athenian tradition is itself, however, a problematic entity. A reading of *On the Peace*, for example, shows that the nature of the tradition was up for grabs: it was no easy thing to decide precisely which paradigmatic Athenian achievement of the past one wanted to use as a model for the present.[32] For Isocrates, as Konstan observes, the tradition was the rule of merit, identified with the Solonian constitution. In the *Areopagiticus*, it is the Areopagus Council. For Isocrates, as for Plato, the elite will form the governing brain of the operation, although qualifications for that elite differ in each case.

Through the analogy between city and soul, Isocrates constructs an even progression from the inner self, up through social relations, to civic relationships. Just as internal deliberation maps onto public persuasion, so the soul and the guiding rational principle of the human body map onto the political forms that regulate civic discourse.[33] When this continuum works properly, it follows that self-interest becomes civic interest.[34]

For Isocrates, mental weakness among the Athenians means that they do not understand this, and it is the task of his *paideia* to help them do so. Isocrates' privileged position outside the hurly-burly of everyday forensic and legislative wrangling allows him to view the operations of consistency more efficiently than active assembly speakers.[35] This external perspective also gives him a panhellenic viewpoint. Isocrates sets up the entire Greek (and even the barbarian) world as audience and monitor of Athenian intellectual, moral, and political consistency. The larger Greek audience observes Athenian internal constitutional, cultural, and educational practice, and also its behavior in the larger Greek context. In order to stress the centrality of his educational mission to Athenian life, Isocrates implies that Greek judgments of Athenian educational culture are based on observing how the Athenians behave towards himself and his school.[36]

Unfortunately for Isocrates, the Athenian public does not, in his opinion, treat him well, and their attitude is symptomatic of larger problems. The *polis* does not act consistently. The Athenian reputation for culture and for panhellenic leadership is threatened by confusion and inconsistency (caused by greed and selfishness) and Isocrates implies that mental confusion in the world of civic politics is at the core of Athens' current woes. As we shall see, the confusion is evident in the gap between words and deeds, in forensic and other varieties of internal civic practice, in the Athenian attitude to rhetoric, and in foreign policy and the panhellenic arena.

Isocrates refers frequently to this disorder and describes it in a number of ways. As we have seen above, he will sometimes talk about opposition or contradiction (*enantiōsis, tanantia peri tōn homoiōn*) or about making an anomalous judgment. Sometimes he will use the terminology of irrationality (*alogia*). One of his favorite terms is "confusion" (*tarachē*). He uses it, or words derived from the same stem, at least forty-nine times in a variety of different contexts. Most of these instances do not refer to the particular sort of confusion at issue here (confusion arising from inconsistent judgments and actions), but represent a more general turmoil—most often political.[37] It is significant, however, that Isocrates' model for what is wrong with Athens is "confusion." The implication is that a good teacher can clear confusion away, and Isocrates plainly has himself in mind for this important role. A survey of passages from the *Antidosis, Panathenaicus,* and *On the Peace* will demonstrate how current practice threatens the Isocratean ideal of consistent behavior on a civic and panhellenic level and results in confused disorder.

Let us first examine Isocrates' problems with Athenian law. Isocrates begins his self-defense in the *Antidosis* by criticizing the Athenian legal system and the extent to which it is dominated by slander. Slanderers are deceivers, and Athens has often had occasion to repent decisions made in haste (19). The defendant, therefore, should be heard in goodwill and not in anger. In other matters, the Athenians are said to be the mildest of all the Greeks, but in court cases they do the opposite (*tanantia,* 20). Here, then, is inconsistency. The Athenians condemn states where men are put to death without a trial, but do not realize that they are doing the same thing when they do not listen to a case impartially (22). When an Athenian is on trial, he denounces the sycophants, but not when he is on a jury. Those who have sense, however, should be the kind of judges of others they would wish to meet with when on trial themselves (23). Isocrates implies that when one acts on behalf of the city, one should apply the same standards one would as a private person. The problem is not only with the judges, but with the laws themselves. At *Panathenaicus* 144 Isocrates contrasts the code of laws established by the forefathers with the current laws. The latter are "full of confusion" (*tarachēs*) and "contradictions" (*enantiōseōn*).

In the particular context of the *Antidosis,* the inconsistency of the Athenians plays itself out both on the forensic and cultural level (in the Athenian attitude toward rhetoric). The detractors of rhetoric condemn in others the rhetorical skill that they would most like to achieve (244–249). Isocrates describes the disposition of such detractors as "confused" (*tetaragmenōs*, 245); he speaks again of their mental confusion (*tarachē*) at 249. Earlier in the speech he had stated that the attitude of the Athenians would be irrational (*alōgias*, 165) if they penalized him when he had spent his means upon them, whereas those who had paid money to him (for his teaching) were well disposed. A similar topos appears at *Panathenaicus* 15. The populace judges Isocrates confusedly (inconsistently) and absolutely irrationally (*tarachōdōs kai pantapasin alogistōs*). They blame the popular orators, yet they put them in charge, whereas they praise Isocrates' discourses, but are envious of him because of those very discourses.

The clear implication is that intellectual approbation should bring personal approbation and political power, and yet it does not. The two are disjoined. Now, in Isocrates' idealized rhetorical world, style mirrors substance: his poetic prose causes pleasure, and many of his followers think that experts in this genre are wiser and better and more useful than those who speak well in court (*Antidosis* 47–48). Yet his detractors think that he has never had an equal in giving pain to the city (*Antidosis* 35). This is a variety of the same disjunction, and it should warn us how far the Isocratean model is from Athenian practice. For it is perfectly possible to give a speech in artistic prose whose content is unacceptable and unpleasing, and this is the situation in which Isocrates finds himself. Just as he assumes continuity between inner and civic self, and between internal and civic deliberation, he assumes continuity between his own elevated and admirable style and what he sees as its elevated and admirable content. The question we must ask is, does his audience accept this continuity?

So far, the examples cited have dealt with Athenian inconsistency within the world of the *polis*. The Athenian attitude towards Isocratean education is symptomatic of a wider political malaise stemming from confused criteria of judgment. I want now to move on to the panhellenic realm, where we will find the same intellectual idealized continuum stretching out into the panhellenic sphere. This was predictable, given that Isocrates sets himself up as external to normal political practice, and makes the larger Greek realm the audience for Athenian internal policy. At *Areopagiticus* 9, Isocrates declares, "I am at a loss . . . whether you have arrived at such a degree of misperception that you don't notice what kind of confusion (*tarachē*) the city is in." Isocrates labels the inconsistent thinking of the Athenians *tarachē.* As an example, he notes that the Athenians give thanksgiving for actions that alienate their allies and all Greeks. Why? Because their *politeia* cannot cope (they need to return to the democracy of their forefathers). We recall that the *politeia* is the soul of the city. Lack of sound judgment (11) internally leads to external troubles and an interruption of the quasi-natural progression that, according to Isocrates, should make Athens the hegemon of Greece.

It is not only difficulties associated with the *politeia* that disturb relations between Athens and the rest of Greece. As I have already noted, the Athenian attitude to Isocratean rhetoric also contributes. At *Antidosis* 299–304 Isocrates moves from a consideration of Athenian inconsistency with regard to intellectual culture to incoherent foreign policy. It is important to note how seamlessly the latter arises from the former. The argument runs like this: some Greeks are well disposed towards Athens, while others think the city is uninhabitable because of the villainy of the sycophants. Yet the Athenians are more pleased with those who bring an evil reputation on the city than with those who cause it to be praised. The solution? They must cease from this confusion (*tarachēs*), take a more favorable view of philosophy, and not hold an opinion about it that is opposite (*enantia*, 302) to that held by the rest of the Greeks. Note how Isocrates slides effortlessly back and forth between the areas of foreign relations and attitude towards his *paideia*. This slide effectively makes the reception of Isocratean education diagnostic of Athenian cultural and political health.

Athenian incoherence is even more the point in *On the Peace.* The Athenians "are disposed to the utmost confusion" (*tarachōdestata diakeisthe*, 9), partly because they are deceived by those who speak with a view to their gratification (10). Isocrates deals at length with the nature of this confusion, which exists both in the external and internal sphere. The Athenians praise their ancestors but do the opposite to what they did (41), and employ mercenaries to commit acts they would not even forgive in their children (45). They govern the city with a greater degree of confusion (*tarachōdesteron*) than those who have just founded a city (49).

Some of this is worth quoting in full. Thus: "We are most experienced in words and deeds, yet we are so unreasonable that we change our decisions on the same issues within the same day" (52). When the Athenians reacted to the Peace of Antalcidas, they recognized that it is not just for the stronger to rule the weaker, and this is, in fact, the principle of the current *politeia* (69). But now they desire a maritime empire. They agree with what

Isocrates says about the rule of despots, but not with what he says about the maritime empire.

"What you see in the case of others, you fail to recognize in your own case. And yet this is not the least sign of sensible men, if they plainly discover in all similar situations the same actions (*tas autas praxeis epi pantōn tōn homoiōn phainōntai gnōrizontes*). You have never yet cared for any of these things, but you consider tyrannies to be difficult and painful not only to others but to those who possess them, yet you consider the rule of the sea the greatest of goods, although it differs from monarchy neither in what it does nor in what it suffers." (114–115).

All these passages make the same argument: the Athenians use different standards in different situations and this means that their decisions and policies are incoherent. Similar situations call for similar decisions. We should note also how civic, Hellenic, and personal realms stack up one on top of the other. He compares condoning the acts of children to condoning those of mercenaries, hatred of tyranny as a *politeia* for Athens to approval for it as a panhellenic policy. Concomitantly, he contrasts disapproval of the rule of the stronger as a principle for the Athenian *politeia* and as a panhellenic principle when Athens was weak to approval of it when Athens is strong.

The passages surveyed here show that the demand for consistency and the rejection of confusion operate with regard both to public and to private deliberation, and are crucial for successful thought, rhetorical performance, and civic policy. This entire intellectual apparatus is predicated, I have suggested, on a series of moves that bring soul, city, and Greece into a close relationship. The move into the realm of the soul is important because Isocrates can then tar confusion and inconsistency in the civic and panhellenic realm with the brush of psychic disturbance and madness. By pointing out the Athenians' confusion, Isocrates educates them to rise above it and adopt his *paideia* as the principle by which they run their lives.

Michael Leff (this volume) suggests that I have done Isocrates' program and *oeuvre* an injustice by confounding "rhetorical consistency" (where principles are generated through an engagement with particulars) with formal or fixed consistency (an abstract notion), and thus that I have measured Isocrates by standards that were more philosophical (in the Platonic sense) than rhetorical. On this model, Isocratean shifts reflect different rhetorical contingencies. Could there be a "prudential" or "situational" rather than a moral consistency, one that would allow self-interest and the shifting of priorities when expedient? If so, the Athenians could be acquitted of the mistakes catalogued above, and Isocrates would escape the charge (which I shall make in my final section) that he fails to abide by the principles he enunciates. Surely the Athenians cannot be asked to give up "the most fundamental agonistic principles that define, then as now, actual political life."[38] The answer to this last point is both yes and no. Isocrates believes, as Plato does not, that reasoned political debate by citizens gives the city the best chance of making a correct decision: "How could people judge well concerning the past or take counsel about the future, if they do not scrutinize the arguments of opposing speakers and provide themselves as an impartial audience for both sides?" (On the Peace 11; cf. Antidosis 21). He also, however, wants to alter, along the lines suggested above, the intellectual and moral structure within which such debate takes place, since current practice does not conform to this ideal.

There are occasions when Isocrates' discourses put forward what might be thought a concept of prudential consistency. At Panathenaicus 30, he describes the "educated" (pepaideumenous) as those who make good use of the things that occur on a daily basis, whose judgment successfully masters opportunities, and who, for the most part, can make an accurate guess as to what is expedient. In the Archidamus, when the Spartan king argues for war rather than peace, he states that nothing along those lines is either good or bad. The important thing is how one uses opportunities and general circumstance (50). I shall return to these "kairotic" skills in my final section. I submit, however, that there is nothing in these passages that contradicts the stronger model of consistency that (as I argue) Isocrates constructs. One must always be prepared to deal with changing circumstances and with contingencies that arise, but one should do so within a larger structure. The problem with Athenian practice, as Isocrates sees it, is that this is not the case. Although it may well be that twentieth-century rhetorical studies have discovered and fruitfully applied a more pliant rhetorical conception of consistency,[39] I argue that this is plainly not the consistency Isocrates was talking about. In the passage from On the Peace discussed above, Isocrates argues that it is not just for the stronger to rule the weaker and that this principle is foundational for the Athenian politeia. The Athenians should not desire a sea empire, nor is it even expedient (69–70). Later on, he argues that the desire for monarchic power is inconsistent. There is no trace in this argumentation that in some circumstances such power is acceptable, nor that the Athenian citizen body is a vastly different entity from a king, nor that it is bad to be the object of kingly rule but desirable to exercise it. When Isocrates criticizes Athenian policy, he does not suggest varying our standards of consistency or propriety depending on whether we are at home or in the law court, engaging in personal meditation or writing to an important dynast. On the contrary, if what I have been arguing is correct, Isocrates wants us to behave in precisely the same way in all those situations. I imagine it is true that no political orator could pass this test. But it is Isocrates, not I, who demands that he should do so.

Hoist by His Own Petard?

Our educator's plan for reforming rhetoric and thus politics and ethics is radical.[40] It is synoptic, whereas Athenian political and judicial practice was determinedly piecemeal. The assembly and the courts made essentially opportunistic decisions on a multitude of different occasions. In his history, Thucydides had the Corinthians immortalize the Athenians as restless innovators who can never stay still and are always greedy for more (1.70). Their mutability is so much of a *topos* that Isocrates can use it to support his own arguments, as we have seen. Isocrates is proposing a dramatic transformation of the democratic *ēthos* as practiced in the late fifth century and in his own time. It would not readily have been apparent to the Athenians that they should employ the same principles towards the other Greeks as they did in internal politics. The whole point of being a citizen of an ancient Greek polis was to have more rights than those who were not citizens. Even in the modern world "Do unto others" is a principle honored more in the breach than in the observance. For the Athenians, certainly, observing it would have run counter to another important principle, the maximization of pleasure. It is human nature, Isocrates admits, always to be insatiable (*aplēstōs*) with respect to seeming advantage (*pleonexias*) (*On the Peace* 5–7; see esp. 7).

In this final section of my paper, then, I shall maintain that, in spite of his breadth of vision, Isocrates' educational project is undermined by his engagement with the very rhetoric to which he owes his success. Although Isocrates tries to distance himself from the weaknesses of Athenian culture, his orations display internally those very vices he condemns in his fellow citizens. Greed, desire, freedom, and insatiability—all of which result in inconsistency—characterize both his prose and Athenian policy; he himself is a product of the city's education in Athenian culture. Additionally, we may observe a tension between consistency and opportunism in the relationship between his orations conceived as wholes.

As is well known, the various orations do not agree with each other either in what they recommend, or in their attitudes to, for example, the Peace of Antalcidas. This has led some to suggest that the speeches should be read as rhetorical exercises rather than political advice. So, for example, Harding argues that *On the Peace* is one member of a *merely* epideictic antilogy. Its hawklike counterpart would be the *Archidamus*.[41] There is a tension between the speeches as rhetorical paradigms and as political discourses. Although sympathy for Isocratean rhetorical achievement may tempt us to see inconsistencies of this type as expression of a flexible response to *kairos* and differing contexts, I ask that we hold Isocrates to the same standards he imposes on others. Let us examine first the problem of inconsistency internal to individual speeches, and then the inconsistency between speeches.

We are all familiar with Isocrates' habit in his later speeches of lamenting his old age as the cause of a lack of polish in the discourse at hand. So too, we sometimes run across the *topos* whereby he will briefly (or not so briefly) change direction, along these lines: "Whereas I originally thought x, now y comes into my mind." I give two examples. First (and most briefly), at *Panathenaicus* 95 ff. the orator comments that his feelings are changing: he had intended to speak conciliatingly about Sparta, but now he loses self-control because of the number of topics that have flowed into his mind. Second, at *Antidosis* 310 ff.:

> I am at a loss how to arrange the many *logoi* that have come to me. For I think that each one of the things I have in mind would seem appropriate in itself, but if I spoke them all now, they would give both me and my listeners trouble. Indeed, I've been afraid of this even in the case of what I have already said, in case some such experience happen because of their number. For we are all so insatiable with regard to *logoi*, that we praise opportuneness and say there's nothing like it, but when we think we have something to say we forget moderation, and always adding some little point we cast ourselves into utter inopportuneness. In fact, as I say and recognize this, nevertheless I still wish to talk to you.

On the one hand, these passages present the old trick of the speaker overwhelmed by sincerity and the force of his convictions, as well as the bounty of his inventive genius (we may well think of Pindar here). Clearly, we are meant to be impressed by the copiousness of his talent. We are expected to be sympathetic to digression because we have all been brought up in the same rhetorical culture, one that prizes freedom and novelty. On the other hand, there is a difficulty. These orations, although they mimic oral form and its occasionality, are intended for written circulation and private reflection. What is more, Isocrates tells us on two other occasions how he wants us to read him. The crucial thing is not to run through the whole speech in one sitting, in case it is too long or we get bored, but to study it piecemeal (*Antidosis* 12; *Panathenaicus* 136–137). Once we accept that the live audience is only an enabling fiction (and intended by Isocrates to be so understood), it follows that there is no need for an author to worry about tiring his audience, and even less reason to buy into the fiction of the author carried away by passion. The *topoi* don't quite fit. Nor do Isocrates' protestations fit with advice I quoted from the *Letter to the Children of Jason* that the orator conceives the speech as a whole and then makes everything else cohere.

One might attribute this incoherence merely to the fiction of spontaneous delivery and an unavoidable awkwardness in the transition from oral to written delivery and dismiss it were it not for the vocabulary in the *Antidosis* passage: we are all "insatiable (*aplēstōs . . . echomen* 311) with regard to *logoi*." The words here are identical with those Isocrates uses in condemning Athens' imperial greed: it is human nature always to be insatiable (*aplēstōs echomen, On the Peace* 7) with respect to seeming advantage. But if the rhetorical, political, and ethical realms map on to each other, then the same insatiability for discourse that allows Isocrates to expand and Athens to be the center for the teaching of rhetoric makes Athens institutionally greedy and unlikely to listen to Isocrates' advice.[42] Just as Isocrates portrays himself as free to change his mind about his approach when the mood strikes him (and in pursuit of rhetorical advantage), so the Athenians chop and change when deciding about the policies of the city. So, then, neither Isocrates nor the Athenians always live up to the ideal that one formulates a goal and reasons, or writes, consistently with it. When they please or when circumstances change, so do they. Isocrates hopes that reading and listening skills can develop into a civic *praxis*, but he is swayed by the intellectual culture of his *polis* even as he seeks to transform it.

We can reinforce this conclusion by observing the use of confusion-vocabulary to indicate the possible effect of an Isocratean digression. At

Panathenaicus 74 ff., Isocrates debates whether or not he should launch into his digression on Agamemnon, a figure dear to his own heart. He observes that when one speaks about matters outside the given subject, they can seem to be confusing (*tarachōdeis*, 74). At the end of the digression, he realizes that many will criticize him for having said more than he should (84). Nevertheless, even though he has perhaps disregarded *kairos* and the symmetry of the speech, he chose to give Agamemnon his due (84–86). We are meant to conclude that Isocrates may not have been so disproportionate as he makes out, or at least that it was in a good cause. Still, *tarachē* descends when the speaker is faced with the gratification of an immediate desire. *Pleonexia* (greed or insatiability; note *pleonazōn*, 85), *tarachē*—the characteristic Athenian vices install themselves as emblems of the noble liberty of the orator. He is a very *democratic* speaker. He would only be ashamed if he had indulged himself inadvertently.

What of external confusion and inconsistency? How do we deal with the contradiction between *Archidamus* and *On the Peace*? There, at least, two different personae are speaking, the Spartan king and "Isocrates." What of the Peace of Antalcidas, endorsed in *On the Peace*, and condemned elsewhere? Takis Poulakos finds in such indeterminacy an acknowledgment of the inadequacy, the contingency, of any particular political ordering, and identifies this as a profoundly democratic strand in Isocratean thought.[43] To an extent, I agree, but it should be clear by now that Isocrates himself finds this democratic strand profoundly problematic, because a good democracy, good citizens, good pupils, will maintain the principle of consistency that guarantees ethical, intellectual, and political virtue.

There is another aspect to this problem, one which Konstan touches upon in this volume and which I have discussed elsewhere. This is inconsistency—or perhaps, to be kinder, indeterminacy and *amphibolia*—as an aspect of Isocrates' panhellenic mission.[44] His audience is never merely an audience of Athenians, but looks towards kings and despots, and even oligarchs in Sparta. In such circumstances, indeterminacy and *amphibolia* can be a sign of moderation, as Isocrates himself points out (*Panathenaicus* 172). One tells different versions of the aftermath of the Seven against Thebes depending on the political situation. After all, the Isocratean orator must be a master of *kairos*, opportunity, and *kairos* is a fleeting thing. Perhaps discretion is the better part of consistency.

I believe that we cannot so easily rid ourselves of the tension between consistency and opportunism, for this is a tension that lies at the heart of

Isocrates' educational mission. Athens has become the center of rhetorical education because the rewards of rhetoric are greatest there and the opportunity for practice is readily available (*Antidosis* 295 ff.). Its political culture, that is, the culture of the law court and assembly, encourages the orator who can move with the crowd and take its measure. "Kairotic" skills are at a premium. If Isocrates is to educate his pupils for success, he must encode in his works a number of different political situations, which the students can model and adapt when necessary. This applies to non-Athenian as well as Athenian students. I think that one reason Isocrates' longer works are so meandering is precisely their status as paradigms, which imposes a certain inclusiveness in order to prepare the student for all eventualities. Thus we find many places where Isocrates mentions and defeats a potential objection, or briefly sketches a subject for the benefit of future speakers and gives an example. A certain indeterminacy is inherent in the function of the speeches as educational paradigms. The good orator adapts to *kairos*, while of course (we hope) holding fast to ethical principle. He must be adaptable and opportunistic, and again, these are fundamental traits of the Athenian character, which enable the development of rhetorical culture there. We should remember how Isocrates lists Athenian *eutrapelia* as an enabling factor in the development of oratory at Athens (*Antidosis* 296). The Loeb translates this as "flexibility of mind."[45] It means, literally, that the Athenians turn, or change, easily. This returns us to the same problem I have been sketching, that the conditions that make Athenian rhetoric possible are at odds with Isocrates' own idealizing view of rhetorical culture, characterized as it is by control, focus, and consistent ethical purpose. Isocrates' centrifugal tendency towards intellectual and rhetorical diffusion, dictated in part by the demands of pedagogy and in part by his native rhetorical culture, exists in uneasy tension with his overall purpose: endorsement of the rule of the best in panhellenic interests.

Conclusion

I started this paper with a dichotomy. Athens' renowned dedication to intellectual culture (as represented in Pericles' Funeral Oration) sits ill with the many protestations of Plato and Isocrates that the Athenians do not want to listen to the kind of rhetoric that is rationally grounded and good for them. They approve rather those who speak with a view to their immediate pleasure and gratification. Only some kinds of intellectual culture are acceptable, it seems. I explained this dichotomy by elaborating the model of Athens as teacher/educator. The city does indeed teach a civic and rhetorical culture, but (according to Plato and Isocrates) it is one based on hedonism and opportunism, and it does not leave room for competing *paideiai*. Plato's response is to withdraw from political life. Isocrates too withdraws, but only far enough to give him space to model a different kind of audience and civic education. He thinks that he can restore to the democracy the love of wisdom that Pericles spoke of. His *paideia* is based on the principle of consistency, which starts its operation inside the individual soul, and then extends itself smoothly up through the levels of *polis* and Greece as a whole. One implication of this principle is that ethics, rhetoric and politics stack neatly and unproblematically on top of each other. By adopting the principles of Isocratean rhetoric, the Athenians (and others) will become good citizens. Yet since Isocratean rhetoric is identified with politics, the rhetorical operations of Isocrates' orations have implications for the consistency of his political and ethical agenda. Rhetorical diffusion implies political and ethical flaws.

Isocrates wants Athens to adopt his *paideia*, but he shows that he has learned the lessons taught by the city all too well. He sets up an alternative *paideia*, but it is colored by the rhetorical culture he wants to escape. How could it fail to be? Could any form of rhetorical education escape this? Isocrates, like his audience, has been educated by the city. Like the citizen in Protagoras' Great Speech, he has absorbed as axiomatic certain societal assumptions. These are the traditions David Konstan talks about in this volume. Isocrates trusts that all will be well if we merely follow through the logic of such tradition. The Athenian tradition, however, is opportunistic and is based on adopting the course that seems best at any given moment. It is unclear how this coheres with a centralized and governing intellectual principle. Isocrates' version of *paideia* falls between the Platonic rejection of the education offered by the *polis*, and the *polis*' demand that its citizens think within the boundaries it has set up. As is often the case with those who try to make a middle ground, Isocrates ends up being regarded with suspicion by both sides.

Notes

1. So in T. Poulakos 1997 and in his paper in this volume.
2. Ford 1993: 50. Ford notes that Isocrates arrived at this position with political and social motives.

3. Yunis 1996.

4. Loraux [1981]/1986: 91–97; 141. But see also Morgan 1998: 106.

5. Ober 1989: 159–160.

6. See Blank 1985; Ober 1989: 166–172.

7. Morgan 2000: 140.

8. Corruption was one of the charges leveled against Socrates at his trial, and it is notable that when Isocrates gives a justification of his life in the *Antidosis*, he chooses to do so by pretending that he has been accused of the same crime. See Nightingale 1995: 28–29, and Ober's essay in this volume.

9. Cf. Ober (1998: 235–259) for a similar analysis of the Platonic material.

10. Passages defending Isocratean education and eloquence occur in *Against the Sophists*, *Antidosis*, and *Panathenaicus*.

11. On Plato's vision of Athens as a "theatocracy" devoted to the pleasures of performance, see Wallace 1997. At one extreme, the relationship of flattery and pleasure between speaker and *dēmos* can be compared to that between *erastēs* and *erōmenos* (Connor 1992: 97–98).

12. Loraux [1981]/1986: 144–145.

13. As was the case with Pericles who, in Thucydides' paradoxical phrase, "restrained the multitude freely and was not led by them more than he led them" (2. 65).

14. Ober (1998: 255–256) has further remarks on Isocrates' panhellenic perspective. See also Morgan 2003: 184–186.

15. Usener 1994: 46.

16. I am indebted to David Depew for this formulation.

17. On the instructive potential of rhetoric as a way of overcoming the limitations of mass deliberation, see Yunis 1996. As Yunis points out, Thucydides portrays Pericles as the exemplar of the educating orator (74–75). Commenting on Isocrates' own time (but with reference to Demosthenes), Yunis notes the potential for unlimited mass communication provided by publication: orations intended for a reading audience allow the orator to aspire to a candor not usually available in the Assembly (246–247).

18. See Batstone 1986: 97–98 for Isocrates' lack of a detailed or fixed methodology. See also Cahn (1989) on Isocrates' "doctrine of nontechnical instruction" (137).

19. Cooper 1986: 89 rebukes Isocrates for his failure to respond to foundational questions. While it is true that Isocrates has no interest in justifying his pedagogy in terms that would have satisfied Plato (Batstone 1986: 99), this does not mean that he does not espouse rational principles he deems *practical*.

20. See also, *Panegyricus* 6: πῶς οὐ χρὴ σκοπεῖν καὶ φιλοσοφεῖν τοῦτον τὸν λόγον; *Antidosis* 121 (of Isocrates' pupil Timotheus).

21. Nightingale 1995: 13–59.

22. cf. Batstone 1986: 102–103.

23. Cleon's arguments come closest to doing this, but it is clear that his rigidity is regarded negatively.

24. Vlastos 1983.

25. I am aware that the distinction between public and private in classical Athens is a contentious topic. Nevertheless, the difficulty of specifying the scope of such a distinction, added to Isocrates' elision of it, strengthens my argument.

26. For this idea of thought as internal deliberation, see also Plato, *Sophist* 263e.

27. Isocrates often criticizes his audience for not applying in public the standards they expect in private. At *On the Peace* 4 he complains that the Athenians abhor slanderers in private, but put their public trust in them (cf. 13, and the contrast between past and present politicians at *Panathenaicus* 139–140). His rhetorical strategy in these passages is to shock the audience by pointing out that, so far from applying standards of superior individual behavior in the case of politicians, they actually invert those standards.

28. Wallace 1994: 146.

29. The desire for a coherent principle of order is not unique to Isocrates. Farrar's interesting study of classical Athenian politics in Protagoras, Thucydides, and Democritus, proposes that these three thinkers believed that "such order as there is in the world is not transcendent, but immanent. Knowledge is knowledge of the order implicit in interaction or of the elements making for constancy and stability in change" (1988: 43). Isocrates' principle of consistency is not dissimilar to the desire for "knowledge . . . of the elements making for constancy and stability."

30. For a short introduction to the problematic nature of the analogy in the *Republic*, see Annas 1981. Gill (1996: 240–320) gives a detailed and convincing interpretation of the "personality unified by reason's rule" in the *Republic*. On the personalization of the student-teacher relationship, see Cahn 1989: 135.

31. Morgan 2003. See also *Panathenaicus* 138.

32. Morgan 1998: 115 re *On the Peace* 36–37. In the same oration, Isocrates narrates the mayhem that befell the Spartans once they pursued a sea empire: "They did not keep the laws they took from their ancestors nor did they stand by the character that they had before, but supposing that they could do anything they liked they entered into a state of great confusion (*tarachē*)" (*On the Peace* 103).

33. Morgan 2003.

34. The Stoics seem to have taken a version of this continuum even further. The principle of right reason operates at both the individual, the civic, and the cosmic level (Schofield 1999: 67–74).

35. Heilbrunn (1975: 157; 160–161) comments perceptively on how Isocrates presents his avoidance of a public career as a condemnation of Athenian democracy.

36. See *On the Peace* 41; *Areopagiticus* 79–80; *Antidosis* 224–226, and (in particular) 295–302.

37. So, for example, *Panegyricus* 6; 134; *Areopagiticus* 76; *Panathenaicus* 164. This generalized usage is paralleled in Demosthenes (see *On the Peace* 1), who uses *tarachē* vocabulary in the region of twenty times. Plato uses this vocabulary much less frequently (ca. 14 times), most often of general psychic and intellectual confusion.

38. David Depew, in personal communication.

39. Cf. Leff, this volume.

40. On the scope of Isocratean *philosophia*, see Cooper 1986: 86. I cannot agree with the evaluation of Yunis (1996: 18, n.40), who states "I am not aware of a single argument on our current problem [the "education" of the *dēmos* by orators] which is original to him or for which he offers a theoretical perspective."

41. Harding 1973. For a response, see Moysey 1982 and Morgan 1998: 116.

42. Compare Cleon in the Mytilenean debate, Thucydides 3.37–39. He combines the *topoi* of Athenian changeability with their mad passion for *logoi*. They are defeated by the pleasure of listening, and are more like the *audience of the Sophists* than people deliberating about the city.

43. This volume.

44. On Isocratean *amphibolia*, see further Bons 1993; Morgan 2003: 187–188.

45. Norlin's translation in Isocrates 1929, ad loc.

PART FOUR

Isocrates and Aristotle

7

DAVID DEPEW

The Inscription of Isocrates into Aristotle's Practical Philosophy

Did Aristotle Have a Close Encounter with Isocrates?

THERE is a doxographical tradition that when the seventeen-year-old Aristotle first came to Athens he studied for three years with Socrates (*Vita Marciana* 3). Now that is plainly impossible. Socrates died in 399, while Aristotle was born in 384 and arrived in Athens in 367. It is not impossible, if "Socrates" is a mistake for "Isocrates," as Anton Chroust has argued that it is (1973). It is significant in this highly speculative connection that Aristotle, having "transferred," as we would put it, from Isocrates' school to the Academy, made a name for himself by lecturing publicly on rhetoric. In that role, he would have been in a good position to confute Isocrates' rhetoric-based conception of education, which he presumably knew firsthand.[1]

Aristotle would have been prepared for this task by having cut his teeth, as all young Academics did, on *Socratikoi logoi*, which served as instruments for dialectical training within the Academy (Kahn 1996). By devising imaginary conversations between well-known, and in some cases well-hated, personages whose fates were antecedently known to the audience (since they lived as long ago as the 1930s now seem to us), Plato asked his Academic pupils to appreciate subtle links between character traits, conversational style, and dialectical ability. It is probably in this way that Aristotle first encountered Plato's *Phaedrus*, which contains some condescending, and possibly ironic, praise of the young Isocrates. Isocrates is said to be more philosophical in temperament than Lysias, the other focal orator in this dialogue (*Phaedrus* 279a). But, as in the case of figures such as Alcibiades, Charmides, and Critias, one must bear in mind that early promise is not always fulfilled, and that what begins well can end badly—if the burdens, as well as the pleasures, of philosophy are not correctly taken up.

Aristotle's earliest extant works, such as the *Gryllus* and the *Protrepti-cus*, give us glimpses of his stump speeches on behalf of the Academy. In spite of sustained efforts to see in them intimations of the philosopher of the *corpus Aristotelicum*, these works exhibit little more than the boiler-plate sublimatory rhetoric of Plato's middle period, which their author would have mastered in the course of his own dialectical education. The puzzle is that during Aristotle's formative period the theory of Forms as we find it in *Phaedo, Republic*, and *Symposium* had already been set up as a target for Academicians, including the elderly Plato himself (Düring 1960). It would appear that Aristotle participated wholeheartedly in this revisionist project *intra muros*, perhaps even while he continued to give or circulate (like Isocrates) *extra muros* the eloquent exoteric speeches for which he became known in antiquity.

Yet Aristotle's close encounters with the school of Isocrates, however they may have unfolded, whether directly or at a distance, seem to have left a mark. For in the course of developing his own philosophy Aristotle took it upon himself, perhaps uniquely among his peers, to produce a philosophical account of rhetoric—a "rhetoric within the bounds of reason," as Kant might have put it—and to encase this account of rhetoric within a wide-ranging philosophy of "human affairs" (*ta anthrōpina*). This philosophy of the human sciences, as I will try to show, exhibits more traces of Aristotle's encounter with Isocrates than the limited number of overt references to that figure in the Aristotelian *corpus* might suggest.

I will argue for three points in this connection. First, Aristotle's philosophy of human affairs—by which I mean the doctrines about *praxis* contained in *Politics*, both versions of *Ethics*, and less directly the subordinate *technai* discussed in *Rhetoric* and *Poetics*—can plausibly be read as a critique, more sustained and systematic than it is normally thought to be, of Isocrates' views about topics which, in a text that clearly has Isocrates' *Antidosis* in its gunsights (*Nicomachean Ethics* [EN] X.9.1181b15–16), Aristotle calls "*ta anthrōpina,*" human affairs (*EN* VI.7.1141b9; X.9.1181b15). Second, in criticizing Isocrates Aristotle pays him a backhanded compliment. He cooptively incorporates within his own philosophy of human affairs the meanings that Isocrates (but not Plato) assigned to key terms, notably *phronēsis*. At the same time, he constricts the conditions of applicability of these terms in a distinctly non-Isocratean way, subordinating practical reason (*praxis*) to theoretical (*theōria*) reason, and in turn subordinating technical reason (*technē*) to practical. Having done so, Aristotle uses this picture to launch a sustained and explicit criticism of Isocrates' claim to be able to teach political science (*politikē epistēmē, EN* X.9.1181a1–1189a19).

My final point concerns this critique of Isocrates. Aristotle's ontotheological privileging of *theōria* over *praxis*, and of *praxis* over *technē*, is not as consistent as he believes with the autonomy he proclaims for *praxis*. Aristotle's interpretive framework is thus vulnerable to a rebuttal by Isocrates, or on his behalf by contemporary appropriators of *praxis*-philosophy and of rhetoric as a "theory of civic discourse." It is Isocrates, I conclude, who might justly be said to be entitled to the last word on the subject, even if he didn't get it.

Philosophia in Isocrates and Aristotle

My point of departure is the claim that to Isocrates' mind there is no limit to the range of an explicitly deliberative, or practical, model of rationality and discourse. If we think or speak at all, he argues, we deliberate—at least where we are not chattering away in the empty, eristic way he accuses the dialecticians in the Academy of doing (thereby making *them* the Sophists and *himself* the philosopher). "I do not think it is fitting," Isocrates writes in *Antidosis,* "to confer the name of *philosophia* on anything that does not help us speak or act (*legein, prattein*) in the present" (*Antidosis* 266).[2] His reason soon becomes clear. Deliberative reason defines for Isocrates the nature and limits of human wisdom (*sophia*):

> Since it is not in the nature (*physis*) of humans to have scientific knowledge (*epistēmē*), the possession of which would enable them to know (*eidenai*) what is to be done or said [with respect to future actions], from what is left I consider to be wise (*sophos*) whoever is able out of his opinions (*doxais*) to chance upon (*epitugkanein*) what for the most part the best [course of action and speech], and I consider a philosopher whoever is able by study quickly to get hold of this sort of practical wisdom (*phronēsin*) (*Antidosis* 271).

This presumption in favor of reason in the deliberative mode reflects a traditional Greek sense that (in spite of constant meddling by the gods, whose ability to shape the future responsibly is compromised by a freedom from death that renders them a bit stupid) humans themselves, especially when

gathered together into *poleis,* are autonomous agents in a *kosmos* that neither systematically supports nor opposes their projects. These are projects
for which humans are responsible all the way down; they are praiseworthy
and blameworthy for outcomes as well as intentions. This picture of humans as autarchic agents was transmitted from the epic and lyric poets to
the Attic tragedians. It was reaffirmed by Sophists like Protagoras, whose
defense of the poetic tradition (against philosophers of Parmenidean line-
age) and of the autonomy of public discourse in a world where *"anthrōpos*
is the measure of all things" is predicated on this very point.

This background understanding of the human condition, and especially
of the role of discourse as a deliberative instrument, was picked up by Isocrates. Distancing himself from ambulance-chasing logographers, whom he
conceded to fall under the weight of Plato's harsh criticism of Sophists (*Antidosis* 2), Isocrates boldly attempted to seize back the term *philosophia*
from the word-wrangling dialecticians, reapplying it to his own reflective,
aestheticized brand of published first-person prose, which was designed
mimetically and performatively to induce a literate and reflective appreciation in his readers of the interests of their *polis* and of Greek culture as
a whole (T. Poulakos 1997; Haskins 2001; Haskins, this volume). Isocrates
invents for this purpose a form of written epideictic that incorporates and
subverts judicial and deliberatory rhetoric, taking distance from the harsh
particularity, and to his mind unreflectiveness, of actual judicial and deliberatory practice. He appropriates the term *philosophia* to name the long-
range, reflective, but still practical, stance that he commends and purports
to teach.

At a crucial juncture in the argument of *Politics VII–VIII,* Aristotle too
uses the term *philosophia* in a sense that does not restrict it to apolitical
intellectuals. Having denied that in an ideal state everyone should be presumed capable of engaging in *theōria,* at *Pol.* VII.15.1334a32–34 he remarks that nevertheless all the citizens will "be especially in need of
philosophia, temperance (*sōphrosunē*), and justice (*dikaioisunē*) to the extent that they are in a position to engage in leisure activities (*scholazousin*)
in the midst of an abundance of such good things" (*Pol.* VII.15.1334a32–
1335a4). That is clearly a sense of *philosophia* comparable in its breadth to
Isocrates'.

I think we are justified in saying that this claim about the virtues necessary for the proper use of leisure harks back to Pericles' remark in the
Thucydidean Funeral Oration that the Athenians are superior to the Spar-

tans because "we philosophize without softness" (Thucydides, *Peloponnesian War* 2.40.1). The term "philosophize" refers in this passage to the public display and appreciation of fine things and to the habit of engaging in public criticism of words and deeds. In the Funeral Oration, these qualities serve as a marker of the well-balanced Athenian life in contrast to the overemphasis on brutal *gymnastikē* in Spartan culture. So too in Aristotle. Just before his remark about the need for *philosophia* in leisure, we find Aristotle engaging in a passionate tirade against the Spartans, in which they are said to be deficient in the ability to practice the virtues appropriate to peace and leisure time, and so must cultivate war not as a matter of justice, but simply to keep from going flabby (*Pol.* VII.14.1333b10–1334a10). This, Aristotle infers, led to their downfall. He generalizes the point by saying that any state whose legislator does not make the virtuous use of leisure time, *diagōgē en tē scholē*, including provisions for *mousikē*, the aim of his educational system will have to suffer the fate of Sparta:

> The lawgiver of the Lacedaemonians . . . legislated everything with a view to domination and war. This view, which is readily refuted by *logos*, has now been refuted by facts as well. Having lost their empire, we see that the Spartans are not happy and that their legislator cannot have been good . . . The reason is that he did not educate them to be capable of being at leisure . . . They lose their edge, like iron, when they remain at peace. (*Pol.* VII.14.1333b12–13, b22–b23; 1334a8–10, trans. Lord, rearranged slightly).

In his insistence that peace is better than war, that *mousikē* is the better half of the *mousikē-gymnastikē* dyad that makes up *paideia* or education, and that all citizens should possess some degree of leisured *philosophia* in order to live well or happily (*Pol.* VII.7.1333a31–37), Aristotle is party to the same contrast Pericles had drawn. It is a view to which Isocrates, too, is party. They all stand on roughly the same Athenocentric ground. Admittedly, in his panhellenic solicitations for unity, Isocrates is less critical of Sparta than Aristotle. Nonetheless, he too employs anti-Spartan commonplaces in both *Panegyricus* and *Areopagiticus* when he praises Athenians for using their leisure and wealth "to devote themselves to horsemanship, gymnastic, hunting, *and philosophy*" (*Areopagiticus* 45, my italics; see *Panegyricus* 47).

Yet there are significant differences between Isocrates and Aristotle within their shared commitment to citizenly *philosophia.* Isocrates' *philosophia* is oriented toward deliberation about what is good for the city in the long run, Aristotle's toward enhancing virtuous leisure activities (*diagōgē en tē scholē*) for their own sake (*Pol.* VIII.3.1338a9–12; 5.1339b14). This difference shows up in their contrasting accounts of the relationship between citizenly *philosophia* and *paideia.* Isocrates implies that adult *philosophia* is continuous with *paideia.* Aristotle does not.

Stimulated by rhetorical performances like his own, Isocrates' ideal citizen is continuously to re-educate himself in the art of practical deliberation by reiteratively reidentifying himself with the aims of his *polis* among other *poleis* and of Greece in relation to the barbarian Other (*Antidosis* 192; 214–216). By contrast, Aristotle's brand of leisured *philosophia—diagōgē en tē scholē*—is construed as a successor to *paideia,* not a continuation of it, in which adults are to devote themselves to all sorts of leisured learning (*mathēsis*)—including the learning one can derive from the hermeneutics of tragic plots as set forth in *Poetics*—by using the fixed moral habits and identities they have presumably acquired at earlier stages in their moral development as a platform from which to cultivate whatever intellectual virtues of which they are severally capable (Depew 1991).

There is a still deeper discontinuity between Aristotle's and Isocrates' conceptions of the *philosophia* that all adult citizens should possess. For Isocrates, *philosophia* of this sort is *philosophia* itself. There is no other; as we have seen, it is equivalent to human *sophia* (*Antidosis* 271). All citizens can have it, moreover, although to different degrees, depending on their native talent and their explicit training. For Aristotle, on the other hand, not all citizens who know how to use their leisure well, and so possess citizenly *philosophia,* possess, or even can possess, the political science (*politikē*) that constitutes the supposed raison d'être of Isocratean *philosophia.* Even more importantly, those who possess Aristotelian *politikē* do not on that account necessarily possess *sophia.* Aristotle reserves the honorific term *sophia* for the theoretical science that he calls theology or "first philosophy," and that we call metaphysics (*Metaphysics* I.2.983a1–10; *EN* VI.6.1141a16–19). Those who have practical or technical knowledge are not, for Aristotle, wise. For Isocrates, by contrast, *only* such persons are wise.

In Aristotle's scheme, first philosophy studies divine things (*ta theia*). The contrasting systematic study of human affairs (*ta anthrōpina*), both the ethical and legislative principles of good *praxis* and subordinate *technai* like rhetoric and poetics, is not even "second philosophy." Second philosophy comprises the *theōria* of natural, as distinct from eternal, objects—humans included, to be sure, but as animals among, and compared to, other animals. No, a philosophy of human affairs, *ta anthrōpina* (an objective, not a possessive genitive, since Aristotle proposes to make *ta anthrōpina*, including the practice of cultural *philosophia*, the object of a systematic inquiry aimed at teaching legislators and statesmen what arts and sciences should be cultivated in their *poleis*) is only "third philosophy," although as far as I know Aristotle does not use this phrase. Accordingly, Aristotle writes in *Nicomachean Ethics*, in what I am strongly tempted to claim is a direct reference to Isocrates' explicit assertion of the contrary, "It is clear that wisdom (*sophia*) cannot be the same as political science (*politikē*) (*EN* VI.7.1141a28–30).

Aristotle gives the following warrant for this conclusion. "It would be absurd," he writes, "for someone to think that political science (*politikē*) or practical wisdom (*phronēsis*) is the most noble thing, seeing that human beings are not the best things in the universe" (*EN* VI.7.1141a20–22; cf. *NE* VI.7.1141a35–b1). Aristotle's firmness on this anti-anthropocentric point derives from two intertwined sorts of confidence, one theological and ethical, the other epistemological.[3] For reasons I will review in the following paragraphs, Aristotle is sure that an anthropocentric perspective—the perspective I earlier ascribed to Greek poetic wisdom, to the sophistic movement, and to Isocrates—will undermine the very possibility of ethical judgment because it necessarily blurs the distinction between intrinsic and instrumental goods. Given the importance of ethical judgment, it is a good thing, then, that epistemologically Aristotle is confident about something that Isocrates explicitly denies at *Antidosis* 271, namely, that at least some humans, by cultivating a studiously impractical and purely contemplative form of knowledge, can enjoy at least glimpses of God, whose life of leisured activity and studious indifference to human affairs provides a model by which ethical education, virtuous practice, and theoretical accomplishment *for their own sake* can be measured (*Eudemian Ethics* [*EE*] VIII.3.1249b15–25; *EN* X.7.1177b19–a8).

From these Aristotelian ethical and epistemological principles, it virtually follows that practically wise rulers—rulers who have been wised up by the Lyceum, for example—must be able to distinguish clearly between activities that are intrinsically good, such as those of God and those who study him, and activities that have merely instrumental worth. Anyone who fails to recognize that human affairs (*ta anthrōpina*) are not the highest object of human reflection will be unable to do this. Only by contemplating the god of the philosophers, who engages in no instrumental actions at all, but whose contemplative activities are the very measure of inherent value, can we have cognitively secure access to the ontotheological framework within which what is inherently good about human activity—the performance of virtuous activity for its own sake—can be cleanly separated from human activities that have only instrumental worth. Failing this, humans will necessarily regress to the meddlesome gods of the mythical epics and to the ideological cover they afford to no less meddlesome politicians—and rhetoricians. By this severe standard, as we will see, Aristotle finds Isocrates wanting.

Admittedly, Aristotle takes the study of *ta anthrōpina* to be autonomous from the theoretical sciences in at least one important sense. There are practically wise people (*phronimoi*), such as Pericles, who are no good at theoretical reflection; and conversely theorists who have no practical judgment, like the proverbial Thales, who was laughed at by a servant girl when he fell down a well while trying to look at the stars (*EN* VI.5.1140b8–11; 7.1141b2–8). It is the former who should rule. To postulate this autonomy of practical reason is of enormous consequence for Aristotle. It is what preeminently distinguishes his view of political science (*politikē*), which is closely related to practical wisdom (*phronēsis*) (*EN* VI.8.1141b23–24), from Plato's ill-conceived doctrine of philosopher kings. Unlike Plato, Aristotle does not think that good political practice is reducible to *theōria* technically applied by experts or by slumming apolitical intellectuals, as Plato does in *Republic;* or that humans should regard themselves as robot-like "toys" (*paignia*) of the gods, rather than as fully autonomous agents, as Plato does in the *Laws* (*Laws* 804b); or that *mousikē*, drama, and *rhētorikē* as actually produced by the free workings of culture, rather than as redesigned by Plato, are a threat to either the good life or to good rule.

None of this is enough to deny, however, that for Aristotle the autonomous sphere of *praxis*, and therefore the scope for *eupraxia* or well-performed activity, is in its very essence circumscribed by the fact that some humans can and do have theoretical knowledge, both theological and natural; and that this kind of knowledge is higher than practical activity and political knowledge. From this fact, it follows that those who in virtue of having *phronēsis* are fit for rule in good states will exhibit their practical wisdom above all in this: they will acknowledge, as Pericles did, that, even if they cannot engage in *theōria* themselves, they will honor those who cultivate the *bios theōrētikos* as living a higher way of life than their own, practical or political life (*bios politikos*); will protect them; and will make the cultivation of leisure activities that approximate to the *bios theōrētikos*— *philosophia* in Aristotle's broad sense—the very point of the constitution (*EN* X.7.1177b5–26; see Depew 1991).

In this way, Aristotle's rulers look *up toward theōria*, not down from it, as Plato's do. When they look up what they see is a god who, although he is the best thing in the universe and the most active in the sense of self-actualized, "engages in no externally and instrumentally good actions at all" (*Pol.* VII.1.1323b23–25; 3.1325b29–30). If practical men do not regard this state of existence as higher than any that can be achieved by practical wisdom, Aristotle warns that the busy-ness (*a-scholia*) in which practitioners of the *bios politikos* are necessarily immersed will degenerate into an instrumentalism that will make the virtuous actions done for their own sake on which high-minded nobles (*kalōkagathoi*) pride themselves difficult to identify and even more difficult to attain (*EN* X.7.1177b1–1178a10; *EE* VIII.3.1249a15–17). Warning the potential rulers who study with him against this descent into instrumentalism—including the higher instrumentalism implicit in the Platonic claim that good politics is technically applied *theōria*—is, in my view, the main burden of Aristotle's *Ethics* and *Politics*. It is the fundamental proposition in what he calls political science (*politikē*). Its correlative burden is to disabuse those leading the *bios theōrētikos* of the contempt for the *bios politikos* or *praktikos* that they usually cultivate in response to the pervasive busy-body-ness (*polupragmosunē, panourgia*) of practical politicians. For when it is constrained by a proper relation to divine things, those who engage in the *bios praktikos* are in a position, Aristotle says, "to achieve much that is noble" (*Pol.* VII.3. 1325a33–34).

In the light of this discussion, we may see more clearly why Aristotle thinks that a good constitution, to the extent that it is good, must be oriented toward the proper use of leisure that has at its pinnacle the theocentric contemplative wisdom that only some can attain, but that also includes under the wider sense of *philosophia* all sorts of intrinsically valuable yet useless forms of learning, including those afforded by art. Only under these conditions, Aristotle argues, can a scale of values be maintained in the *polis* that teaches people in their daily life to distinguish what is inherently fine, including good political activity, from what is merely instrumentally good, or vulgar, or even vicious.

A good case can be made out that under the influence of men like Demetrius of Phaleron this Peripatetic program for politics was, through the force placed at its disposal by the Macedonian military, put into practice in cities like Alexandria, with their museums and libraries. Aristotle's Lyceum thereby proposes to take up where Plato's Academy, discredited by its ineffective and imprudent meddling in politics based on a false conception of the theory-practice relationship, had left off in its efforts to re-educate Greece so that it would be worthy of the domination of the barbarians on which the panhellenic crusade shared by Isocrates and Aristotle is predicated.

Phronēsis in Isocrates and Aristotle

The distance Aristotle takes from Plato in countenancing a relatively autonomous sphere of political practice is equal to the distance that Aristotle is willing to move toward Isocrates' stress on deliberative reason. He meets Isocrates, as it were, halfway. My primary evidence for this judgment is that Aristotle's use of the term *phronēsis*, or practical reason, to name the architechtonic virtue of the sphere of *praxis* reflects *Isocrates'* definition-in-use of that term, not Plato's.[4] It is Isocrates' notion of practical wisdom that is enshrined in Aristotle's account of human things, although it is then circumscribed within a theocentric framework which Isocrates, in his sophistic anthropocentrism, does not countenance, but which Aristotle takes as a necessary precondition for separating what is noble in the sphere of practice from what is not.

I can begin to show this by recalling an old, and now largely resolved, scholarly quarrel. All parties to this quarrel recognized that Plato uses the term *phronēsis* indiscriminately for both practical and theoretical wisdom, albeit with a bias toward the latter, whereas the Aristotelian *corpus*, especially *EN* VI, carefully restricts that term to practical reason: the engagement of the moral virtues with particular, contingent circumstances through the use of deliberative rationality (*bouleusis*) to determine good actions (*praxeis*) (Jaeger 1948: 239–243; Natali 2001). That Plato should not have discriminated between these two uses of intelligence is not surprising. Many of his dialogues retain the Socratic identification of virtue with knowledge, and even when this identification is weakened by the admission that good judgment is dependent on a good upbringing, as it is in *Republic* (Irwin 1977), Plato does not go out of his way to recognize two different *kinds* of knowledge, practical and theoretical, let alone the third kind that Aristotle mentions, *craft knowledge* (*technē*). Many of what Plato calls *technai*, in his later dialogues especially, are what Aristotle would call *praxeis*, governed by *phronēsis*.

On the basis of this perception, Werner Jaeger set out to demonstrate that Aristotle's earliest writings, such as the *Protrepticus*, exhibit this generalized Platonic usage, and that the first version of his ethics, the *EE*, does as well. Aristotle's own conception of an autonomous practical reason, *phronēsis*, appears, according to Jaeger, only in the presumably late middle books of *EN* (Jaeger 1948). In the vast literature responding to Jaeger, it is generally conceded that the *Protrepticus* does exhibit this indiscriminate meaning of *phronēsis*. This tells us very little, of course, if texts like this were rhetorical performances on behalf of the Academy, as I have already suggested they may have been. Neither does the fact that the generalized meaning seems to persist in the *Topics*, since the identification of knowledge and virtue is, precisely, a *topic*—a claim on which dialectical reasoning can be exercised (Natali 2001). Still, Jaeger has definitively been shown to be wrong in assimilating *EE* to the view expressed in the exoteric speeches. *EE*, no less than *EN*, restrictively identifies *phronēsis* with practical wisdom and contrasts it with theoretical intelligence, if not quite as clearly as *EN* VI does (Cooper 1975: 136–139; Kenny 1978; Natali 2001: 6–10).

The argument that *EE* and *NE* both restrict *phronēsis* to practical wisdom is as follows. Jaeger's argument for the persistence of a generalized Platonic intelligence (*phronēsis*) in *EE* was that at the crucial climax of that version of Aristotle's ethics—a version that, *contra* Kenny (1978), I consider earlier than *EN* for any number of reasons[5]—Aristotle affirms the Platonic spin on *phronēsis* when he says that the measure of external goods for the person is "whatever choice of goods of the body, or money, or friends, or other goods will best foster the contemplation of god" (*EE* 8.3.1249b16–18). But in saying this Aristotle does not imply that theorists, as theorists, can make such choices. Theorists as theorists do not, by Aristotle's own account, make any choices (*prohaireses*) at all. Only those who deliberate do that. What Aristotle means is that those who deliberate *well*, or exhibit the virtue of *phronēsis*, measure their choices of external goods in all matters that involve intrinsic worth, both theoretical *and practical*, by reference to the transcendent value of theoretical wisdom (*sophia*). (See *EE* 8.3.1249b9–19 and *EN* 6.13.1145a6–11, where Aristotle says that *phronēsis* does not give orders to *sophia*, but for its sake [Cooper 1975: 136–139; Dunne 1993: 241–242].) This is substantially the same view that is found at the end of *EN*.

Nor does Aristotle, in either text, recommend to rulers the asceticism and indifference to external goods (*ta hekta*) that is conventionally associated with the *bios theōrētikos* and is consistently maintained by the Stoic tradition. Rather, Aristotle simply notes that no one can make good judgments about political matters unless the god of the philosophers is generally perceived as the highest object of knowledge and reverence. For only then can the right amount of external goods—neither too much nor too little—be employed in pursuing one's practical ends virtuously. Otherwise, external goods such as health, wealth, beauty, fame, and so forth, will become de facto ends, rather than necessary means, and reason will degenerate into a utilitarian instrument for acquiring those goods. This general principle, which I have been reporting as Aristotle's considered view, is already articulated in *EE* (*EE* VIII.3.1249b1–25). It is expressed, moreover, by way of a decidedly *non-Platonic* usage of the term *phronēsis*, which, as in *EN* VI and X, restricts it to practical reason (although not yet couched in a vocabulary as well adapted to eschewing instrumentalism as the conceptual vocabulary of *EN*).[6]

Instead of trying to find precisely where to draw the line between a young, Platonizing Aristotle and a mature, supposedly "empiricist" Aristotle, Jaeger and the scholars who followed him would have done better to have inquired where the deliberation-and-choice oriented usage of *phronēsis* to which Aristotle cleaves might have come from (or minimally with what existing conception it agrees). My suggestion is that it comes from (and explicitly agrees with) Isocrates' conception of the term.[7]

Consider again the following passage from *Antidosis:*

> Since it is not in the nature (*physis*) of humans to have scientific knowledge (*epistēmē*), the possession of which would enable them to know (*eidenai*) what is to be done or said [with respect to future actions], from what is left I consider to be wise (*sophos*) whoever is able out of his opinions (*doxais*) to chance upon (*epitugkanein*) what is for the most part the best [course of action and speech], and I consider a philosopher whoever is able by study quickly to get hold of this sort of practical wisdom (*phronēsin*) (*Antidosis* 271).

In the last line, Isocrates, like Aristotle, sees *phronēsis* as deliberative intelligence deployed in pursuit of what is in one's best interest (*EN* VI. 5.1140b10–12; VI.8.1141b25–35; *Antidosis* 207). It deliberates about what needs to be acted on by the deliberating agent himself and specifies what course of action to adopt under a particular set of circumstances. It is what we call "common sense." *Phronēsis*, so construed, stands in contrast to the nondeliberative universality of scientific knowledge (*epistēmē*), quite apart from whether humans can have any such thing or not. In orienting *phronēsis* to practical insight, both Aristotle and Isocrates are in agreement with general Greek usage (see the LSJ lexicon). In this connection, Plato's assimilation of *phronēsis* to what Aristotle calls *epistēmē* appears as an attempt to legislate meaning, driven by the Socratic tendency to assimilate deliberation to theoretical insight. Isocrates' identification of *phronēsis* with deliberative rationality constitutes a reflective validation of what the many unreflectively presume, but with an explicit anti-Platonic contrast to theoretical intelligence added. Aristotle agrees. Nonetheless, Aristotle differs from Isocrates in a crucial respect. While both make a firm distinction between the spheres of scientific knowledge and practical reasoning, Aristotle affirms that some humans are capable of the former, whereas Isocrates explicitly denies it. As a result, Aristotle denies the universality of *phronēsis*, its status as the *only* accessible kind of human intelligence.

For Isocrates, the scope of *phronēsis* is as wide as it is for his old antagonist Plato. It is just that Plato's bias in favor of universal *theoretical* knowledge as constituting *phronēsis*, and hence *philosophia*, has been switched by Isocrates in favor of the universality of *practical*, deliberative knowledge and *its* status as *philosophia*. I rather suspect, in fact, that it is just because he merely *reverses*, rather than breaks out of, Plato's epistemology that Isocrates admits Plato's view that human affairs fall within the sphere of variable, aleatory, and stochastic opinion (*doxa*). As Isocrates, in a remarkably Platonic spirit, puts it, "All of the things with which we [as human beings] are concerned evade certain demonstrative knowledge (*epistēmē*)" (*Antidosis* 184). In saying that he can make wise men out of those who study human affairs under his tutelage, assuming only that they have a certain modicum of native talent, Isocrates claims no more than that he wants to be the educator of those who make educated *guesses* (*Antidosis* 185, 189). Aristotle explicitly and categorically rejects in *EN* VI the agreement between Isocrates and Plato about the universality of *phronēsis* as well as their equally odd agreement that thinking about human affairs reduces to mere opinion [*doxa*].

At this point, Aristotle's compliment to Isocrates about the autonomy of *phronēsis* begins to turn into a serious criticism, as I will now try to show. It is significant that the same array of terms—*phronēsis, epistēmē, sophia, doxa, technē*—that figure prominently in Isocrates' *Antidosis* figure just as prominently in Aristotle's treatment of practical wisdom and the other intellectual virtues in *EN* VI. But they figure in it quite differently. I suspect that Aristotle's parsing of the intellectual virtues in this book has Isocrates' *Antidosis* in its dialectical sights more explicitly than it has Plato, and that disagreements about the relationships among these terms that are registered there can serve as proof of what I have been saying about the complex relationship among *phronēsis* in Aristotle, Plato, and Isocrates.

Aristotle affirms, in the first instance, that scientific knowledge (*epistēmē*), which Isocrates denies to humans, is indeed possible for some people (*EN* VI.2.1139a18–b13). This assertion would be pointless if the Academics were his principal targets; they never doubted it. Having said this, Aristotle goes on to deny just as explicitly that *phronēsis* should be called *sophia* (*EN* VI.13.1145a7–11), which is precisely what Isocrates does call it, as we have already seen. Aristotle also explicitly denies that *phronēsis* is reducible to opinion (*doxa*) (*EN* VI.8.1142a7–10; VI.9. 1142b8–9), or to guesswork or conjecture (*euboulia*) (*EN* VI.9.1142b2), or to cleverness (*deinotēs*) (*EN* VI.13.1144a24–29). If these arguments do not have Isocrates as their explicit target, I would be very surprised. For it must be acknowledged that he fits the profile perfectly; even a charitable reader will find in *Antidosis* precisely the identifications of *phronēsis* with wisdom, opinion, guesswork, and cleverness about which Aristotle complains.

Let us consider these arguments in a bit more detail, beginning with Aristotle's views about *epistēmē* and *sophia*. For Aristotle, scientific knowledge (*epistēmē*) consists of noetic intuitions about the first principles (*nous*) that govern a particular disciplinary sphere, which are arrived at through inductive ascent (*epagōgē*) and are then displayed in a sequence of lawlike consequences that flow apodictically from these principles (*apodeixis*) (*EN* VI.6.1140b30–37.1141a19). Scientific knowledge so defined bumps up against *sophia* only when it touches on the science of the divine (*ta theia*). For *sophia* is the "most exact form of scientific knowledge"(*EN* VI.7.1141a16–17); it is "noetic intuition (*nous*) plus scientific knowledge (*epistēmē*) of the most valuable things, with divine *nous* as its coping stone" (*EN* VI.8.1141a16–20). In a world where humans are not the most valuable things (*EN* VI.7.1141a20–22), and in which some of them can get at least a bit of scientific knowledge about the things that are most valuable, Aristotle thinks that it would be *absurd* to reserve the honorific term *sophia* for knowledge of human affairs, as Isocrates does.

Aristotle disagrees with Isocrates, then, about whether humans can possess *epistēmē*. In consequence, he even more categorically disagrees with him that *phronēsis* is equivalent to *sophia*. Nonetheless, he concurs with Isocrates in saying that *epistēmē*, and a fortiori *sophia*, does not name the kind of knowledge we require in order to deal with contingent particulars concerning what is to be done (*EN* VI.8.1142a23–30).[8] That requires *phronēsis*, not *epistēmē*. Aristotle thus agrees with Isocrates that *phronēsis* is the intellectual virtue that governs the sphere of practical reasoning, reasoning under particular circumstances calling for decision and action. At the same time, Aristotle denies what Isocrates asserts *about phronēsis:* that *phronēsis* is *doxa* (*EN* VI.9.1142b7; see T. Poulakos this volume on Isocrates' reasons for saying this); and that, in consequence, it is equivalent to guesswork (*EN* VI.9.1142b2). That is because Aristotle thinks *phronēsis* is as epistemically solid as perceptual recognition (*EN* VI.8.1142a27). If it were mere guesswork, it could not reliably identify or perform actions that have intrinsic worth. *Phronēsis* cannot be acquired, then, as *doxa* can, by mimetic training on a contractual basis, or by educated guessing about how to apply vague rules of thumb to particulars. For Aristotelian *phronēsis* is a distinctive kind of cognition. It is nondemonstrative insight into just the right thing to do in particular circumstances, backed up by its own kind of noetic intuition (*EN* VI.8.1142a27; Dahl 1984).

This form of knowledge, Aristotle asserts, can arise only in persons who have been habituated since childhood into moral virtues and noble values:

> Therefore it is necessary for those who can listen profitably to lectures about what is noble and just to have been brought up in good habits (ethically). For the "that" (*hoti*) is the starting point [of such inquiries], and if this is sufficiently clear to a hearer, he will need nothing of the "why" (*dioti*). Such a person will easily grasp the proper starting points [of practical reasoning] (*EN* I.4.1095b3–8; on the distinction in this passage between the "that" and the "why"—a fundamental distinction in Aristotle's philosophy of science—see Burnyeat 1980).

Aristotle asserts this because for him moral virtue (*aretē*), rather than reducing to a certain set of passions, is a mode of having intentionally constituted experiences that light up the world in a certain value-laden way. It is virtue that makes it possible for reason (*phronēsis*) to identify how, in a specific moment, one must act in a way that embodies a fundamental fact about the world: that some things have intrinsic values, and others do not. This is why Aristotle says that virtue gives the ends and *phronēsis* finds the means (*EN* VI.5.1114oa26). (The point is even stronger at *EE* II.2.1227b22–24, where he says that "virtue *is* the target [*skopos*] that makes our choices correct.") It is also why Aristotle provides a (probably false) etymology of *phronēsis* which makes it mean "preserver of [the moral virtue of] temperance (*sōphrosunē*)" (*EN* VI.5.1140b11–12). Virtue, by giving access through its performance to a world of intrinsic values, controls and reorients the desires we share with other animals.

What lies behind these arguments is Aristotle's clean distinction between intrinsic and instrumental goods. A virtuous person recognizes, in what Aristotle regards as a cognitive rather than a merely opinionated act, the right thing to do here and now in and through his or her habitually fine (*kalos*) way of experiencing things. The good person always acts in a way that respects the distinction between the intrinsically good and the instrumentally good, and brings that distinction to bear on particulars. This perhaps explains why Aristotle is so insistent that no one who has not been brought up in good habits since childhood can have *phronēsis* (*EN* I.4. 1095b8; see Burnyeat 1980). *Pace* Isocrates, mere opinion, which can readily be acquired and just as readily lost in youth and adulthood, is not strong enough to recognize and apply the distinction between the intrinsically good and the instrumentally good, especially under conditions of duress.

From this moral-epistemic high ground, we may be sure that Aristotle would not be pleased by any tendency to identify what is merely clever (*deinos*) with what is practically wise (*phronēsis*) (*EN* VI.13.1144a24–37). Yet Isocrates tends to think of cleverness and *phronēsis* as interchangeable terms, or at least to think of cleverness as the same thing as *phronēsis* when it is viewed from the perspective of admiring audiences rather than deliberative agents. The latter is how Isocrates puts the matter in *Antidosis* when he remarks proudly that he himself is perceived to be clever, and that Timotheus, the eminent but unpopular general who had been his pupil, and who serves as his model of *phronēsis*, is a clever man because as a general he knows with whom to go to war, when to do it, and how to raise and deploy an effective force to get the job done (*Antidosis* 117).

The perceived blurring of the distinction between cleverness and *phronēsis* in Isocrates' *Antidosis* provides a plausible explanation of why Aristotle goes out of his way to say in *EN* VI that cleverness is not equivalent to *phronēsis*, since (he says) a clever man may be bad (*kakos*), while a practically wise man is by definition good, even though on occasion he can, and must, be clever as well (*EN* VI.123.1144a24–36). (Just why Aristotle puts forward Pericles as his model of the *phronimos* may seem obscure until we remember that Aristotle's Pericles is Thucydides' Pericles, and that the Thucydidean Pericles supports Aristotle's conviction that *philosophia, mousikē,* and *scholē* stand at the pinnacle of civic values and norms. It is possible that Aristotle's choice of Pericles is meant to contest Isocrates' choice of Timotheus, who exhibited no such sensibilities.)

In general, we may say that traits that appear as moral defects to Aristotle appear fairly often as virtues in Isocrates. Thus in specifying what character traits those who put themselves under his tutelage must studiously cultivate, Isocrates says that they must above all have a burning desire for recognition. They must have a certain *pleonexia* or urge to seek advantage over others, albeit *pleonexia* "of the good sort," he assures us (*Antidosis* 275–276). For Aristotle, by contrast, *pleonexia*, grasping for power, *always* names a vice, and a burning desire for recognition names the moral defect of those who mistakenly want to be honored quite apart from knowledge of whether they deserve to be (*EN* I.5.1095b23–30; II. 1.1107b29–32).

Aristotle and Isocrates on Political Science

So far I have been arguing that Aristotle's sustained effort in *EN* VI to distinguish *phronēsis* from opinion, guesswork, cleverness, and personal advantage may have Isocrates as an explicit (though perhaps not exclusive) target. At the very least, we may conclude that the views expressed in Isocrates' *Antidosis* fail to match Aristotle's criteria for *phronēsis*. Confusions and conflations of this sort, Aristotle implies, testify to an insufficient discrimination of the morally fine from the merely instrumentally good. But we need not remain content with these suspicious correlations. For this very issue is directly broached in Aristotle's argument in *EN* X to the effect that anyone who fails to distinguish political science (*politikē*) from rhetoric (*rhētorikē*) cannot be judged to possess or be able to teach the former (*EN* X.9.1181a12–19). There are overwhelmingly persuasive textual reasons to think that this argument is aimed at Isocrates, and to infer that the source of his confusion on this point is, for Aristotle, Isocrates' prior failure (which we have just reviewed) correctly to discriminate *phronēsis* from character states that merely resemble it. To this argument I now turn.

The thrust of Aristotle's argument is as follows. If the conceptual distance is collapsed between political science and rhetoric, a vulgar orientation toward instrumental values will necessarily flood into the space of political decision-making, thereby conflicting with and undermining the possibility of a genuine political science. Aristotle insists on this because he holds (1) that *politikē* depends on the same cognitive capacity, and character trait, as *phronēsis* (*EN* 6.8.1141b23);[9] (2) that this practical cognitive capacity is not the same capacity as that of the technically intelligent person (*technites*) (*EN* VI.3.1140a2); (3) that technical forms of knowledge are instrumentally related to ends; (4) that if the ends of politics are to be attained technical forms of knowledge must be subordinated to the decision making of political agents who possess practical reason (*EN* I.2.1094a27–b5);[10] and (5) that rhetoric is a technical form of knowledge (*Rhetoric* I.2.11357b26). It follows from these five propositions that conflations of *politikē* with *rhētorikē*, if they are institutionalized in the discourse of a state, will open that state to an inappropriate stress on instrumental values. For the inherent instrumentality of *technē*, which means it can be exercised in a value-neutral way, will refashion *phronēsis*, and hence *politikē*, after its own image.

Aristotle is convinced that *phronēsis* and *politikē* cannot be possessed or exercised in this way and still remain faithful to their essence or perform their proper functions (*EN* VI.8.1141b23–24). As we have seen in the preceding section, what it means to be a practically intelligent person is habitually to perform the noble for its own sake, that is, to do it for reasons having to do with the intrinsic worth of what is done, quite apart from its consequences (which is not the same thing as saying that a good act isn't aimed at something good or to deny that it presumptively achieves a good result). It is precisely in view of this constraint on what can count as *phronēsis* that political science (*politikē*) cannot be an art, and so cannot be identical to rhetoric. Although it thinks on a bigger scale and has a scientific dimension, *politikē* rests on the same character state as *phronēsis* and apprehends the same intrinsic values. *Politikē* (*EN* VI.9.1141b24) cannot be an art (*technē*), and so cannot be identical with rhetoric. By contrast, an art is a capacity of realizing opposites. The sign of the artful doctor, for example, is that he or she knows how to kill you as skillfully as how to cure you. So too in the art of rhetoric, which is a capacity for arguing opposite positions. Accordingly, the practitioner of an art may be badly motivated without compromising the claim that it is an *art* that is being practiced. But it is quite otherwise with *phronēsis* and *politikē*. These cannot be pursued for bad ends and still be the kinds of capacities they are.

This is not to deny that the *artful* quality of an Aristotelian *technē* depends on pursuing goods internal *to that art*. Garver (1992; and this volume) has shown quite clearly that it does. What it means is that, because of the different ways in which means are related to ends in technical and practical reason, there is an instrumentalism lying at the conceptual or definitional, and not merely the psychological, heart of any *technē*. For Aristotle, this instrumentalism must be constrained by the pursuit of intrinsically good actions if good politics is to be practiced—and if the internal goods proper to an art are to be realized as consistently as good politics requires that they must be. Anyone who conflates *politikē* and *rhētorikē*, accordingly, or *a fortiori* subordinates the first to the second, must run afoul of the subordination that Aristotle requires.

There are textual reasons for concluding that Aristotle has Isocrates explicitly in mind in pressing this point at the end of *EN* X. Scholars have long been unanimous in identifying the following passage in the argument of *EN* X.9 as aimed directly at Isocrates:

> Those sophists who advertise [that they teach about politics] appear to be a long way from being teachers; for they are altogether ignorant about what sort of thing *politikē* is, and the sorts of things it is about. For if they had known what it is, they would not have taken it to be the same as rhetoric, or something inferior to rhetoric, or thought it an easy task to assemble laws with good reputations and then to legislate. For they think they can select the best laws, as though selection did not require understanding (*sunesis*), and as though correct judgment (*krinai orthōs*) were not the most important thing, as it is in *mousikē* (*EN* X .9.1181a12–19, Irwin translation, slightly amended).

We know that Isocrates is Aristotle's target in this passage because he cites Isocrates' proposal about laws in *Antidosis* 79–83 as an instance of

what we can expect from someone who only *believes* himself to possess political insight. Isocrates' proposal is that it would be easy to collect Greek
laws, find out which ones are most highly regarded, and put them into effect in every *polis*. One theme of Aristotle's accusation seems to be that
Isocrates substitutes mere reputation for experienced judgment as a criterion for discerning which constitutions are best (*EN* X.9.1181a20–22). (The
argument is rather like those raised by academics against rankings of top
graduate schools based on surveys sent around to professors asking them
what they *think* to be the best programs. Needless to say, the majority of
those who are sensitive to this methodological flaw come from universities
whose programs don't make the list.) Behind this accusation, however, lurks
Aristotle's recognition that for the Isocrates of the *Antidosis*, *phronēsis* is
doxa, opinion, rather than a genuinely cognitive moral discrimination. It is
this substitution of mere *doxa* for habit-based insight into moral particulars
that underlies Aristotle's indictment of Isocrates' for his one-size-fits-all approach to recommending laws to the Greeks, with its assumption that one
constitution will be best for all states.

From this Aristotle infers that Isocrates cannot *possibly* possess political science. Aristotle says that different laws will improve different states at
different times, just as artful doctors will recommend differently for different patients at different times (*EN* X.9.1181b3–9). Fine discrimination under particular circumstances is required if a good legislator is to turn deviant
states into correct ones, which is the overriding aim of the possessor of *politikē*. But fine discrimination depends on the close, mutually supportive relationship between *phronēsis* and political science. *Phronēsis* provides the
political scientist with the perception of moral facts on which his science is
based; political science gives to the legislator and governor a range of lawlike, though not exceptionless, relationships on the basis of which good,
value-laden choices must be made. This is one of the main points of Aristotle's *Politics*. Perhaps Aristotle began the laborious job of assembling his
famous collection of one hundred and eighty-five constitutions, of which
only the *Constitution of the Athenians* is extant, in order to show that he
could do a better, more discriminating—in short, more practically intelligent—job on constitution-making than Isocrates because he, Aristotle, actually possesses *politikē*, while Isocrates does not.

Assuming that Aristotle does have Isocrates in mind in *EN* X.9.
1181a12–18 as someone who conflates rhetoric and politics, we may infer
that Aristotle's further claim to the effect that anyone who conflates rheto-

ric and politics cannot be said to possess or to teach *politikē* may find its ultimate warrant in Isocrates' conflations of cleverness, ambition, and desire for recognition with *phronēsis*, which Aristotle attacks in *EN* VI. For to the extent that Aristotle is successful in associating political science with *phronēsis*, and in turn dissociating *phronēsis* from opinion, conjecture, cleverness, and *pleonexia*, we may find in Isocrates' failure to make the latter set of discriminations grounds for the following conclusion: Isocrates, in Aristotle's view, does not possess the concepts and values that underlie *phronēsis* and so cannot possess *politikē*, depending as it does on the same values. These conflations all fail to keep the inherently instrumental goods of an art sufficiently subordinate to the intrinsic goods whose pursuit defines the fundamental principle of Aristotelian political science.

Isocrates Vindicatus

It may seem to the reader that I have explicated Aristotle's critique of Isocrates with a zest that might suggest that I commend it. It is true that I am greatly disposed to favor Aristotle's view that *praxis* consists in the habit of realizing intrinsically noble values and that the various *technai*, having no such intrinsic orientation to the good, must be subordinated to, and oriented toward, good political and moral *praxis*. Nonetheless, I am not as certain as Aristotle that the distinction between intrinsically and instrumentally good actions is altogether wanting in Isocrates.

My reconstruction of the premises of Aristotle's argument allows us to see that Aristotle's argument about the *praxis-technē* relation is dominated by his views about the *theōria-praxis* relation. Aristotle, as we have seen, requires the good politician to recognize that the *bios theōrētikos* is inherently superior to the *bios praktikos*, since in the absence of this recognition the distinction between inherently good action and merely instrumental action will collapse. Two points can be made against this claim. The first is that this may not be true; it may be possible to distinguish between the inherently and instrumentally valuable, and to subordinate the technical to the practical, without privileging *theōria*. In distinguishing himself from the logographers and sophists, Isocrates may in fact be making this exact distinction. A second objection bears on the conditions under which Aristotle's thought can be appropriated by moderns. If Aristotle is right that the *bios theōrētikos* provides a source of values on which good practice is in some sense dependent, those who are eager to leave Aristotle's ontotheological foundationalism behind and at the same time to retain and recommend his moral theory can easily run into some very heavy weather. This vulnerability is particularly salient for us today, when even the most ardent advocates of Aristotle's virtue theory, such as Alasdair MacIntyre, find it difficult to rest their case on a return to Aristotelian metaphysical foundationalism and to its essentialism about "natures," human and otherwise. MacIntyre would like to believe that one can retain most of Aristotle's virtue theory while dispensing with his metaphysical and scientific backing for these views (MacIntyre 1981).[11] My argument, using Isocrates as its mouthpiece, poses a challenge to this hope by suggesting that Aristotle's conception of good action (*eupraxia*) is hostage to *theōria*, whereas Isocrates' is not.[12]

Aristotle's main idea, as I have shown, is that unless the leisured life of the god of the philosophers is set up as a model of intrinsically good human action, and in consequence good action (*eupraxia*) is *paradigmatically* viewed as action devoid of any external conditions and external consequences (*Pol.* VII.1.1323b23–25; I.3.1325b28–30), interventions in the sphere of human affairs (*ta anthrōpina*) must necessarily be compromised by a stress on the external aims to which we direct merely instrumentally good, and often burdensome, actions. This utilitarian stress on means to external ends will, Aristotle is certain, come at the expense of the intrinsic moral worth of actions as expressions of good character. Under such conditions, he goes on to claim, practical rationality will necessarily be conflated with technical rationality, which is inherently instrumentalist. In this connection, Aristotle asserts that the art of rhetoric will be confounded with the morally fine decision-making that is required of the good political agent. On these grounds he proceeds to indict Isocrates as having an inadequately conflated view of both political science and of rhetoric.

One way of undermining Aristotle's argument will certainly not do. This is to say that he regards virtuous action, undergirded by moral habits, purely as *means* to a life of philosophical contemplation (Kraut 1989; Dunne 1993).[13] Such an instrumentalist conception of the value of practical reason is inconsistent with Aristotle's claim that the life of an engaged political agent and householder "realizes much that is noble" in its own right. It is true that Aristotle, unlike Plato, recognizes that *phronēsis*, rather than theoretical reason itself, must arrange practical matters if theoretical *sophia* is to be maximized. But nothing follows from this fact that compromises the moral worth of the practical activity of legislating and governing with this end in view.

A more accurate way of stating the relation between philosophical reflection and practical reason is to say that Aristotle lays it down as a fundamental theorem of political science itself that the inherently good values proper to the politically engaged life of practical reason (*bios politikos*) can be realized only if the life of contemplation is held up by the politically engaged person *himself* as inherently superior to his own life of politically engaged rationality. The "second best" way of life is not on this account devalued. On the contrary, it is only when the *bios theōrētikos*, which is exemplified by the life of god, is treated as inherently superior to the life of political and householding engagement that the practitioner of these skills will be able confidently to discriminate between the intrinsically good and the instrumentally good on any given occasion. And so he will realize the noble in action, without compelling him to maximize *theōria* at the expense of *praxis* in his own life, or in the life of the state in which he is a *politikos* (Depew 1991).

It is *this* rather powerful Aristotelian claim that Isocrates must rebut, and not a weaker, Platonizing substitute for it. Naturally, he often chooses the easy way out, playing off the weaknesses of the Academy. If he had been forced to confront Aristotle's more powerful argument, however, Isocrates would not necessarily be devoid of some relevant means of persuasion. He might have noted, for example, that Aristotle uses a bit of conceptual legerdemain to advance his argument. He claims that the leisured life of god, and of his philosophical imitators, which in normal usage (and the usage of Hellenistic philosophers, such as the Epicureans) is viewed as inactive in comparison to the busy life of finite beings like us, is actually more active than any sort of human life (*Pol.* VII.3.1325b13–26).

Aristotle probably thinks this because he stipulatively identifies good action (*eupraxia*) with his own metaphysical notion of actualization (*energeia*). God is pure *energeia*. Hence he is purely active (*praktikos*).[14] This is an equivocation, however, which arises from the philosophical habit of asking conceptual definitions to substitute for ideas whose meaning is already fixed by their ordinary uses. We may unmask this fallacy by recognizing that Aristotle's model of god's life, rather than being the model of fine action, is actually an idealization of the "fine and good life" of the Greek nobleman (*kalōkagathos*). It achieves its rhetorical purchase with its audience only because values that have already been ascribed to the ideal of *kalōka-gathia* are transferred to a theoretical god, who thereupon appears as an object of appreciation just because he comes to resemble a culturally validated icon.

From this angle, it seems that the ascription of nobility to god's leisured life is actually parasitic on the value already placed by the audience on the life of a *kalōkagathos* gentleman. There is no reason to think that a noble Greek who happens to know nothing of the god of the philosophers cannot make the crucial distinction between intrinsic and instrumental goods. An actual, living *kalōkagathos* gentleman must perform many instrumentally good actions *in the very act* of maintaining his nobility. He must be clever, for example, in the very act of exhibiting *phronēsis;* and he must exhibit a certain concern for his reputation *(doxa)* without either being or appearing vulgar. Isocrates realizes this. By erecting a fully leisured god as the model of intrinsically good action, on the other hand, Aristotle runs the risk of devaluing, rather than upholding, these admirably strenuous components of the *kalōkagathos* life by demoting them to the status of external trappings or psychological traps.

He doubtless does so in order to ground the strong cognitive status he demands of practical insight *(nous praktikos)* in the noetic intuition of the *bios theōrētikos*, thereby dissociating *phronēsis* from opinion and guess-work.[15] The actual result may be to undermine the settled meaning of the term *doxa* within the performative sphere of Greek culture, where it refers to one's reputation and tacitly to the moral seriousness required to defend and preserve it. Aristotle's theoretical *bias* can thus devalue the ways in which concern for one's reputation for virtue is a stimulus to the acquisition and display of genuine virtue. Isocrates does not run this risk. For as T. Poulakos argues in this volume, even though he is affected by the Platonic reduction of *doxa* to mere opinion, he still preserves much of the traditional meaning of *doxa*.

There are points where Isocrates explicitly recognizes this weakness in the Academic-Peripatetic position. In *Antidosis*, he asserts that burning ambition, concern with one's reputation, and even a certain eagerness to seize the main chance *(pleonexia)*, far from detracting from the ideal of noble action, will actually stimulate those who would "act and speak well" to conform their behavior to the ancient norms of noble high-mindedness *(kalōkagathia)* rooted in the epic tradition. Isocrates writes:

The man who wishes to persuade people will not neglect virtue, but will above all bend his mind (*nous*) to how he can attain the good repute (*eudokimein*) of his fellow citizens. Who does not know that words seem more true when spoken by men of good repute? . . . To the extent that someone's desire to persuade his hearers is strong, then, just to that extent will he zealously strive to be *kalōkagathos* and to enjoy the good repute of his fellow citizens . . . As to the question of seeking advantage (*pleonexia*), it is the most difficult of those about which I have spoken . . . None are at a greater disadvantage in life, however, than men [who do evil things to gain advantage] . . . On the contrary, those who are most pious and most conscientious in their services [to the gods will receive] the best from their fellow human beings both in their households and in the public sphere, and will be thought to be the best among them (*Antidosis* 278–282).

Presumably, Aristotle would not have been much moved by such protestations. For he would undoubtedly have seen in Isocrates' identification of acting well with speaking well, in this passage and in many other places, a misguided attempt to infer what is required for good *action* (*eupraxia*) from what is required for good public *speaking* (*eulegein*). By subordinating *technē* to *praxis*, and more specifically *rhētorikē* to *politikē*, Aristotle contests this conflation. Nonetheless, the theocentric presuppositions of his own subordination of rhetoric to *politikē* are counterproductive enough to encourage those who would speak on Isocrates' behalf to look for means by which he might have held his ground.

One way of disrupting Aristotle's train of thought might be the following. Aristotle's conception of political science requires *praxis* to constrain *technē* in the same way that *theōria* is to constrain *praxis*. To do this, however, Aristotle must not only separate the moral worth of an action from its external conditions and consequences, but the artful quality of rhetoric from its actual conditions of employment. The artfulness of rhetoric is said to reside in argument (*logos*), and in particular in the way in which appeals to reason manifest the *ēthos* of a virtuous and reasonable speaker who addresses, indeed hails into existence, a would-be virtuous and reasonable audience (Garver 1992). Aspects of rhetorical practice that do not fall within this charmed circle are treated as inessential to its rational, artistic core. Something like this also goes on in Aristotelian poetics. Aristotle prizes the rational skill that is exercised and further developed when a reader works through the motivational logic of the plot of a tragic script. But in poetics, no less than in rhetoric, what had constituted the performative force of a ritualized social practice is reduced to an external husk (Haskins 2001).

Just why Aristotle treats poetic and rhetoric this way is murky. He certainly intends to tell the young rulers who would study "philosophy of human affairs" under his tutelage that they are responsible for "what arts are practiced their states" (*EN* I.2.1094a35–b2). In contrast to Plato's repressive attitude toward his own cultural inherence, he also appears to tell them that they may accept a traditional canon of art works, as well as the highly developed practice of public speaking that has been spontaneously produced by their culture. Still, Aristotle's attempts to rationally reconstruct rhetoric and poetics within the framework of a theocentrically grounded philosophy of human affairs, and to devise a recondite set of methods for interpreting and judging these productions, expresses, at best, a slightly contemptuous toleration of social practices which, although they are deigned to have a rational core, are in the end judged incapable of doing either much good or much harm in their native setting. There is more Platonism in this than meets the eye. More important in the present context is the fact that it is difficult to see Aristotle advocating in his *Rhetoric* or the *Poetics*, as he is often reputed to have been doing (Kennedy 1991; Farrell 1993; Garver 1994), anything that *we* would recognize as an "art of civic discourse," especially one that does full justice to the precipitous autonomy that, as Nietzsche recognized, has fallen to our lot now that we have been cut off from the theological and metaphysical bases of our founding culture.

Eighteenth-century virtue theorists are instructive on this topic. Virtue was as important to figures as different as Lord Shaftsbury, Adam Smith, and Edmund Burke as it was to premoderns; utilitarian calculi and formalist rule-based moral technologies had not yet been devised. But eighteenth-century virtue theorists, including rhetorical theorists and practitioners, were all terrified by the potential of both religious and philosophical dogmatism to stir up and justify violence, and so asked the emerging discourse that we call aesthetics to do the warranting work for virtue theory. Some contemporary advocates of aesthetic education as a route to a virtue-based moral and political education, such as Martha Nussbaum and, in a different way, Hans-Georg Gadamer, have trod this path once again, thereby issuing challenges to proceduralist, rule-based versions of ethics and political liberalism that are often more persuasive than those of other *praxis*-theorists and communitarians (Nussbaum 1986; Gadamer 1977). Nonetheless, writers like Nussbaum and Gadamer have made what seems to me a mistake in trying to give us an aestheticized *Aristotle* as a model for contemporary practice. If Greek exemplars are to be sought, a more plausible approach would be to take *Isocrates'* conception of the relationship between *philosophia* and *ta anthrōpina* as a starting point for envisioning the connection between virtue-based morality, political wisdom, and humanistic learning today.

As various contributors to this volume have persuasively argued, Isocrates is much more plausibly construed as an aestheticist moralist than Aristotle. Although he faced the same questions that preoccupied Aristotle, he recognized in the behavior of the ideal Greek *kalōkagathos*, and in the poetico-rhetorical tradition that transmitted this ideal, an aesthetic dimension that had normative force and a performative dimension that he believed could be perpetuated in a literate world. It is to Isocrates that contemporary virtue theorists might direct more of their attention. By doing so, we might discover that the scene of fourth-century Athenian discourse was not nearly as indifferent to our own concerns as might be suggested by the inordinate amount of attention that scholars and cultural critics have paid to the Academic and Peripatetic legacy.[16]

Notes

1. I do not adopt the view (which seems to have sprung from a remark of Cicero's at *De Oratore* 3.35.141) that Aristotle confronted Isocrates by producing a rival handbook for rhetoricians. Like Eugene Garver (this volume), I do not think of Aristotle's rhetoric as a handbook at all. It is a "philosophy of rhetoric," and, as such, part of Aristotle's project in the human sciences. But I do not infer from this that Aristotle does not wish to confute Isocrates. I will be producing evidence that the confrontation occurs along a much broader front than the pedagogy of rhetoric.

2. All translations are my own, unless otherwise noted.

3. I stress this anti-anthropocentric aspect of Aristotle in order to qualify views such as those of Sedley (1991), who argues that Aristotle's extension of teleological reasoning to the *kosmos* as a whole commits him to anthropocentrism. From his own point of view, and in a world where there were many genuine anthropocentrists, Aristotle was at least attempting to be anything but.

4. This point has been made recently by Carlo Natali (2001: 25), although only in passing and without developing it.

5. Kenny (1978) argues that the middle books of *EN* are the missing books of *EE*. I disagree. I take *EN* in general, including *EN* VI, to be a rewrite of the whole of *EE*, registering the effect on the human sciences of a new ontological framework that is also found in *De*

Anima and *Metaphysics* VII–X. The middle books of *EN* reflect that change. We can only guess at what the middle books of *EE* contained.

6. It is true that in *Eudemian Ethics, phronēsis* is represented as a moral virtue among other moral virtues, and indeed as a mean between busybodiness (*panourgia*) and innocent simplicity (*euētheia*) (*EE* II.3.1221a12), and not as an intellectual virtue, as in *NE* VI. Aristotle seems to have changed his mind about that. My point here is a different one. It is that in *EE, phronēsis* is represented as governing human action just as exclusively as it is in *EN* VI. Just why it is not yet represented as an intellectual virtue, as it is in *EN* VI, is a good question, but not one I attempt to answer here.

7. It is possible, if only barely, that the reverse of this claim is true—that Isocrates adopted Aristotle's usage of *phronēsis*, and then universalized it. This is not either chronologically or textually plausible. Isocrates' *Antidosis* was written, by his own testimony, in 354–353. Thus Aristotle would have known this text long before his departure from Athens in 348, and before the production of any of the works that served as texts in his Lyceum, which was founded only after his return to Athens in 335. It is unlikely, then, that even an early version of any *Ethics* existed before his departure from Athens. Textual arguments against this possibility are even more convincing. There are no allusions in Isocrates' texts to Aristotle, although there are plenty of them to Plato's Academy. But there are many allusions in Aristotle to Isocrates. For these reasons, I set aside the possibility of an Aristotelian influence on the formation of Isocrates' conception of *phronēsis*.

8. This does not mean that there is for Aristotle no science (*epistēmē*) of politics. Although the point is still in dispute, contemporary commentators are coming around to the view that Aristotle does countenance sciences whose generalizations are secure enough to sustain the typical movement from *epagōgē* to essential definition to demonstrative *apodeixis*, but that hold in particular cases only "for the most part." Such a science is set forth in Aristotle's *Ethics* and *Politics*. See especially Anagnostopoulos 1994 and Reeve 1995. My own inclination is to think that an appreciation of "moral facts" acquired in the same way that the man of action acquires them is a necessary, but perhaps insufficient, condition for understanding the principles of political science.

9. I prescind here from the difficult question of precisely how to discriminate *phronēsis* from *politikē*. It is clear that whatever Aristotle means by saying they have a different "being," he is confident that they are, or rely on, the same characterological state (*EN* VI.8. 1141b23–24).

10. "Politics ordains which of the arts should be studied in a state, and which each class of citizens should learn, and up to what point they should learn them; for even the most honored capacities (*dunameis*), such as generalship, household management, and rhetoric, are subordinate to it" (*EN* I.2.1094a28–b3).

11. This view is closely related to attempts to retain Hegel's theory of practical reason or Objective Spirit even while decapitating his system of its basis in Absolute Spirit. (Taylor 1975 is a good instance of the genre.) Contemporary appeals to Aristotle as a model for contemporary practical reasoning are often undertaken by people who, like Taylor, Gadamer, and MacIntyre, are quite aware that Hegel himself was explicitly trying to

rewrite Aristotle's *theōria-praxis-technē* doctrine for modernity. Recently, MacIntyre has modified his views about Aristotle's biology.

12. Another, no less desperate, approach is to think of modern biology, in the form especially of sociobiology, as underwriting the same claims about human nature that Aristotle makes, and then to use this as a basis for contemporary normative political prescription. The most well developed and well argued version is Arnhart 1995. For my part, I have nothing against getting an "ought" from an "is." I have considerable doubts about sociobiology; about its consistency with Aristotle's approach; and about whether the resultant politics can ever get clear of its ideological contamination with conservative causes. No matter how much advocates of this position would like, political thought, as Aristotle recognized, does not take place in a vacuum.

13. Dunne's (1993) instrumentalist position is not as clear cut as Kraut's. He affirms, as I do, that for Aristotle practical reason functions autonomously. He also affirms, as I do, that "Aristotle places a higher value on the exercise of the theoretic faculty than on the exercise of *phronēsis*" (241). Yet he infers from these premises, invalidly and falsely in my opinion, that "Aristotle . . . instrumentalizes [*phronēsis*] in the service of theoretic reason" (241). Dunne's treatment of the *phronēsis-technē* distinction presents more difficulties. It is based on taking ordinary crafts as paradigms of *technē* (249). Dunne then sees complex crafts such as rhetoric and medicine as more like context-dependent *phronēsis*. He infers from this that Aristotle's concept of *phronēsis* itself is "not very deeply embedded in the core" of Aristotle's architectonic, and indeed is somewhat confused in its identity conditions. But Aristotle does not take ordinary crafts as paradigms of *technē*, simply as analogues and examples. In fact, he takes medicine as a fully developed, hence paradigmatic, example of an art, and concentrates on its cognitive, more than its "productive," aspects. Aristotle's treatment of rhetoric should be placed in this epistemic context as well. Dunne also takes *phronēsis* and *epistēmē* to be mutually exclusive, which they probably are not.

14. For a diagnosis of this fallacy, see Depew 1991.

15. I think it is not an accident that the threat of "intellectualism," which privileges the theoretical over the practical life by making theory its instrument, is approached most problematically and notoriously at the end of *EN*. I think this impression is a side consequence of Aristotle's newly found intellectualist conception of *phronēsis* in *EN*, and of his insistence that a practically wise person, such as Pericles, must recognize that the theoretical life is intrinsically higher than the political life.

16. I wish to thank audiences at the University of Iowa and Northwestern University for valuable criticisms of earlier drafts of this paper. I appreciate detailed suggestions and comments from Dilip Gaonkar, Eugene Garver, Michael Leff, and Carol Poster.

8

Philosophy, Rhetoric, and Civic Education in Aristotle and Isocrates

Language as Teleological, Not Instrumental

PLATO puts into Protagoras' mouth a myth about the origins of the arts and virtues. This myth, along with the *logos* or account that follows it, serves as a common framework for understanding very different conceptions of the nature of rhetoric and several of the issues about politics and language that anyone interested in civic education has to confront. Prometheus stole from Hephaestus and Athena "wisdom (*sophia*) in the practical arts together with fire. . . . The wisdom they acquired was for staying alive; wisdom for living together in society, political wisdom, they did not acquire, because that was in the keeping of Zeus" (*Protagoras* 321d). At that first technological stage, humans developed "speech and words" (322b), but not the art of politics, which includes the art of war. Taking pity on people who possessed technology but no justice, Zeus sent Hermes with justice and a sense of shame (322c). Language developed in the context of the arts, I suppose especially for transmitting the arts and exchanging their products. There are all sorts of arts, and each of them has a way of talking associated with it. Language precedes the gift of justice and piety, and is itself quite a minor actor in Protagoras' story. Protagoras' myth and argument are designed to advertise the goods he wants to sell. As he continues, he will have to tie linguistic facility and political excellence together, but it is important that they have distinct origins.

Human beings receive the productive arts from Prometheus, and language is a by-product of the arts. People are innocent recipients of stolen divine property. Justice and shame are, unlike the arts, gifts of Zeus. Everyone must share in these gifts so that everyone can live together. While the arts are necessary for living, justice and shame are necessary for living together. Still, justice and shame have no special relation to discourse. As Isocrates says (*Nicocles* 5–9), "There is no institution devised by man which the power of speech has not helped us to establish." If language is as omnipresent as that, there is no special connection between it and justice.

Protagoras uses the myth to show that everyone in a *polis* must have justice and shame. He then has to explain why, if everyone has justice and shame, and passes them on to the children, there is a place in the *polis* for professional teachers of these things. The more justice and shame are universal endowments, the less room there is for experts. Protagoras argues himself out of this bind by comparing himself to a teacher of Greek. Everyone speaks Greek; everyone teaches Greek by speaking it; yet there are professional teachers as well (328a). The equality of Hermes' distribution of justice can coexist with Promethean inequality of *technē*. There is no special association of justice with discourse in the myth, but there is instead a special analogy between teaching justice and teaching language.

Greeks who called non-Greek speakers "barbarians" would appreciate this connection between justice and the possibility of living together with facility in the language of nature and truth. Language is useful, and has its origin in the domain of the crafts, not of political wisdom, and so it is conceived instrumentally by the Sophists. Yet when Protagoras abandons myth for *logos* he alludes to the civilizing powers of the Greek language. The relation of these two sides of language, explicit and implicit in Protagoras' discourse, is as unstable as the relation between the two sides of rhetoric, as neutral power, and rhetoric as civilizing force, one that, Protagoras says, was surreptitiously practiced by Homer, Hesiod, Simonides, and others (316d). There is no special association of justice with discourse. But there is a special analogy between teaching justice and teaching language.

The Sophists trade on these two sides of rhetoric, the instrumental and the civilizing. Their art would not be worth buying unless speakers could use it to advance whatever purposes they have. An art which only permitted speakers to tell the truth would have much less exchange value. And yet such an art would be admired and praised, while the art of advancing any cause has a much more doubtful moral status. Thus Hippocrates at the beginning of the *Protagoras* wants to learn from the Sophists, but he is horrified at the idea that he might become one, or be mistaken for one. Such a discrepancy between the act of teaching and the content of what is taught is bound to create trouble. Plato can refute the Sophists with ease because they need to profess the neutral version of rhetoric to their students and the culturally ennobling version of rhetoric to a wider public. His refutations point out the contradictions between these two visions of rhetoric offered by the Sophists.

Protagoras' analogy between teaching rhetoric and teaching Greek displays these two sides of rhetoric. No language can only express truths. The devil, after all, can quote scripture, in Greek. Greek, like any language, allows its speakers to say all sorts of things. On the other hand, to speak Greek is to be civilized. If it is not the language of the gods, it is the language of Homer and other divinely inspired men. The fact that devils can speak Greek does not mean that speaking Greek is any less civilized and civilizing. The fact that people who do not know anything about justice, or who advocate unjust policies, can speak freely and well does not mean that speech about justice is any less the mark of being fully human.

The Sophists were torn between two concepts of rhetoric, a neutral one which they, as specialists, were uniquely prepared to teach, and a culturally constitutive one that is the property of all citizens. Takis Poulakos calls these two conceptions Protagorean and Gorgianic, and that may be right, but both are present in Protagoras' great speech. Both have to be present if one wants both to teach and to practice rhetoric: Callicles has no such problem because he only wants to persuade, not to teach others to do the same (e.g., *Gorgias* 482d, 487a–b). Reconciling these two is a problem for all students of both politics and rhetoric.

One might think that this tension in the sophistic position is not all that interesting, since the Sophists were intellectually empty—at least that is what Plato taught us—so it is no surprise that they would quickly get entangled in contradictions. But this tension points to a real problem that anyone interested in civic education must face. How are a generally shared competence and a particular expertise compatible? How can something both be useful for a variety of purposes, and also contain its own ends and values, or at least be oriented to good social ends?

The paradox that makes Protagoras declare himself a specialized professional teacher of a universal art is no embarrassing self-contradiction that simply shows that the Sophists have an unsustainable position. The paradox lies within the phenomena themselves and must infect any attempt to come to grips with an art of rhetoric and its place in the *polis* and in civic education. The same paradox animates Plato's picture of Socrates. Socrates is a gadfly, a unique individual whose role is as an outsider and yet as the only true politician in Athens. He predicts that Athenians will regret his execution. At the same time, he denies his own uniqueness, and replicates that denial in his practice of talking to anyone. He refuses to become available as a model for imitation. He does not accept pay, and he does not accept responsibility for those who try to imitate him. He says that he knows nothing at the same time that he expresses confidence in his own virtue, a pair of beliefs that are, at least, in tension with one another once Socrates also asserts the identity of virtue with knowledge. Note too the lines from Thucydides that T. Poulakos quotes: "The best counselors are the intelligent, and the best at listening to and judging arguments are the many" (6.39.1).[1] The two strands present in *Protagoras*, the one that says that justice is a universal possession and the other that makes the art of eloquence a matter for expertise, are here made into the respective virtues of hearers and speakers.

Aristotle and Isocrates face the same challenge. Aristotle and Isocrates agree that rhetoric is a practical art. It is an art which produces conviction (*pistis*). It is a practical art because it is amenable to practical assessment, as something that can be done well or badly, like human actions. It can be judged ethically and not only in terms of the results it produces. For both Aristotle and Isocrates, the idea of a practical art combines the Gorgianic and the Protagorean, the competitive and the civilizing sides of rhetoric. If rhetoric can be explicated as a practical art, then the dispute between Plato and the Sophists can be circumvented.

Isocrates thinks that he has reconfigured the relation between philosophy, eloquence, and practical wisdom so that the dispute between Plato and the Sophists has been overcome. Aristotle simply dismisses that controversy. Isocrates' strategy is to locate himself in relation to the positions of Plato and the Sophists. Aristotle's is to ignore them. I will draw contrasts with Aristotle as I proceed, but for Isocrates the instrumental and the civilizing aspects of rhetoric coexist, and a practical art of rhetoric exists, when doing well and speaking well are identical. In the first place, he claims that training in eloquence is the best education for virtue. Second, his own rhetorical performances connect speaking well and doing well by constructing his discursive productions in such a way, with all the self-references, that they demand ethical evaluation as well as simple assessment in terms of the quality of the policy advocated or the person defended or attacked.

Both Isocrates and Aristotle were accused of writing handbooks to compete with the Sophists to teach people how to speak effectively.[2] But Aristotle and Isocrates both oppose handbooks for rhetoric, since to conceive of rhetorical education as a handbook is to make rhetoric into a productive rather than a practical art. Isocrates, instead of a handbook, writes speeches of self-presentation and direct practical intervention. Epideictic rhetoric directs attention to the speaker as well as to what he is talking about, and his own peculiar kind of *epideixis* invites ethical assessment. Aristotle shows how rhetoric is a practical art by articulating its workings from the inside. He shows that the concentration on argument makes rhetoric a rational procedure which embodies the values of *phronēsis*. Although it is wrong to confuse rhetorical excellence with *phronēsis*, there are good reasons why people tend to do so, while no one confuses medical excellence or skill in any other craft with political wisdom. For Aristotle, it is just because rhetoric is a practical art that we can avoid conflating it with *phronēsis*. Aristotle makes rhetoric a practical art because he distinguishes between speaking well and acting well, while Isocrates' rhetoric as a practical art depends on their identity.

Aristotle tells us that art is a virtue (*aretē*). It is one of the intellectual virtues that are good conditions of the thinking part of the soul (VI.4. 1140a9–13). Rhetoric in particular is a virtue not only because it brings into good condition part of the soul, but because it is a useful practice. It is one of the noblest of arts (*Ethics:* I.2.1094a29–b4). Thus far Aristotle and Isocrates are indistinguishable. But, for Aristotle, while the art of rhetoric is a virtue, proficiency in rhetoric will make no one wiser (*Rhetoric:* I.2. 1356a32–34) and there is a sharp boundary between rhetoric and political knowledge. Only in degenerate states does rhetoric pass itself off for wisdom. The better the *polis*, the more rhetoric functions in the subordinate role it should occupy. Only in good states should we expect the Aristotelian rhetorician to best defeat the sophist. The crux of the difference between Aristotle and Isocrates concerns how Aristotle bars and Isocrates admits these inferences from rhetorical to practical excellence.

Both Isocrates and Aristotle ally eloquence and justice more intimately than the Prometheus myth does. Speech comes into existence alongside the arts and prior to justice for Protagoras, but Isocrates makes the power of speech the source of all arts and virtues:

> We are in no respect superior to other living creatures; nay, we are inferior
> to many in swiftness and in strength and in other resources; but, because
> there has been implanted in us the power to persuade each other and to
> make clear to each other whatever we desire, not only have we escaped the
> life of wild beasts, but we have come together and founded cities and made
> laws and invented arts; and generally speaking, there is no institution de-

vised by man which the power of speech has not helped us to establish (*Antidosis* 253–255; see too *Panegyricus* 48 *Nicocles* 5–9).

In an echo of the Protagoras speech, Isocrates says that "among the ancients, it was the best *rhētores* who enjoyed the highest reputation and brought the greatest benefits to the *polis*" (*Antidosis* 231). "Habituating himself to contemplate and appraise [the most illustrious and edifying] examples, he will feel their influence not only in the preparation of a given discourse but in all the actions of his life" (277).

Aristotle's literal epitome of the Prometheus myth makes the connection between language and justice much stronger than Protagoras has it, and enables him to face the paradox in a novel way. Language and justice come into existence together:

> Man alone among animals has speech (*logos*). The voice (*phonē*) indeed indicates the painful or pleasant, and hence is present in other animals as well . . . but speech serves to reveal the advantageous and the harmful, and hence also the just and the unjust. For it is peculiar to man as compared to other animals that he alone has a perception (*aisthēsis*) of good and bad and just and unjust and other things [of this sort]; and partnership in these things is what makes a household and a city (I.2.1253a11–18).

While for Aristotle language and justice come into existence together, excellence at speaking about justice is not the same excellence as the virtue of acting justly. Aristotle does not agree with Isocrates' hopes for uniting *eu prattein* and *eu legein*. The ability to teach people how to speak about good and bad and just and unjust has nothing to do with an ability to teach people how to act well. To say that rhetoric will make no one wiser is equivalent to saying that virtue cannot be taught. The art of rhetoric is subordinate to politics, not a substitute for it or a part of political education.[3] On the subordination of rhetoric Aristotle is one with Isocrates, who says:

> Those who are willing to obey the instructions of this philosophy would be aided far more quickly towards equity (*epieikeia*) than toward rhetoric (*rhētoreia*). Let no one think that I am asserting that justice can be taught; for I am absolutely sure that there is no *technē* capable of implanting justice and temperance into those ill-formed by nature for *aretē*. But I still believe

that education in political discourse would give students the most encouragement and practice (*Panathenaicus* 21).

Aristotle's and Isocrates' relation to the Sophists generates a new paradox. For both Aristotle and Isocrates, the ability to use language is essentially tied to perception and partnership in the good and the just, and yet rhetoric is not the gateway to political wisdom for either of them. For the Prometheus myth, the ability to use language develops independently of political wisdom, yet in Protagoras' *logos* that follows it rhetoric is the foundation of all wisdom and power, including political wisdom and power. The job of the Sophist is to make compatible Protagoras' *mythos* and *logos*, the competitive and the civilizing sides of rhetoric. The job of both Aristotle's and Isocrates' *polis* will be to make compatible the equality and inequality that together comprise justice; rhetorical or philosophical excellence will have to be able to contribute to that project. For Isocrates, philosophical eloquence makes the inequality of leadership compatible with the democratic equality of the audience.

What is Aristotle's solution? Aristotle's association of *logos* with justice and the good in *Politics* I shows that language is not a neutral tool. All the arts are powers for opposites, as doctors can kill or cure, a *topos* anticipated in Gorgias' *Helen* (14) and developed throughout Plato's dialogues and Isocrates' self-defense speeches. Plato, Isocrates, and the Sophists would all agree that because rhetoric can and must be used to effect purposes outside itself, it is therefore a neutral instrument. That is, for the Sophists, rhetoric's power and attraction, and, for Plato, rhetoric's threatening and fraudulent nature. For Isocrates, it is the power of what he calls philosophy to argue both sides of a question, which makes it both philosophically refined and practically valuable. This ability to argue both sides of a question will be for the Romans, who followed Isocrates on this point, what unifies eloquence and philosophy.

It does not follow for Aristotle from the fact that an art is a power for opposites that it itself is a neutral instrumentality. Rejection of that inference is a profound insight on Aristotle's part. It separates him from the Sophists and Plato, as well as Isocrates, with whom he otherwise seems to agree. Arts can be oriented to the good while still being powers for opposites. Aristotle's standard example of an art is medicine, and rhetoric is compared to medicine, not to a tool or a game as in later conceptions of instrumental rationality or later conceptions of the goods of practices. Aristotle's rhetoric can and must be used for purposes outside the art itself, and yet this is an art with ends and values of its own. Here Aristotle separates himself from Plato, Isocrates, and the Sophists.

Language is not a tool or a neutral instrument, and neither is any of the other arts. Aristotle agrees with Plato and the Sophists that rhetoric is always used to achieve some end that is given to it, but he denies that rhetoric itself is therefore a neutral tool. Even though medicine can be used to kill or cure, it is *about* health. Language is naturally oriented to the truth, so that it is easier to win if a speaker has the right on his side. It is both cause and effect of Aristotle's lowering the temperature of this debate that Aristotle thinks rhetoric not much of a practical threat, and is not a grand theoretical problem as Plato has it. For the same reasons that rhetoric is not a practical threat, he does not think it offers the practical advantages praised by Isocrates.

It may be for this reason that the *Politics* has nothing to say about rhetoric, this in spite of the lines T. Poulakos quotes from Vernant: "The system of the *polis* implied, first of all, the extraordinary preeminence of speech over all other instruments of power. Speech became the political tool par excellence, the key to all authority in the state, the means of commanding and dominating others." [4] Speech is a central condition for the *polis*, as my quotation from *Politics* I.2 shows. Deliberation and judicial processes are among the central activities of the citizen, and so come in for extended discussion in the *Politics*. But the art of rhetoric as such is absent from the *Politics*.

Language is not a neutral tool. None of the arts is a neutral tool, although all arts are used to achieve ends outside themselves. *Technē* is defined as a rational power of making (VI.4.1140a11). That sounds innocent enough, and in its context the stress falls on the last word as Aristotle contrasts making with doing and thus *technē* with *phronēsis*, the rational power of doing. I want to emphasize the word "rational" instead. A rational power has to have a rational object. For me to know something, I have to have the appropriate relation to a rational object, to something knowable. Persuasion is not a rational object and so cannot be the end of an art. One cannot know what will work in a given case.

"The fact that pleasure is not the product of a craft is quite reasonable; for a craft does not belong to any other activity either, but to a capacity" (*Ethics* VII.12.1153a23–25; cf. MM 1208a31–b2). Finding the available means of persuasion in a given case is a search for a rational object, just because Aristotle limits those available means to argument. He stresses the difference between searching for the available means of persuasion in a given case and sophistic definitions of rhetoric as the power of persuasion, a difference that others might think paradigmatic of Aristotle's penchant for unnecessary precision. The same difference between internal and external ends, between doing everything in one's power and external success, is definitive of all the arts. It is a condition of rationality that an art have its own internal end, something that can be known and chosen. The Aristotelian rhetorician succeeds when he has found the available means of persuasion, and that is a rational end. It is an end internal to the practice of rhetoric.

The sophistic rhetorician has only one end, whatever particular kind of winning is assigned to him. The Aristotelian rhetorician has two ends, one the internal end of his art, and the other the external end towards which his artful performance is directed. He tries to persuade, to achieve the external end, by aiming at the internal end, finding the available means of persuasion and constructing an argument. Rhetoric, like any art, is instrumental by having its own end. It never occurs to Aristotle to think that because rhetoric is an art and an instrument it is therefore neutral, an inference that seems almost irresistible to everyone else. The role of rhetoric in civic education will be radically different because of this conception of rhetoric as instrumental because it has its own end. Reason, while an instrument, is never neutral, nor is language. Nor is rhetoric. Aristotle's own contribution is to show that having an internal end is a condition of being an effective instrument. Looking more closely at Aristotle's conception of rhetoric and its relation to *phronēsis* will lead to a greater understanding not only of his own work but of Isocrates'.

Rhetoric and Political Wisdom

Plato's dispute with the Sophists poses two alternatives. Either rhetoric teaches virtue, and rhetorical practice embodies virtue; or rhetoric is worthless. Like Plato, Isocrates thinks that rhetoric is empty verbiage, and so recommends another verbal art called philosophy to replace it—an art of words and thought that will lead to good and successful deeds and to a good life. The impracticality of Plato's discourse in Isocrates' eyes makes Plato the Sophist and Isocrates the philosopher. Plato and Isocrates define philosophy in very different ways, but each contrasts philosophy with sophistic rhetoric, not only as ways of using and conceiving language, but as ways of life.

Plato, Isocrates, and the Sophists all agree in rejecting a strong distinction between theory and practice. Anything that is not practical is *impractical*. Civic education for each of them depends on the unity of theory and practice. Aristotle, by contrast, thinks that the distinction between theory and practice preserves the legitimacy and autonomy of each. This stance allows him to see nobility both in theoretical activities without practical use and in practical activities in spite of the fact that they are directed towards external ends. The distinction of theory and practice allows a reorientation of leisure and so of the relation between philosophy and politics.

Corresponding to Aristotle's strong distinction between theory and practice is a strong boundary between rhetoric and politics. He is not a participant in the debate that pits both Plato and Isocrates against the Sophists. Characteristically, he tries to eat his cake and have it too. Rhetoric is one of the most noble of arts. Rhetoric is useful, and he says that the good man who is outdone in argument by a skilled rhetorician has only himself to blame (*Rhetoric* I.1.1355a20−22). On the other hand, facility in rhetoric makes no one wiser. It is only ignorant audiences and ignorant and self-deceived speakers who would mistake rhetorical skill for political wisdom (*Rhetoric* I.2.1356a27−30).

Practicing rhetoric will make no one wiser, Aristotle says, and excellence in the art of rhetoric is no sign of the presence of *phronēsis*. Aristotle therefore has nothing to do with Isocrates' claim that the "power to speak well is taken as the surest index of *phronēsis*, and discourse (*logos*) which is true and lawful and just is the outward image of a good and faithful soul *agathēs kai pisteō*" (*Antidosis* 255). Plato's Protagoras had earlier advertised his art as one that will allow citizens to have the "most power on public affairs both in speech and in action" *prattein kai legein* (319a). That thesis, picked up and amplified by Cicero and Quintilian, is central to figures throughout the history of rhetoric who seek to make eloquence the key to citizenship. If that tradition does not originate with Isocrates, his is the earliest fully developed case for the connection between eloquence and citizenship that has survived.

But Aristotle's rejection of the thesis is different from Plato's. While rhetoric is distinct from political virtue, the practice of rhetoric is, for Aristotle, compatible with citizenship, as it is not for Plato. Because rhetoric is distinct from political virtue and makes no one wise, Plato thinks it has no value at all and is incompatible with citizenship and virtue. Justice Holmes famously said that a "man may live greatly in the law as well as elsewhere."[5] Aristotle would say something similar at this point. Rhetoric is not *phronēsis*, but one can practice rhetoric and exercise *phronēsis* at the same time in the same act. To do something artfully is no bar to doing it virtuously. So he can count among the goods listed in the *Rhetoric* the "capacity to speak and to act, for they are productive of many goods" (I.6. 1362b14–15).

For Aristotle, unlike Plato, Isocrates, or the Sophists, rhetoric, and *technē* in general, has relative value. The others either think that because it has relative value, it has value (Isocrates and the Sophists), or that because it has only relative value, it does not have real value (Plato). Art is defined in the *Ethics* as an intellectual virtue, a rational capacity for making. Rhetoric is good, noble and useful—so long as it is subordinated to political science. Anyone who takes Plato's dialogues with the Sophists and their students seriously must worry about the stability of such a solution. Civic life must be carefully defined if rhetoric is to keep within such bounds, if it is to stay useful and noble without such power going to its head and making it think that because it can speak persuasively and intelligently about justice, it can settle political questions about justice. Isocrates solves the problem by substituting philosophy for rhetoric. Aristotle solves it by subordinating rhetoric to politics. Americans with a recent experience of a professional actor convincing citizens that persuasiveness means political ability must worry about how Aristotle could ever hope to prevent such border violations.

How does Aristotle pull off such a trick? I suggest that there are three unique features of Aristotle's configuration of rhetoric and politics that are especially worth emphasizing in this connection. The first is a noninstrumental conception of language, which I discussed in the first section of this paper. The second is a sharp distinction between theory and practice to which neither Plato nor Isocrates nor the Sophists would consent. That has been the subject of this section. Finally, Aristotle, thus armed, reconceives the art of rhetoric as a mode of *praxis* as well as a mode of making, a practical art. While Aristotle seems one with Isocrates here, the noninstrumental conception of language and the distinction between theory and practice will make Aristotle's conception of rhetoric as a practical art very different from Isocrates' development of the same idea.

Rhetoric, Theory, and Practice

Aristotle differs from both Plato and Isocrates by his sharp distinction between theory and practice. That distinction has consequences for his conception of *technē*, and the relation between art and civic practice, and so, ultimately, for civic education. Because of the difference between theory and practice, an art of rhetoric is not a threat to politics. Without a separation between theory and practice, as in Plato, Isocrates, and the Sophists, rhetoric must be either a threat or a boon. (In Isocrates' case, it is both. The sophistic discourse that is impractical is a threat to both politics and civic education, while his own philosophy is a boon to the state.) Where Aristotle distinguishes theory from practice and Plato assimilates them, Isocrates reverts to the earlier Socratic dismissal of natural science in favor of a concentration on the ethical.

For purposes of action, Aristotle says, experience is no worse than art. "With a view to action experience seems in no respect inferior to art, and men of experience succeed even better than those who have theory (*logos*) without experience" (*Metaphysics* I.1.981a13–15; cf. *Ethics* VI.1141b12–23). As I mentioned before, Aristotle offers no guarantees that possessing his art of rhetoric will make anyone more eloquent. But take away the "view to action" and experience is inferior to science. In both making and in doing, experience is superior to theory without experience. In theoretical science, theory is superior to experience. The trouble is that, in certain respects, the *Rhetoric* is more like an Aristotelian science than one might think from his assertion that facility in rhetoric makes no one wiser about anything.

How does Aristotle know that there is an art of rhetoric? The first paragraph of the *Rhetoric* seems to regard the matter as simple:

All people, in some way, share in both [rhetoric and dialectic]; for all, to some extent, try both to test and maintain an argument [as in dialectic] and to defend themselves and attack [others], as in rhetoric. Now among the general public, some do these things randomly and others through an ability acquired by habit, but since both ways are possible, it is clear that it would also be possible to do the same by [following] a path (*hodos*); for it is possible to observe (*theōrein*) the cause why some succeed by habit and others accidentally, and all would at once agree that such observation is the activity of an art [*technē*] (1354a3–11).

If that is how he knows that there is an art of rhetoric, then its existence carries no implications for improving practice. The opening inference is echoed later, in III.10: "It is possible to create [urbanities and well-liked ex-

pressions] by natural talent or by practice, but to show what they are be-
longs to this study" (1410b7–8). There is no implication there that the
present study will be a third source, along with nature and practice, of the
ability to create these stylistic virtues. Even if there is an art which uncov-
ers the causes of natural or empirical success, its connection to practice is a
further question. Knowledge of causes is not by itself empowering. An art
of rhetoric will not necessarily make anyone a better speaker.

The situation is completely different for theoretical knowledge. Knowledge (*epistēmē*) differs from experience. We think that we know when we
know the cause. Knowledge of causes makes *all* the difference. Knowledge
of causes is what makes rhetoric an art, but in that case there is no guarantee that such knowledge will improve practice. The person who has an art is
wiser than the one who acts by experience alone (I.1.981a24–30)—in this
case wiser about persuasion rather than about politics. But wiser is not
equivalent to more effective. Rhetoric resembles the sciences in not prom-
ising that possession will make someone more effective practically, but it
differs from science in making no one scientifically or practically wiser. The
possessor of the art of rhetoric is doubly disqualified from practical wisdom.

The value of Aristotle's *Rhetoric* lies not in the improvements it offers
to rhetorical practice, but in the understanding of rhetoric it offers to statesmen who need to regulate the practice of all the arts and sciences in the *polis* (*Nicomachean Ethics* I.2.1094a27–b5). The art of rhetoric has little to
offer to practitioners because the practical experience of rhetoric already offers all the rhetorician needs. Someone who persuades through art knows
what he is doing. He is not on that account more persuasive. If this art of
rhetoric has a role in civic education, it must be far more modest than Isocrates and a long line of successors would have it. Even if Aristotle should be
included in Josiah Ober's claim that the "content of several of Isocrates'
speeches makes it quite clear that by the mid-fourth century (if not before),
if one claimed to be an intellectual—a practitioner of *philosophia*—one
must also be as critical of the rule of the people." Aristotle differs from both
Plato and Isocrates in not offering philosophy as a cure for democracy.[6]
Good legislation and civic education, that is, training in the virtues, are all
the cure that democracy needs.

Civic education and philosophy have nothing to do with each other; on
that point, Aristotle sides with Callicles against both Plato and Isocrates. I
have never seen Aristotle accused of being an anti-intellectual. But for him
philosophy does not play this educative role in the good life of the *polis*. Phi-

losophy is necessary because unless the legislator and virtuous person recognize that philosophy is a better activity than politics, that, as he puts it, "man is not the best thing in the universe" (VI.7.1141a20–22; see also 1141a34–b2), politics itself will be degraded into an economic life of acquisition and conquest. Philosophy is one thing; civic education another. Isocratean philosophy and civic education are the same (see *Antidosis* 192, 214–216), while the Platonist becomes a citizen of another state. Aristotle thinks that to valorize philosophy as Isocrates does is to remove the connection between habituation and civic virtue, while Isocrates thinks he has solved that problem by finding room for philosophy within civic practices. Given Aristotle's account of rhetoric and of democratic deliberation, there is no room for theory or philosophy because democratic practices are already rational. Deliberation, and therefore rhetorical deliberation, produces the best practical policies, and so does not need further help from philosophy. The solution to political problems is better legislation, not better politicians, as it is in Isocrates.

The Sophists, Plato, and Isocrates all argue about philosophy and politics as ways of life. Isocrates' lines: "I would advise you men to spend some time on [gymnastic of the mind, grammar, and music], but not to allow your minds to be dried up by these barren subtleties . . . I hold that men who want to do some good in the world must banish utterly from their interests all vain speculations and all activities which have no bearing on our lives" (*Antidosis* 268–269; see too *Panathenaicus* 27–28). This remark echoes the criticism leveled by Callicles, that philosophy makes a man inexperienced (*apeiros*) in the things that will make someone *kalos k'agathos* (484c–d); he becomes unmanly (*anandros*) (485d).

Aristotle distinguishes theory from practice. Practice is subordinate to theory, since man is not the best thing in the universe. Theology is nobler than *phronēsis*. But while practice is subordinate to theory, Aristotle's *polis* is no theocracy. *Theōria* gives no orders to politics. Practice is subordinate to theory, but within its own sphere *praxis* is autonomous. It has its own values and makes its own decisions. None of that is new to people who study Aristotle. But I maintain that the same relation obtains between rhetoric and politics as that asserted between politics and theology. Rhetoric is subordinate to politics. But within its own sphere rhetoric is autonomous. It has its own values and makes its own decisions.

The politician makes his own decisions in the best way, although the good politician is mindful of the fact that, since man is not in fact the best

thing in the universe, politics is inferior to theology. Similarly, the rhetorician makes his own decisions in the best way when he recognizes that rhetoric is not politics but is subordinate to it. Subordination without reduction
is one of Aristotle's most subtle achievements, both the subordination without reduction of politics to theology and of rhetoric to politics.[7] The example of Isocrates shows that one can cross the boundary between rhetoric
and politics, and hence be a Sophist by Aristotle's account, without any an-
tisocial or immoral motivation.

In practice, this means that the good rhetorician does his job well not by
bringing in political considerations, on the hypothesis that since politics is
better than rhetoric, the more someone thinks about politics rather than
rhetoric the better he and his decisions will be. Instead, the good rhetorician
does his job well by doing his own job well. The rationality of rhetoric allows it to proceed autonomously without constant political oversight. The
good of the rhetorician is to find in any given case the available means of
persuasion.

Aristotle shows that this function is equivalent to limiting one's persuasive appeals to argument. That is, the good rhetorician manifests his subordination to politics not by orienting his persuasive appeals to the right ends
dictated by politics, but by limiting them to the right means, dictated by the
art of rhetoric itself. That the good rhetorician manifests this goodness
by limiting herself to the right means, rather than limiting her appeals to
good ends sets Aristotle off from everyone else who worries about the relation between rhetoric and politics, between rhetoric's availability for ends
outside itself and its civilizing power. The good rhetorician limits herself to
argument; "good" in this sentence means something more than technical
prowess and something less than moral goodness. Holmes captures this
sense of the good rhetorician:

> I confess that altruistic and cynically selfish talk seem to me about equally
> unreal . . . if you want to hit a bird on the wing, you must have all your
> will in a focus, you must not be thinking about yourself, and equally, you
> must not be thinking about your neighbor; you must be living in your eye
> on that bird.[8]

The twin subordinations of politics to theology and of rhetoric to politics
provide data for those who want to believe that Aristotle is merely replicat-
ing and so providing ideological justification for traditional aristocratic and

oligarchic hierarchies of class. The subordination of politics to theology is a model for subordinating craftsmen to men of leisure, who alone can afford to engage in politics. Rhetoric has to be kept in its place so that parvenus can be kept in theirs. Aristotle's tactics of subordination are in this case of a piece with Isocrates' own strategy of preserving democracy through eloquent elite leadership.

I think that the opposite is the case, that Aristotle actually severs the ties between theology, politics, and rhetoric and their social connotations. "It makes much difference what object one has in view in a pursuit or study; if one follows it for the sake of oneself or one's friends, or on moral grounds, it is not illiberal, but the man who follows the same pursuit because of other people would often appear to be acting in a menial and servile manner" (*Politics* VIII.2.1337b17–21; see also III.4.1277b2–7, VIII.6.1341b11–14; *Rhetoric* I.9.1367a30–31; *Ethics* IV.3.1124b31–1125a2). Rhetoric, like the other arts, can be an activity fit for a citizen or a slave, depending on its purpose. Directly contrary to how an oligarchic ideologue would have it, one can simultaneously be a good rhetorician and a good citizen. The good rhetorician can at the same time be the good citizen because being a good rhetorician means confining oneself to the right means, argument, while being a good citizen means directing one's persuasive powers to the right ends.

I take rhetoric here as a model for the arts in general. The relation between rhetoric and politics shows something of how good citizenship is related to the excellent practice of a variety of particular practices and skills. I mentioned that Aristotle develops his conception of the art of rhetoric through a comparison to the art of medicine. In the *Ethics* too the constant term of comparison for ethics is medicine. Earlier I cited Holmes' remark that a man may live nobly while practicing law, and now we can see how Aristotle would explicate that fact. To do something artfully is no bar to doing it virtuously because "artfully" refers to how the act is done, its limitation to argument or, generally, to rational methods, while "virtuously" refers to its purpose, the act being done for its own sake.

Earlier I noted that for Aristotle no art, including rhetoric, concerns the particular. Ethics and *phronēsis* are about the ultimate particular, and so there is an unbridgeable gap between rhetoric and *phronēsis*. For Isocrates, as for many later rhetoricians, the concept of *kairos* or appropriateness to the occasion, bridges that gap. *Kairos* is the Isocratean rhetorical equivalent of the ethical engagement with the particular which Aristotle thinks is impossible for the arts. Hence in the *Antidosis* Isocrates denies a separation of theory and practice in order to advance his own program of philosophy. The name "philosopher," he says, should not be given to "those who ignore the things that are necessary" but only those who "learn and practice the studies which will enable them to manage wisely their private households and the commonwealth of the city, since it is for the sake of these things that one should work, philosophize, and do every act" (284–285).

On the score of the autonomy of *praxis* and of rhetoric, Aristotle is in a sense at one with Isocrates. Isocrates' epideictic performances display his skills through extensive quotations from his earlier speeches. The speeches are thus designed both to persuade and to illuminate the principles of persuasion. That is Isocrates' strategy for establishing the autonomy of rhetoric and *praxis*. Aristotle instead shows this autonomy by showing that even instrumental speech has internal values. All rhetoric, including *epideixis*, aims at persuading an audience, but it is liable to evaluation not simply in terms of success but in terms of its own rationality. But where Isocrates thinks that moral and political autonomy stands and falls with anthropocentrism—and here Isocrates is with both Plato and the Sophists—Aristotle has a new theology in which moral autonomy depends on the relation of people to gods. Previously the relation of people to gods had to destroy moral autonomy because of the putative nature of the gods. Aristotle's gods make possible a distinction between theory and practice that allows human action to be autonomous without having to take place in an anthropocentric universe. This reorientation allows Aristotle to distinguish the contemplative life from the political life without making contemplation antipolitical.

Rhetoric and Civic Education

I said that there were three unique features of Aristotle's *Rhetoric* which allow him to confront the paradox of eloquence that so upset the Sophists in Plato's dialogues, and confront it in ways that separate him from Isocrates. First, language and rhetoric are not neutral instruments. The fact that something can be used for purposes outside itself does not mean that that thing cannot have purposes, values, and ends of its own. Instead, Aristotle shows that being useful for a variety of external purposes presupposes that an art have its own internal ends and standards. Next, theory and practice are different, and consequently an art of rhetoric will not improve practice and so poses a threat to the autonomy of practice and the autonomy of ethics and politics.

Finally, the *Rhetoric* creates an apparent paradox of its own, that rhetoric is a practical rather than a poetic art, to be evaluated not only by what it accomplishes but by how it operates. As I mentioned, this is a paradox to which Isocrates too would consent, and its elaboration is especially useful in understanding both Aristotle and Isocrates. The *Rhetoric* shows that engaging in artful rhetoric is an activity fit for citizens, a thesis Isocrates seeks to make through the example of his own productions. The activities central to rhetoric, deliberation, legal argument and judgment, and *epideixis*, are the activities central to citizenship (*Politics* III.1.1275a22–33, 1275b15–16). Similarly, the *Politics* shows that *technai* properly oriented and conceived are useful in civic education and are compatible with civic activity. (See the lines I just quoted from *Politics* VIII.)

In the first chapter of the *Ethics* Aristotle says that when the "ends of the actions are the activities themselves" (I.1.1094a18) they still can be subordinated to further ends. Practical arts are rational capacities for the making of which are valued, and judged, and subordinated to the ultimate value of the good life, as activities and not simply for the products they produce. The products of rhetoric not only have a place in the *polis*, so too does the activity of rhetoric itself.

There are two lessons for civic education that the *Rhetoric* offers, one negative and the other positive. Both are quite different from Isocrates. Aristotle himself draws neither of these consequences of his own argument because he has no overt discussion of the place of the art of rhetoric in the *polis* or in civic education. The negative moral of the *Rhetoric* is that the difference between civic and banausic activity is not identical to the distinction between *praxis* and *poiesis*, and certainly not identical to the difference between two classes of action and person as conventionally conceived. The practice of some of the arts, including rhetoric, can, as Aristotle says at the beginning of the *Ethics*, be "noble" (I.2.1094b2).

The positive moral is that rhetoric is a civic activity when it is limited to argument. To act rationally is to have an internal end to aim at. Rhetoric becomes a civic activity when it is rational. Only rational activity can be practiced for its own sake and so can be part of a good life. Rational powers of making can be part of the good life; irrational methods, no matter how successful, cannot. The rationality of Aristotle's rhetoric is very different from the rationality of Isocrates' philosophy.

In an important way, these two Aristotelian morals are not much. They shouldn't be. In a strict sense, there is no such thing as civic education for

Aristotle, not if civic education is thought to be anything other than moral education. While the city is "made one and common through education" (*Politics* 1262b36–37; cf. 1310a12–18), "the regulations laid down for the education that fits a man for civic life (*pros to koinon*) are the rules productive of virtue in general" (*Ethics* V.2.1130b23–27; cf. II.1.1103b5–6; *Politics* VIII.1.1337a17–18). We become virtuous by developing good habits as directed by good laws. Civic education and education for virtue or moral education are identical. Education is central to the unity of the *polis* and to the development of citizenship. Since the city is a heterogeneous multitude, it "must be made one and common through education" (II.5.1263b36–37).[9] We become good citizens by becoming virtuous people. Rhetorical education has no special and essential role in such development.[10] While Isocrates' discourses about rhetoric are designed to contribute to civic education and civic virtue, Aristotle's are not.[11] Thus Isocrates maintains, as Aristotle never would, that the "stronger a man's desire to persuade his hearers, the more zealously will he strive to be honorable and to have the esteem of his fellow citizens" (*Antidosis* 278).

In another way, I think that Aristotelian rhetorical education and practice do offer something for civic education. Because of some very strong assumptions about the natural character of the *polis*, there is no room for an art of rhetoric to contribute to civic education or civic virtue in the *polis* Aristotle envisions in the *Ethics* and *Politics*. Civic education consists in the habituation by which we become morally virtuous by performing morally virtuous actions and learn to rule by being ruled. But in the absence of those assumptions, or in the absence of the *polis*, the *Rhetoric* offers some useful and challenging resources for us.[12]

I certainly think that Isocrates is more directly applicable to today's problems of civic education than Aristotle. But in more indirect ways Aristotle does offer some resources. Today, rhetoric is less subordinate to politics and more constitutive of it. From the beginning, I noted the inherently dual nature of rhetoric—as a competitive device for self-assertion and as the tie that binds communities together. Each of these taken separately generates a traditional and characteristic defense of rhetoric, what Lanham calls the weak and the strong defense.[13] In the weak defense of rhetoric as neutral instrument, which is the natural accompaniment for rhetoric as competitive self-assertion, apologists for rhetoric say, with Protagoras and Gorgias, that rhetoric is a mere tool and should not be blamed for the bad uses people make of it. Isocrates uses that *topos* at *Antidosis* 251–252, *Nicocles*

3 – 4, and elsewhere. The strong defense, associated with the conception of rhetoric as the means of binding communities together, goes on the offensive and claims that rhetoric is in fact a moralizing and civilizing activity, that, e.g., arguing both sides of a question makes men free. This defense is also at work, for example, in *Antidosis*. "To speak and think well will come together for those who feel a love of wisdom and of honor" (277).

Aristotle gives glancing reference to both these defenses in the first chapter of the *Rhetoric*, but I think he provides material for a more interesting defense as he integrates the two faces of rhetoric, the agonistic and the community founding, much as the *Politics* is dedicated to integrating equality and inequality in its complicated inquiry into justice. There is no specifically rhetorical education because of the way moral and political education work. Aristotle blocks the Isocratean inference from speaking well to acting well because he offers his own pathway towards acting well, a far less intellectual and more political pathway. We learn to rule by being ruled. There is no shortcut to becoming a ruler and no education specific to the ruler. We learn to rule by being ruled. Similarly in ethics, we become autonomous and learn to do things for their own sake by doing good things for ulterior reasons. We become virtuous in the first instance by performing virtuous actions because of fear, shame, or other emotions. Acting virtuously eventually becomes habit forming. There is no education or other means of development specific to *phronēsis*, Aristotle's intellectual virtue concerned with conduct. We become *phronimoi* by developing the virtues of character.[14]

These formulas that we learn to rule by being ruled and become virtuous by doing virtuous acts might make things seem too simple. We all know many people who are good at following orders but who never learn how to rule, and people who can never do something for its own sake, but only for the sake of further reward. If we in fact learn to rule by being ruled, the experience of being ruled is itself no guarantee that we will learn to rule. It is at best a necessary condition. Therefore it is fair to ask: What breaks down when being ruled does not lead to an ability to rule? What breaks down when performing virtuous acts for ulterior reasons leads not to virtue but to nothing better than the ability to act for increasingly remote ulterior reasons, not virtue but the self-control that we call delayed gratification?

I think that the answer is easier to see on the political side than on the individual side. Whether being ruled teaches one to rule depends on how one is ruled. People who were once ruled slavishly, now freed can themselves only rule others despotically, and relate to people only as master or slave. I have had colleagues who could be masters and who could obey orders, but were incapable of relationships involving friendship and equality. Similarly, it is easy to see how people who were brought up to do good things for ulterior reasons could only progress in the sense of responding to more and more abstract and remote reasons that were still distinct from the good acts themselves, waiting and hoping for a reward in heaven.

Consider Aristotle's Spartans who are shameful because they are "good while occupied at war but slavish while at peace and leisure" (*Politics* VII.15. 1334a38). They are good at doing what is necessary to acquire good things, but lack the virtues for "doing the best things and enjoying all that brings blessing" (a27–28). Those given a slavish education become slaves. They might be able to be despots as well, but not citizens. Without the specifically political relationships of friendship and equality, we can achieve self-control but not virtue. "To promote friendship is thought to be the special task of the art of government" (*EE* VII.1.1234b23–24).

I see a place for rhetoric in the development of the ability to rule and to do things for their own sake. Being persuaded rhetorically is an education in mutuality. Being persuaded is the right kind of being ruled that leads to ruling and acting autonomously. Rhetorical relations between ruler and ruled assure that by being ruled politically we learn to rule politically. Aristotelian rhetoric, limiting itself to argument, is an education in mutuality.[15]

Being a good citizen is hard because mutuality is difficult. Such mutuality is a condition for moral education to lead to virtue. "Men seek friendship on a basis of superiority more than that on one of equality; for in the former case they score both affection and a sense of superiority at the same time" (*EE* VII.4.1239a22–23; see VII.6.1241a32–34). "All *technē* and education wish to supply what is lacking in nature" (*Politics* VII.17.1337a1–3). There is no *technē* which can make people into political animals. But civic education is necessary for people to fulfill their nature as citizens. The family is natural in a way civic life is not, so that no one needs an education in order to be part of a family, even though families of course are tied by friendship.[16] "Rule over the free differs from rule over slaves no less than that which is free by nature differs from that which is slave by nature" (*Politics* VII.3.3125a27).

The original tension I detected in the Prometheus myth recurs here in the very idea of political rule: for a speaker to be worth listening to, she must have something I do not have, whether it is knowledge or virtue. How is the equality that civic persuasion requires compatible with the inequality that makes something persuasive? Where Isocrates relaxes this tension in the direction of finding a place for eloquent leaders within democracy, thereby demoting the power of the *dēmos,* Aristotle's sense of reciprocity in the *polis* keeps the tension intact. Doing things for their own sake requires mutuality. It requires a community in which people come to rule and learn to rule by being ruled. That is why man is a political animal: one cannot learn to do things for their own sake without learning how to live in a political community. Both Isocrates and Aristotle limit the role of democratic deliberation, Isocrates by his attention to the power of rhetorically adept leaders, Aristotle by a parallel focus on the statesman-legislator, who is to insure that states will be ruled by laws rather than men as much as possible. "On any important decision we deliberate together because we do not trust ourselves" (*Ethics* III.3.1112b10–11). And similarly for Isocrates: "The same arguments which we use in persuading others when we speak in public we employ also when we deliberate in our own thoughts" (*Nicocles* 8; see *Antidosis* 256–257). Isocrates' limitation of democratic deliberation by eloquent leaders carves out a large place in civic education for his own practices, while Aristotle's stress on the rule of law leaves him, and other intellectuals, nothing to contribute to civic education.

The limitation of rhetoric to argument offers some difficult and therefore useful lessons in mutuality and reciprocity. This limitation shows just how hard mutuality is. At first the limitation to argument seems to be an unfair restriction, trying to persuade with one hand tied behind one's back, operating at a disadvantage compared to the Sophist who will do anything to win. Aristotle develops rhetoric as a practice with its own internal goods, while others will see the limitation to argument as a set of conventions only contingently connected to the external end. These conventions are seen as rules of a guild designed to exclude other people, such as emotional outsiders who could also compete for the achievement of the external good.[17] But in the right political circumstances, the rhetorician can come to see the limitation to rational methods as liberating rather than restricting. Rational rhetorical persuasion is a model for the right relation within the soul between reason and desire: reason persuades desires, and persuades through reason. "The soul rules the body with despotic rule and the intellect rules appetite with political or royal rule" (*Politics* I.5.1254b3).

If I limit myself to argument, I can engage in relations of friendship, justice, equality with the hearers. In the language of the *Rhetoric,* only by limiting myself to argument can I have *ethical* relations with my audience, since the only artistic form of *ēthos* is one created through argument. Without such limitation to argument I must be the audience's master, or slave. Callicles discovered that I can think myself the master of the audience while really being its slave.

By limiting the art of rhetoric to argument, Aristotle has made the practice of rhetoric rational. But by confining the excellence of rhetoric to the means of persuasion, and saying nothing about the ends to which rhetoric is put, he has avoided moralizing the difference between good and bad rhetoric. He thus need not deny the competitive and controversial side of rhetoric that comes from the diverse ends that rhetoric serves. The equality that comes in the limitation to argument coexists with the inequality that comes from the diverse ends to which argument is put. Because the artful rhetorician has two ends, he can integrate the two sides of rhetoric that for so many others are incompatible, requiring either the weak or the strong defense of rhetoric with their divergent implications for civic education.

In rational persuasion, speaker and hearer share a reason, and there is a certain sort of reciprocity and equality between them. That does not mean that the speaker does not know more than the hearer, nor that the speaker is not trying to win the hearer over to his own cause. Similarly, political rule is distinguished from despotic rule by a certain equality between ruler and ruled. That equality does not preclude the ruler giving orders and the other citizens obeying them, but the connection between ruler and ruled is a rational one. Where the ruler has *phronēsis,* the ruled have right opinion, a condition absent in the person ruled despotically. Friendship between ruler and ruled is possible, while that is impossible in the relation between despot and slave, just as *eunoia* is one of the ethical means of persuasion in rhetoric (*Rhetoric* II.1.1378a10–14). In that sense, practice in artful persuasion is a model for the mutuality of citizenship. Artful persuasion is a model for the coexistence of equality and inequality that is the center of politics. On this point, Isocrates seems to hold the same view. In *Concerning the Team of Horses,* he has Alcibiades' son argue for Alcibiades' loyalty (*eunoia*) on the basis of what he did for the *polis* and how he suffered with it (39–42).

When Aristotle's way of thinking is removed from the *polis,* there remains a sort of civic education that has more affinities with Isocrates' teaching than the more political side of Aristotle. Aristotle could depend on public practices of praise and blame, punishment and reward, to do most of the work of civic and moral education. I am suggesting that the *Rhetoric* offers resources for people to move, as Isocrates has it, from *eu legein* to *eu prattein*. But differences remain. On my reading, the *Rhetoric* outside the *polis* contributes to moral and civic education by exhibiting mutuality and demonstrating the connection between rationality and reciprocity. Isocrates' civic education is more individualistic, less political and civic. It is training for leaders. Aristotle maintains that we learn to rule by being ruled. Speaking well leads to acting well via justice and friendship, not hegemonic leadership. Isocrates will preserve the *polis* by transforming it into a civic body subordinate to eloquent and prudent leaders.

"When there is something that exists for the sake of another, and this other is the end for the sake of which the first is, then they have nothing in common save by way of making and receiving" (*Politics* VII.8.1328a27–29). In Aristotle's art of rhetoric, the speaker and hearer do have something in common: the reasons and argument they share. The reasons we share are what Aristotle calls *homonoia* in the *Ethics*.[18] Such political friendship is the *ēthos* of the *polis* (as Aristotle explores it in *Rhetoric* I.8) and the *ēthos* of the speaker. The Aristotelian speaker can still try to win over his audience, but his relation to the audience is not purely instrumental. How to draw the line between instrumental and reciprocal relations, how to treat someone as an end and not merely as a means, is difficult and contested. The *Rhetoric's* limitation to argument is a lesson in making those distinctions. It is a lesson in equality and friendship.

Conclusion

Plato's Protagoras argues himself into a corner with his *mythos* and *logos*. Since being virtuous is a condition for living in a *polis*, all citizens not only have to be virtuous. They must all teach virtue. Protagoras seems to have argued himself out of a job. Aristotle agrees with the Prometheus myth, as opposed to the *logos*, that there is no such job as a teacher of virtue. Civic education is done by the laws, much as Socrates' accusers claimed. It is done by habituation governed by shame and other emotions, not argument. We come to rule by being ruled, and to be virtuous by performing virtuous acts. Writing and reading the *Rhetoric*, engaging in rhetorical activity in the assembly and the law courts, and educating one another for citizenship are three distinct activities.

Isocrates, by contrast, accepts the *logos* of Protagoras, not the myth. His own discursive performances bridge the boundaries Aristotle erected, and so his speeches are supposed to be models of such bridging. Parallel to the *Rhetoric*, Isocrates' speeches tell the legislator about the place of intellectual and persuasive activity in a *polis*. Parallel to deliberative and judicial rhetorical activity, Isocrates' *epideixeis* are acts of leadership designed to move a *polis* to a good decision. Parallel to civic education, they not only speak to citizens but transform them by supplying civic motivations, civic pride, and loyalty.

Aristotle and Isocrates are one in aiming at practical arts of discourse, ways of using language that are at once practical and artful. Aristotle's separation and Isocrates' unity of theory and practice, Aristotle's teleological and Isocrates' instrumental and celebratory conceptions of language, these generate different conceptions of the practical arts of discourse, and therefore different models of civic education. Their competition sets the *topoi* for discussions of civic education today. And yet in one respect I wonder whether neither Aristotle nor Isocrates can help much with modern problems of civic education. Aristotle says at the start of the *Rhetoric* that the laws should decide as much as possible, and that deliberation and legal judgment, and so rhetoric, should be practiced only when the laws must be silent (*Rhetoric* I.1.1354a31–b7). Isocrates similarly restricts the role of the public by substituting political leaders for Aristotle's statesmen-legislators. Neither Aristotle nor Isocrates, nor anyone else, talks about a practical art of discourse, call it rhetoric or philosophy or anything else, for the *audience*. Aristotle may be more explicit than Isocrates on this, but both presume that the Athenian audience does not need an education in making rhetorical judgment that it does not already have by its experience of citizenship. Today one must wonder whether it is not more important to formulate an art of rhetorical judgment for hearers than an art of rhetorical persuasion for speakers. That would be civic education for our time.[19]

Notes

1. Quoted in T. Poulakos 1997: 68.

2. See Cole 1991.

3. On the other hand, Ober (1998) concludes his treatment of Isocrates by noting that "in a society that did not focus centrally on *logoi* and lacked a well-defined class of *logos*-makers, Isocrates would be irrelevant and would have no *paideia* to teach, and so would enjoy no fame, and could claim no special purpose for his profession. . . . Without the popular audience's ultimate authority over perceived reality, absent their desire to hear fine-crafted speeches, the rhetor (and thus, a fortiori, the teacher of rhetoric) would have

no role to play in society." (287). Here I think Aristotle and Isocrates part; see also Ober, this volume.

4. T. Poulakos 1997: 65.

5. Holmes 1992: 219.

6. Ober 1998: 252.

7. David Depew and I agree that Aristotle's world depends on maintaining strong distinctions between human and divine, between theory and practice, and between *praxis* and making. He thinks that all these distinctions are unstable in the sense that they require constraint to be maintained. Without such constraint, they all collapse, theology into anthropomorphism and bargaining with the gods, theory into practice—true is what is good to believe—and, especially, doing into making, as living well becomes a matter of getting rich. Our disagreement is not large. I think that production needs external regulation, that without the institutional arrangements of the *polis* practical life will degenerate into a life of masters and slaves aiming not at the good but at pleasure. I think that the virtues need no such regulation. *Phronēsis* simply is the *orthos logos* of the virtues and not an external regulator. A tendentious way of making this point is to say that there is a unity of the virtues for Aristotle but no unity of the crafts. Rhetoric is at the same time one of the noblest and one of the most dangerous of the arts. It requires external regulation, as does any art. Aristotle stresses the need for good laws at the start of the *Rhetoric*. These are laws that would make speakers and audiences alike concentrate on argument. But in addition the *Rhetoric* itself is designed to be a contribution to *phronēsis* by articulating the rational aspects of practical reason and persuasion. Making rhetoric a practical art does not reduce *praxis* to making but elevates rhetoric into *praxis*. Aristotle has no need to elevate *praxis* by denigrating the crafts. Instead he elevates *praxis* and demonstrates its autonomy by showing how even the arts, to the extent that they are rational, coherent, and effective, rely on internal values. Thus he elevates *praxis* by elevating the arts. The more rational the arts are, the more the rationality and autonomy of *praxis* is evident.

8. Holmes 1962: 122–125. Quoted in David Luban 1997: 1556.

9. See the lines that follow: "It is odd that one [Socrates] who plans to introduce education and who holds that it is through this that the city will be excellent should suppose that it can be corrected by things of this sort [Socrates' regulations about property and common wives and children], and not by habits, philosophy, and laws" (1263b37–1264a1).

10. I find no evidence for Carnes Lord's (1996) intriguing suggestion that rulers and other citizens need different forms of education, and that the *Poetics* is designed to show how tragedies teach the *dēmos* political judgment, while the *Rhetoric* teaches rulers how to deliberate and persuade the *dēmos*. Among other things, while Aristotle asserts that rhetoric is subordinate to politics, there is no parallel claim in the *Poetics*.

11. I agree with Depew's assessment that Isocrates invents and displays a new kind of *logos* "that is to perform functions in a literate culture previously assigned to poetry in an oral world." Isocrates invents a new genre with a practical function. Aristotle's works, though, are not contributions to existing genres or inventions of new ones. They are not literary productions at all. Even considered as forms of argument or modes of inquiry they are not designed to be imitations or responses as Isocrates' are.

12. For Isocrates on habituation, see *Antidosis* 277: The good orator "will select from all the actions of men which bear upon his subject those examples that are the most illustrious and the most edifying, and, habituating himself to contemplate and appraise such examples, he will feel their influence not only in the preparation of a given discourse but in all the actions of his life."

13. Lanham 1993: 154–194.

14. In contrast to Aristotle's synthesis of equality and inequality, see for example Cleon speaking in Thucydides 3.37, quoted in Ober 1998: 96: "Ignorance (*amathia*) mixed with moderate sobriety (*sōphrosunē*) is more useful (*ōphelimōteron*) to the *polis* than cleverness mixed with insubordination. Ordinary men, when compared to the more gifted, actually administer (*oikousi*) *poléis* better." Here democratic equality is incompatible with the inequality of intelligence or virtue, severing Protagoras' *mythos* from his *logos*.

15. "Deliberative politics was the crucial element in the experience by which a *dēmos* constructed itself as a political actor. Deliberative politics was for the *dēmos* a model of political development, and by the same token certain other types of politics—bureaucratic, charismatic, or even representative government—arrest that development. A participatory and egalitarian politics that is deliberative serves the political education of the *dēmos*. It is the nurturing ground of a democratic *paideia* to which Plato's Academy was the self-consciously radical alternative" (Wolin 1996: 66).

16. "The human being is by nature a familial rather than a political animal, inasmuch as the household is earlier and more necessary than the *polis*" (1162b16–19). For more on family friendship, see Belfiore.

17. Stocks 1929: 74–75: "The [tennis] player finds himself indignantly turning away from tactics which would bring certain victory—why? Because, he would probably say, they are not his idea of tennis. Now, considered with reference to victory or any other end pursued in the game, this diversion necessarily appears as a limitation of the means by which they may be secured. The end is not denied, but its ability to justify these means is denied. Thus it is an insistence that an act shall be done in a certain way, a specification of conditions positive and negative. It makes its presence felt as limiting the activity, just as the law of the land enters occasionally as a limit and determination into the lives of its citizens.

"This is how it inevitably appears to one concentrated on the issue and the result. But what is it? and what is its title to interfere? We have already seen what it is, and what has already vindicated its title. The man is actually playing tennis, and the basis of the interference is simply that recognition that this is what he is doing, and the demand naturally associated with it, that he shall really and truly do it. There could be no simpler or more fundamental consideration. For though as an explicit factor in decision the conception of tennis-playing may be an occasional and intermittent visitor, yet no proof or apology is required surely for the thesis that this conception is really the basis and foundation on which all the rest is built. This is the root from which the fruits to which our purposes are directed spring; and if the root is poisoned or cut away, the fruits will soon fail and wither. It is not truly our purposes that are interfered with; they are at best intermittent, dependent on circumstances and opportunity. It is the activity that is the constant factor and continuing form, and it is this that occasionally is endangered by the material in which it finds embodiment. On such occasions the activity asserts itself in self-defense against the danger of self-mutilation or suicide under pressure of events."

18. "*Homonoia* is not merely sharing a belief, since this might happen among people who do not know each other. Nor are people said to be in concord (*homonoia*) when they agree about just anything, e.g., on astronomical questions, since concord on these questions is not a feature of friendship. Rather a city is said to be in concord when [its citizens] agree about what is advantageous, make the same decision, and act on their common resolution" (IX.6.1167a22 – 30). See also IX.6.1167b3 – 4: "Concord, then, is apparently political friendship (*philia*) . . . for it is concerned with advantage and with what affects life." See too *Ethics* VI.5.1140b13 – 19. For one example, in the *Crito* Socrates claims that there can be no common deliberation (*koinē boulē*) with those who think that it is better to commit than to suffer injustice (49d3).

19. I am grateful for the conversations and criticisms by participants at the Isocrates Conference at the University of Iowa, and especially to the organizers and editors, David Depew and Takis Poulakos, and to Depew, for a lifetime of stimulating conversations about these matters.

PART FIVE

Isocrates Then and Now

9

ROBERT HARIMAN

Civic Education, Classical Imitation, and Democratic Polity

THE remarkable accomplishments in classical scholarship during the twentieth century have been accompanied by near-complete abandonment of classical texts as a source for civic education. Most college students never study them, and where used they often are part of a multicultural olio in which they have no special place. The history, literature, philosophy, oratory, art, and political thought of Greece and Rome have never been more accessible or less appreciated.

These pedagogical changes are the result of cultural forces that are generally progressive, and those proponents of classical study who align it with reactionary politics, class-restrictive education, or Tory manners do no one any favor. The question to be faced is whether any part of the civic education based on classical sources can be recovered and put to good use in the new context. Whatever postmodern culture is to be, it will include recuperation of some of the symbolic resources predating the modern era, but in fragmentary or transfigured patterns of appropriation. If the liberal arts education is to continue, it will have to identify the materials and methods that can produce its best product: individuals with the knowledge, values, and communicative skills sufficient for democratic participation and leadership in respect to the problems that will define and test their society.[1]

In the contemporary milieu, imitation itself is barely thinkable as an educational practice. Note how the infrastructure of imitative pedagogy has disappeared, including its many small technologies such as the copybook, the recitation, the class play, the display of portraits and busts, and the attribution or adoption of classical names. One can track where processes of imitation are alive and well by looking to see whose names are being taken or whose pictures displayed. The answer, of course, is in popular culture.

You might be known as the "Michael Jordan" of your garden club, but you won't be called the "Cato" of anything. If classical texts are to provide a civic education for a contemporary democratic society, they will need to be able to operate as models for imitation within that society. In order to discern how that might be done, we ought to examine how classical literature itself provides some guidance regarding imitation. As Isocrates was the preeminent educator of classical Athens, he should be a good test case.

The following discussion sets out an analysis and an illustration. The analysis identifies how several of Isocrates' characteristic claims cohere as a program of imitation, it positions this program as an important element in his larger, "philosophical" project, and it derives a specific inflection for the *logos politikos*. The illustration, which is one attempt to define Isocratean imitation by example, offers a speculative formulation of what an Isocratean politics could be today. Along the way, I also suggest that Isocrates was developing two themes that serve as important regulatory mechanisms in his pedagogy and his political practice: these are the idea of a civic profession and the goal of democratic sustainability. As often is the case with Isocrates, these ideas are what we might call proto-institutional. They are early articulations of social forms that were foreign to the Greek world but subsequently have been proved to be important features of Western culture.[2]

Isocrates' attention to imitation occupies a central place in his arguments on education, as we can see from examining his first educational manifesto, *Against the Sophists*, and his mature summation of his educational program, the *Antidosis*. In each case, we are dealing solely with the question of how one might use language to reproduce a predecessor's verbal skill, wisdom, character, or culture in a manner that would be persuasive—socially competent and politically effective—in one's own world. Although the topics cannot be separated completely, in Isocrates or elsewhere, the focus is not on the question of how literary art is capable of imitating reality.[3]

Against the Sophists can be read as a harangue, as an extended definition by contrast, and as a series of topical arguments. It also provides the outline for a pedagogy grounded in imitation. The key steps are: the focus on the class of educators ("all those who have undertaken to teach"); the assumption of human cognitive deficiency; the principle of proportionality; the principle of trust; the contrast between creative and literal imitation; and the value of institutionalized training (1–6, 10–14 ff.)[4] In addition, there runs as an undercurrent through this pattern the suggestion that Isocratean instruction will impart right character. This softly pedaled claim starts with the gibe about the Sophists not trusting their students, and it is used to secure both an internal summary (8) and the conclusion (21). Thus, the purpose of education is to inculcate a disposition to just conduct and creative problem solving, without fostering the arrogance and rigidity that come from excessive confidence in one's expertise. But I am getting ahead of the story.

The crucial step in Isocrates' rationale for his educational program is the contrast between two types of imitation. This contrast is set out twice in succession: first, in the digression that adds the teachers of political discourse to the Sophists (9), and second, in the resumption of the larger argument where he foregrounds the method itself: "But I marvel when I observe these men setting themselves up as instructors of youth who cannot see that they are applying the analogy of an art with hard and fast rules to a creative process" (12). The key maneuver made each time is to compare the two classes of educators with two levels of linguistic instruction. The other educators "undertake to transmit the science of discourse as simply as they would teach the letters of the alphabet" (10), and "excepting these teachers, who does not know that the art of using letters remains fixed and unchanged, so that we continually and invariably use the same letters for the same purposes, while exactly the reverse is true of the art of discourse?" (12). In each case, rhetoric is set over grammar. The values of exact, literal reproduction (as in the rules of spelling) are subordinated to the values of variation within a range of options for artistic effect (as with the rules of style).

The full significance of this analogy can be discerned from its alignment with another, seemingly spurious argument. Isocrates contrasts himself from other educators by tying his critique of technical knowledge to his defense of high fees (3–8).[5] He disputes the claim that technical knowledge is sufficient for achieving our objectives in life, and he ridicules the payment practices accompanying this claim. In modern terms, when education merely imparts skills, it becomes commodified, the market soon pulls down the price, and the relationship between student and teacher is reduced to an economic contract. By contrast, when education produces qualities (such as resourcefulness) that cannot be commodified, the price should reflect the value of the ends it serves, and other social ties are important if it is to be pursued correctly and produce the right effect. These more responsible relationships are essential for the development of character, which is all the more important since skill can never suffice to provide happiness.

It is difficult not to see *Against the Sophists* as craven. By lambasting the Sophists, Isocrates uses one of Plato's standard rhetorical ploys but with even greater hypocrisy, and isn't he selling out some of his intellectual comrades? Perhaps, but we also know that the intellectual culture of fourth-century Athens was wide open to cheap products, hit-and-run salesmanship, and fraud, in part because there were few institutional gatekeepers. In addition, Isocrates' criticism of this unregulated educational marketplace had deep political resonance. His concluding condemnation of the older Sophists as professors of *polupragmosunē* and *pleonexia* (20) will have still had a sharp bite to anyone concerned about Athens' recent history and present circumstances. I suspect there is another dimension to his manifesto (and his lifelong educational project) that is closely related to both his epistemological and pedagogical differences with the other intellectuals of his day and the political circumstances in which he set out to educate students for civic leadership. This additional difference that he is insinuating can be made evident through a useful anachronism. Isocrates' highly reactive and self-serving attack makes more sense when we read it as a program for a school—for institutionalized instruction and certification—and particularly as an attempt to delineate two different senses of professional work.

"Profession" today can mean either a skilled service for pay—as in "professional athlete"—or a community of experts whose skill contributes to the common good—as in the "legal profession." We don't say the "athletic profession," although professional athletes do little else, and we don't say "professional lawyer" although many lawyers don't practice law. Obviously, both athletes and lawyers are paid, but the payments carry different meanings and there is a clear hierarchy at work. Lawyers who earn too much are suspected of putting private gain above collective interests, but athletes who earn too much are used as examples of how the society is over-valuing entertainment. These differences in usage and attribution are indicative of a pattern of social thinking.

As Burton Bledstein (1976) and others have demonstrated, the rise of the professional ethos in the modern era was very much an instance of the self-assertion of the ascendant middle class.[6] This is the class that reveres professional authority and organization, attempts to restructure society according to linked conceptions of expertise and character, and uses educational institutions as the primary means for social validation and individual success. Consequently, both the class itself and individuals anywhere in the society find that social and material rewards are shaped by a constant tension between "lower" and "higher" forms of professional status. The terms of definition are relatively fixed, including certification, payment for services (rather than as wages), technical expertise, disciplinary autonomy, peer review, and a code of ethics, while the contest for status is never ending. Athens had been experiencing a similar social transformation, and Isocrates was not only middle class but someone who had experienced downward social mobility.[7] While much has been made of Plato's aristocratic background, not enough has been done with Werner Jaeger's (1944) observations regarding the "practical bourgeois character of Isocrates" and his "strong admiration for respectability" that was vouchsafed by one's income.[8] This middle-class character and its associated anxieties must have been at issue in the debate about the Sophists and their art of rhetoric, as that debate was very much about questions of status and it was replete with comparisons among a host of occupations.[9]

I am suggesting that Isocrates was feeling his way toward the distinction between the lower and higher forms of professional identity. In doing so, he was consolidating and elaborating a development begun by the Sophists he supposedly was repudiating. As G. B. Kerferd (1981: 25) remarked, "Protagoras both claimed to be and was a professional. In fact the professionalism of the Sophists in the second half of the fifth century B.C. distinguishes them quite markedly from all their supposed predecessors."[10] Isocrates sets himself over the other teachers of rhetoric not to contest professionalism but to advance his higher order version of the same thing. As Michael Cahn (1989: 128) notes, the problem addressed in *Against the Sophists* is "a professional rather than a moral crisis in rhetoric."[11]

Andrew Ford (1993) sees this social anxiety as crucial to the formulation of Isocrates' ideas of linguistic artistry (and, by implication, imitative use of artistic models). "The attempt to objectify the rhetorician's work on language as a parallel to the artisan's fashioning plastic artifacts was not the inevitable result of the rationalization of the art of speaking, but part of a conflicted attempt to secure a professional standing that could be viewed as rationally based, independent, and a neutral service to the state." In other words, Isocrates was defining eloquence as a "high art" (in our terms) in order "to establish himself as a 'philosopher,' someone above mercantile hucksterism or mere banausic labor." The "major themes of his life and thought on education are linked to his economic place in the city."[12]

These observations all point in the same direction. Isocrates is expanding an emergent form of social identity by defining civic culture as an elevated instance of its commercial practices, rather than as something that is either identical with or wholly separate from those practices. On the one hand, "profession" can be defined in primarily economic terms. A professional athlete is paid to compete in front of spectators. On the other hand, "profession" can be defined ethically: a lawyer is paid for a service according to a professional code of conduct that coordinates self-interest with social responsibility.

The distinction can never be hard and fast; both sides are paid, both involve training, that training is both instrumental and oriented toward some good, members of the lower group often try to raise their status by claiming to have the attributes of the higher group, and members of the higher group often betray its claims about personal character and civic benefit. By developing such a distinction, Isocrates was able to define both the art of rhetoric and education itself as honorable forms of civic practice. The Sophists had made the mistake of settling for the merely economic form of professionalism (which may have been the best they could do, given the social context of the time, the radical implications of their project, and their status as aliens). No wonder that Isocrates subordinates technical instruction and insists that he is teaching *philosophia*.[13] As Jaeger summarized, the "teacher of rhetoric at last achieved the dignity which put him on a level with the philosopher and made him independent of machine politicians."[14] In short, he had obtained the equivalent of the modern law school and its art of jurisprudence.

These several strands of argument in *Against the Sophists* come together when Isocrates makes the difference in imitative method the key distinction between the two forms of professionalization. Low-level professionals (like Sophists or hairdressers) are provided models for imitation which they reproduce exactly. High-level professionals (like Isocrates and his students) also work with exact instruction and the imitation (*mimēsasthai*) of patterns (17–18), but they become proficient in a number of discourses and are judged successful when they excel in performative virtues (*anthēroteron kai chariesteron*). In other words, in civic education the successful reproduction of the teacher's instruction cannot occur without being somewhat different from the teacher's own example. Successful imitation includes judgments of which verbal means to use in previously unspecified situations, as well as qualities of usage that can succeed only if fitted to the distinctive features of the speaker in the specific situation. Because a process of literal imitation is not useful, students have to not only acquire expertise but also learn to use it according to standards of opportunity, propriety, and originality (13), which in turn are resources for civic leadership. The educated speaker rises above both mere technique and merely economic relationships, and this higher character that can be obtained by education—rather than by birth—is best suited to a society that wants to have both markets and respectability.

To summarize, Isocrates' program for civic education is based on a series of aligned contrasts between, on the one hand, the Sophists, technical expertise, literal imitation, the merely economic form of professionalism, and grammar as the paradigmatic discourse, and, on the other hand, his school, civic values, creative imitation, the ethical form of professionalism, and rhetoric as the paradigmatic discourse. The key difference in means is the difference in the kind of imitation used by each, and the key difference in ends is the kind of professional character that is produced: self-interested, petty, and rigid on the one hand, or civic-minded, generous, and flexible on the other (20–22). It is the difference we recognize today between the "hired gun" media consultant and the good jurist. The question remains whether classical texts can nurture the creative imitation that is the key to achieving this superior character.

This question is similar to one that Isocrates takes up in *Antidosis*. What kind of education can both equip and elevate the student? Isocrates' rationale is positioned between a critique of natural philosophy for its inability to guide practical affairs and another attack on the lesser Sophists and sycophants who are too involved in public life and corrupt it with their self-interested meddlesomeness. The answer follows many of the same steps taken before: insistence on human cognitive deficiency (271); compensating attention to proportionality as between payment and value, or between discourses and their ends (276); emphasis on creative imitation that leads to both persuasiveness and right character (277); and contrast between two forms of professional practice (300 ff.). There are several additional elements and alterations as well: he adds his distinction between the two forms of advantage (275, 281–285), which, we might note, corresponds to the distinction between the two forms of professionalism; imitation now is nestled within a cognate process of habituation (277); fame is invoked as a form of validation (one which makes sense if trying to legitimate a practice that is both separate from politics and dedicated to preparing students for political participation); there are somewhat stronger linkages between public and private affairs (285) and between wisdom and speech (294); and, most important, the culture of the city is foregrounded as the essential context for and substance of the program of study (293 ff.).

This mature formulation of Isocrates' ideas puts special emphasis on the concepts of proportionality and habituation, which in turn point directly to the importance of the city. If one sets out to produce honorable discourse, we are told, two challenges must be undertaken. First, the subject must involve questions of the "common good" rather than "private quarrels" (276), for only then will it be large enough to invoke the qualities of an honorable character. Second, the speaker will "select from all the actions of men which bear upon his subject those examples which are the most illustrious and the most edifying; and, habituating himself to contemplate and appraise such examples, he will feel their influence not only in the preparation of a given discourse but in all the actions of his life" (277).[15] In other words, character can't be developed in a cramped space, whether it is cramped because it allows only literal transcription of a *techne* or because it focuses only on private quarrels or selfish ends. It can be developed in the open space of public debate where one is exposed to many voices in a competition that allows only the most accomplished words and deeds to distinguish themselves. These results require not only the preoccupations of public life but also the time required to acquire experience and make sound judgments. Character cannot be developed quickly, but it can be developed over time through reflective, critical study of models of wise action. These models are not directly reproduced, but their attributes are assessed in respect to an ongoing series of tasks and events. The influence is indirect, and it is possible only if one lives within the flow of public life.

This is another example of how Isocrates gave the art of rhetoric the "gift of time."[16] Isocrates slows down the process of imitation, which also allows him to widen its scope in terms of both its objects and its effects. Imitation is no longer a technique for reproducing discourse on demand in a particular time and place. It now is a means of self-fashioning, and it can draw on sources that exceed one's circumstances while it also can influence all areas of one's life. Most important—and contrary to the image of Isocrates as an arrogant blowhard—it follows that no one figure or text could be a sufficient model for such a long-term, extensive discursive practice. But what object of study would qualify as the best means for habituation? The answer comes from the norm of proportionality: *only the city is the proportionate object for such a discourse.* The city provides the context within which one is habituated; its culture is the means and end of imitation.

Although also a conventional appeal for support, Isocrates' celebration of the city of Athens is an extension of his program of imitation. In addition, by aligning imitation with the culture of the city (rather than setting it out as a set of rules), Isocrates resolves a problem regarding his commitment to a single, comprehensive political discourse, or, perhaps, a universal discourse of democratic polity. Even if there could be such a discourse, Isocrates' critique of *techne* and literal imitation insists that it couldn't be reproduced exactly; or, if we begin with Isocrates' emphasis on creative imitation, it would seem that the process of reproduction would soon break up the original discourse into many contingent and perhaps ever more divergent variants; or, if we designate the higher discursive norms (such as timeliness) as the engines of the discourse, we have an excessively formal model that begs questions of substantive guidance. But Isocrates was not a deconstructionist and he did take politics seriously, so we need to ask how his program of imitation could be consistent with his ideal political discourse. Let me suggest that by locating the process of imitation (and, therefore, the best means for the reproduction of right speech and just polity) within the culture of the city, political discourse itself is redefined. The *logos politikos* is not a single code or original text, but a creative process through which many speakers and audiences collaborate to invent ever more eloquent statements of who they are and what they should do. More important, *no one speaker can speak the logos politikos.* It is the voice of the city: polyglot, multifaceted, and openly adaptive to a myriad of new circumstances. It is something that one can't even hear at once—and so there is need for habituation and reflective appropriation. It can be imitated, but only in part; most important, *it can only be imitated, never spoken directly.*

And the final measure of this relationship between teachers, students, and their texts, and between speakers, audiences, and their discourses, is not the success of the individual speaker but the sustainability of the culture. This emphasis on sustainability is crucial to understanding Isocrates' fascination with imitation. Once again, Jaeger provides an important hint. In contrast to the original Sophists, who were nomads and metics, Isocrates fully assimilated rhetoric into the fabric of Athenian life. (This is another reason his middle class position was significant.) "Before it [rhetoric] could become effective," it had to be rearticulated by "an Athenian who, like Isocrates, was fully alive to the nature of his city and the crisis which then confronted it." [17] Isocrates lived through the period in which Athens suffered military defeat and occupation, the loss of empire, tyranny and re-

taliation within the city, the breakdown of civic values, economic exploitation, and social turbulence.[18] If temperamentally conservative, he also knew
that the past golden age could not be reborn—indeed, that it had been one
cause of the subsequent troubles. The crucial issue becomes that of cultural
continuity.

This continuity depends on the continued existence of the city as a great
city, but with its mission now primarily cultural rather than military and
economic. "You [Athenians], yourselves, are pre-eminent and superior to
the rest of the world, not in your application to the business of war, nor because you govern yourselves more excellently or preserve the laws handed
down to you by your ancestors more faithfully than others, but . . . in the
fact that you have been educated as have been no other people in wisdom
and in speech" (293–294).

The model as we have it today comes straight from the Periclean funeral
oration, and as commentators have noted, the project certainly was idealistic. What may not be apparent is that this project is grounded in the specific
practice of flexible imitation of models of civic virtue (and not in technical
mastery of political science or literal adherence to the laws).[19] Continuity is
achieved through the act of imitation, and because literal reproduction of
the models is bound to fail—just as one could not persuade while wearing
fourth-century clothing today—the key is to school leaders in the higher
form of imitation. The key to achieving high-quality democratic discourse
is not to institutionalize a single form of that discourse, but to support those
practices that contribute directly to the sustainability of the public culture.

This commitment of cultural sustainability is thoroughly democratic
not just because Athens was democratic, but because the city was the object
of imitation. Even when enduring Spartan oversight or under the sway of
autocrats, Athens still would be polyglot, interactive, competitive, and artistic, and this character would be fully realized not through political assertion but by becoming the school of Greece. Isocrates' comments on the
glory and trials of the city demonstrate his commitment to democratic government and to justice (e.g., 309, and more generally the discussion of mutual advantage at 281 ff.), just as they exemplify his sense of elitism, but the
common thread tying his many themes together is the primacy of the city
as the context and purpose for education, which in turn is the key to per-
petuating the city. Isocrates is defining democracy primarily as a cultural
practice, and one that works by being a preeminent art among many other
arts.[20] In this context, the identification of rhetoric with "philosophy" and

"culture" is not only understandable, but essential. Democracy is primarily a form of speech that cannot be spoken by any one person. It can be learned well only amidst many voices.

At the same time that he was making the art of rhetoric thoroughly Athenian, Isocrates was hellenizing Athens. The Sophists' nomadic cosmopolitanism remained in his ability to imagine a larger horizon of political intelligibility than the parochial interests of the *polis*. His commitment to sustaining Athenian culture amidst political and economic change—and the increasing separation of individual and political identity—looks somewhat like a commitment to the modern idea of the public sphere. This is one place where the ideas of professionalism and sustainability intersect, which in turn is reinforced by the relationship each has with the practice of writing.[21] Professionalism is a "missing link" between the intellectual, economic, and social elements of Isocrates' conception of rhetoric, just as sustainability is a common thread between his conceptions of rhetoric, politics, and education.

Together these form something like a guild mentality, but one grounded in a sophisticated public audience rather than in institutional procedures.[22] This public also provides an internal restraint on the process of flexible imitation: the successful rearticulation of a model will depend on their response (e.g., as is suggested for the jury interpellated in the *Antidosis*), and this public will recognize that its best interests are served neither by slavish adherence to the past nor wholly individuated self-assertion. More important, this mentality would mediate between the individual and the state, and between states, in a world where states are unable to resist alternating processes of competitive fragmentation and global organization.

Such claims obviously lead to the illustration I promised earlier. The question is, can Isocrates provide a viable model for imitation in the contemporary world? Claims about his educational practice are confounded by his extensive influence in the history of Western education, and perhaps too limiting anyway. Let's take the harder case of identifying an Isocratean model of polity, which also would be an objective of his educational program. The attempt to set out an Isocratean politics turns precisely on his distinction between the two kinds of imitation. On the one hand, imitation can be excessively literal and self-interested: Isocrates becomes a model for elitism, autocratic government, cultural hegemony, and militaristic imperialism. But that places too much weight on the particular circumstances of his actual statements, while it allows too little room for inventive and timely adaptation to the conditions of our own day. Neither his politics nor his rhetoric were fixed templates to be reproduced mechanically.

On the other hand, a more artistic imitation would start with the basic outline of his *paideia*, the goal of the articulate citizen and the program of habituation amidst a broad range of discourses. Add to this his emphasis on creative imitation of models of eloquence and practical wisdom in order to activate the richness and power of the best possible political language. Finally—and we're starting now—we imitate the most distinctive, original feature of his political program: panhellenism. Obviously, a call for a united Greece is of little interest today (unless you live in Macedonia). But panhellenism can be read as more than that, and it has to be if it is to be read with the flexibility and right sense of proportionality required by the Isocratean hermeneutic.[23] Let's describe panhellenism as an attempt to identify a new class of political problems, and to create political harmony by expanding the horizon of politics, and to ensure cultural sustainability amidst large-scale forces of change.[24] What, then, would be the best articulation of this program today?

In a word: ecology. An Isocratean politics would be one that would argue for global political concord to address those problems that the individual states are incapable of solving on their own. These problems include ozone depletion, resource exhaustion, the distribution of wealth and scarcity, population growth and movement, and bio-extinction. Such problems not only affect all states while eluding single state action, but they also are the most comprehensive and historically powerful threats to the political culture of the open society. The best solution to these problems is the extension of democratic practices within each society and across the society of states. And it just so happens that such extensions could be achievable objects of civic education, while the solutions also depend on the cultivation of a stronger civic orientation in both the established professions and the newer areas of expertise. In every case, the Isocratean education would be directed to developing citizens capable of acting together to solve these problems in a manner that would allow for mutually sustainable ecological, cultural, and political practices. And if classical texts are to be used in this regard, it will have to be through a process of imitation that features timely, suitable, and eloquent appropriations to forge a new political language to these ends.

There is an additional consideration regarding this comparison. Isocrates consistently focused on those problems that were endemic to Greek society. For all his talk about the barbarians without, the point was to deflect energies that were otherwise self-destructive.[25] In his day, the debilitating contradictions in Greek life were largely political. (Obviously, the focus for the moment is more on stability than on justice.) In the modern world, they are economic. Specifically, there are too few "checks and balances" that can restrain resource consumption, environmental destruction, and species extinction. There is good reason to believe that modern civilization will not only destroy itself—all others have, so that is no big deal—but that it will take the rest of the planet with it. And need we add that the solution is not to be found through the application of technological expertise? Once again, there is need for an Isocratean education that includes technical mastery but subordinates it to prudential reasoning on behalf of a larger conception of civic life.[26] This is an issue of character, and character is not merely a stable good lending weight to decisions. Character is a form of resourcefulness, and the right character is one that can act in response to the new class of problems facing the polity. This resourcefulness cannot be specified as a fixed set of rules, of course, but the study of Isocrates suggests that it will include creative imitation of models of speech and action.

To conclude, Isocrates teaches us that inventive imitation is an important element of democratic discourse. Democracies by their very nature cannot rely on expertise alone—including legal or constitutional expertise—but they can't succeed if they are always starting over from scratch or if they never develop skilled speakers. The key to developing skilled speakers and sophisticated audiences is to traffic in representative examples of democratic speech and action, and to learn how to use those models adaptively, flexibly, creatively. Polities that are tied to single models and inflexible patterns of imitation (that is, to literal interpretation of those models) are more slavish than democratic in character, and their prospects are limited. We also might consider how the conventional criticism of Isocrates' varied political alliances over his long career is somewhat anti-democratic. Democratic speech developed by imitating the many voices of a pluralistic society presents any speaker with a wide range of resources for addressing a continually unfolding set of unpredictable circumstances.

Such speech has always had its critics. As Josiah Ober (1989) has argued convincingly, "Athenian public rhetoric—with its complex mix of elitist and egalitarian tactics—was a key form of democratic discourse. It stood in the place of an abstract theory of democracy and made theory unnecessary to its participants. It was arguably the failure of the elite to control political ideology that led them to devise and write formal political theory which would explain what was wrong with the system they failed to dominate" (338–339).[27] Democracy, then as now, sees no need to be guided by theorists who in turn see themselves as alienated from its practice. More important, perhaps democratic polity can get by without theoretical direction because it already has a more workable hermeneutical practice: the practice of imitation. Imitation operates as a proto-theoretical machinery within public rhetoric, and the flexibility and inventiveness that is a key part of democratic imitation uses a different cognitive style than the abstract, systematic rationality of political theory. In short, political theory and political imitation are distinct discursive practices, and each is a poor substitute for the other. No wonder that Isocrates gets no respect as a political theorist.[28] He might offer an important model for civic education for just that reason, however.

Comparisons of ancient and modern democracies inevitably are faulted because of the obvious limitations on the use of classical models in the contemporary world.[29] These problems come in part from expecting too much of substantive correspondences. What is needed instead is a strong understanding of imitation. Isocratean imitation is a creative process determined ultimately by the inventiveness of the speaker and the sophistication of the public audience, not by fidelity to the original form. Obviously this performative perspective leaves open the door to demagoguery, which in turn puts a premium on education that can instill a sense of civic responsibility that might regulate self-interest. Education becomes a profession in the ethical sense of that term, in order that it can model the appropriate character for all public practices. This character is developed in part by learning how to speak in the many distinctive voices that make up the city as a whole, past and present. So it is that there is little reason to object to mixing classical texts with those of other periods and genres, while there is good reason to explore all manner of analogies between past and present. However it is done, the objective would be both discursive skill developed through habituation within a pluralistic society and ethical restraint on behalf of the continued sustainability of democratic polity.

Isocrates doesn't theorize these ideas so much as he performs them.[30] His performative excess grates today, but it also can remind us that imitation is an aesthetic concept. It is based on the perception of essential form, it requires craft, it is directed toward its own completion, it begins and ends in pleasure, it is subject to varying standards of taste, and it implies a larger totality. The imitation of classical models seems to imply an aesthetic state as the object for political unity. To the extent that we believe such unified perception to be impossible or dangerous, those models will not be imitated.[31] I believe Isocratean education includes a program for sophisticated imitation that can check its own tendency to become a totalizing discourse. Surely this is the lesser problem, however, when he is not likely to be read at all.

Notes

1. My definition of the liberal arts education draws directly on the rhetorical tradition stemming from Isocrates. See Kimball 1986.

2. It seems that any essay on Isocrates has to creep around questions of the nature and stature of his intelligence. Was he a second-rate philosopher or a first-rate rhetorician (and if the rhetorician, is it still equivalent to the philosopher)? Was he a great writer or merely skilled and successful? The list could go on. As Too (1995: 2) has remarked, for most scholars today he is no more than a "figure of adequacy." I'd like to suggest that such questions and the judgment of mediocrity are symptomatic of a distinctive feature of his intelligence that has been overlooked: Isocrates was a *proleptic* thinker. He worked out early representations of major social and intellectual developments that could not yet be articulated directly in his own culture. As other commentators have noted, these anticipations include the institution of higher learning dedicated to the liberal arts education, the art of prose literature, the public sphere, and the idea of Europe. I also believe he was working out the idea of a profession as an ethical vocation.

3. For review of the history of literary imitation, see Boyd 1980. The major critical work remains Auerbach 1953. For review of the concept in the history of rhetoric, see Kennedy 2001. Both forms of mimesis—i.e., describing reality and crafting one's discourse according to a model—are at work within any literature, as any writer orients toward both world and genre (i.e., reality as it is experienced and the conventions for identifying that experience). The two forms of mimesis came together in Isocrates in the idea that speech can depict action and character. So it is that by imitating the right discourse, the right character can be reproduced (see, e.g., the claim at *Nicocles* 8 and *Antidosis* 256: "discourse which is true and lawful and just is the outward image of a good and faithful soul").

4. See Norlin's (1982) translation.

5. One of the features of the Athenian debate about the sophists that puzzles modern readers is the alignment of commerce and epistemology. Plato and Isocrates alike moved effortlessly between discussions of *epistēmē* or *doxa* and discussions of payment. See Blank 1985: 1–49.

6. See also Larson 1977. For an early influential essay in the sociology of professionalism, see Goode 1957: 194–200. Veysey's (1965) definitive history of the American university confirms the importance of professionalism in the development of that institution. Lest one think we now are beyond discriminations of status, see Fussell 1983. There also is need for qualification. Kimball (1992) would dispute Bledstein regarding the internal development

of the "traditional" professions. Kimball's scholarship is not to be taken lightly, but I believe Bledstein's account identifies broader conditions of competitiveness and social acceptance that continue to shape the organization of knowledge and the practice of everyday life.

7. The debate over the existence and role of a "middle class" in the Greek world has yet to be resolved. Ober (1989: 27–31) provides a review of the arguments. Ober needs to be skeptical of the concept if he is to develop the dialectic of mass and elite, and I agree with his assessment that one should not attribute the social stability of Athens to the presence of a middle class. That argument might suggest that the Athenian middle class was similar in size and structure to those of modern societies, which it clearly was not. On the other hand, the argument against middle-class identity and influence relies on too narrow a sense of linguistic analysis and social theory: In that account, unless political actors use the term to describe themselves (while no others use the term), and unless class members consciously act together to achieve "well-defined political goals" for the class (30), there is no class influence. The fact is that the denial of class interests is a characteristic of middle-class consciousness, while the appropriate term of class identification ("mesoi," "middling," "middle class") might be used by any rhetor in a society in which the middle class does have influence. For the Greek world, we might posit, first, an emergent and generalized egalitarianism coincident with democratization; second, a much narrower middle-class formation that was historically unique, quite different from the modern bourgeoisie, and probably not influential as such; and, third, a less stabilized set of attitudes and anxieties that are characteristic of those doing the entrepreneurial and managerial work of commercial societies. It is this sensibility that both created and was being negotiated through the debates about the status of intellectual work, the commodification of knowledge, the use of education for personal advancement, the accessibility of that education, and other such questions about the Sophists.

8. See 3: 142, 70.

9. There is no doubt that Plato's comparisons of rhetoric and sophistic with occupations such as cooking and retail trade reveal his aristocratic background. See, e.g., *Gorgias* 464b–465e and *Sophist* 231. For my rationale for analyzing status claims to discern a text's fundamental definitions of speaker, subject, and audience, see Hariman 1986. For additional demonstration of the method, see the chapter on Machiavelli in Hariman 1995.

10. See also Jebb 1893: vol. 2. "Isocrates conceives himself as belonging to a numerous and honourable profession, but as distinguished from most of his brethren by certain characteristics which give him a higher moral and intellectual dignity" (39).

11. Cahn goes on to argue that the "institutional reform proposed by Isocrates to solve these problems constitutes his most important innovation" (135). It was not the only possible solution to the problem, however. Garver (1994: 45; 45–51) carefully develops the thesis that "the purpose of the *Rhetoric* is to articulate a civic art rather than a professional one." The labels vary, and there are enormous differences between Isocrates and Aristotle, but Garver and I are working with similar distinctions.

12. See especially pp. 34, 35, and 38.

13. "It is not until the fourth century B.C. that philosophy begins to be treated as a distinct profession. Both Plato and Isocrates sought to 'professionalize' and 'disciplinize' the term *philosophia*, but in decidedly different ways" (Schiappa 1995: 56). See also Havelock 1983: 7–82; Timmerman 1998: 145–159.

14. See vol. 3: 54.

15. See Norlin's (1982) translation.

16. See T. Poulakos 1997: 70.

17. See vol. 3: 50.

18. As he notes at *Antidosis* 317–319.

19. This point was not lost on Jaeger, however. "He clings to the principle of imitation established by his predecessors . . . all his great speeches were meant to be models in which his pupils could study the precepts of his art" (3: 65). The distortion comes in suggesting that he merely reproduced an imitative pedagogy instead of developing it into a much richer educational practice, and in the implication that the speeches were models of a strictly defined rhetorical or literary art, rather than of the art of politics broadly conceived. Where Jaeger sees models of verbal technique, I see a pedagogy for the inculcation of the ethos of the civic professional.

20. Jaeger and Poulakos each recommend emphasis on the idea of culture. See also Forster 1979; Marrou 1956. Timmerman (1998) acknowledges the argument but holds out for keeping philosophy the central term in Isocrates' program. See also Schiappa 1995. For the importance (and expansion) of the idea of culture in Isocrates' legacy, see Smethurst 1953.

21. Habermas (1989) emphasized the importance of writing and reading. For discussion of Isocrates on writing, see Heilbrunn: "Dobesch has shown convincingly the link that exists between publication and panhellenism; the written communication, addressed to the Greek as an individual wherever he may reside, and not to the members of the particular *polis* who may be listening, is the appropriate vehicle for propagating panhellenic ideals. By passing [*sic*] the assembly, the written message helps to undermine the particularism and authority of the *polis*" (1975: 160). Too (1995) provides the most extensive study of the political implications of Isocrates' writing. For discussions of technique, see Usher 1973: 39–67; Bons 1993: 160–171.

22. The development of character via professional education oriented toward habituation within the public culture of the city might have been both distinctive and efficacious in a society maintained more by civic liturgies than by institutional regulation of behavior. For discussion of the importance of liturgy for Athenian democracy, see the essays by Conner and Cole in Ober and Hendrick, eds., 1996.

23. Other proleptic interpretations are possible as well, as with de Romilly (1992: 2–13). De Romilly believes that "The Greek authors can be models, even in their most fragile activities and their repeated failures" (12), and she recognizes that panhellenism was not merely expansionary: "Concord doesn't only suppose that one doesn't encroach on the others' freedom, but that one accepts a number of restrictions for a general advantage" (10). Such definitions are already looking forward, and should not be mistaken for literal accounts of

what panhellenism might have meant pragmatically to Isocrates or others in the Greek world. In that regard, see Flower 2000: 65–102.

24. For discussion of the problem of identifying a new class of political problems, see Marone 1998; Ankersmit 1996. Note also the connection between Isocrates' theme of panhellenism and his rhetorical sensibility. As Gillis (1969) remarks: "These are the two central ideas of Isocrates' life, eloquence and panhellenism, one serving the other" (338). Heilbrunn (1975: 164) also remarks on this unity of theme and style. In the terms of my earlier analysis, the *logos politikos* always has to be reaching towards the proportionate object, and the highest forms of public discourse will be those that address the largest problems and encompass the largest field of action.

25. Heilbrunn 1975: 170.

26. See also Hariman, ed., 2003.

27. See also Farrar 1988.

28. For example: "Isocrates professed to teach a rhetoric that benefited the *polis*, and he is often of use for providing background. But his extensive preserved work reveals few theoretical interests, and I am not aware of a single argument on our current problem which is original to him or for which he offers a theoretical perspective." Yunis 1996: 18n.40.

29. Important texts in the comparative democracy project include Ober 1989; Ober and Hedrick, eds., 1996; Euben, Wallach, and Ober, eds., 1994.

30. T. Poulakos 1997 chap. 5; Schwarze 1999.

31. So it is that Too believes that Isocrates cannot avoid being an exponent of cultural hegemony. I believe Poulakos (1997) has the better read on this question: We need to distinguish between the specific politics of the past era and his commitment to democratic political agency (xi). At her best, Too does the same by focusing on Isocrates' development of the political agency in writing. Poulakos is equally careful about invoking Isocrates today, however. He concludes that "Isocrates' writing gives us one of the final glimpses in the history of rhetoric of community as a unified collectivity, and perhaps the last successful deployment of rhetoric against the forces of fragmentation and the pressures of difference. It is a dream that can no longer be dreamed . . ." (106). Both Too and Poulakos are stuck at the question of whether political imitation requires a grand narrative. As Ankersmit (1996) has argued, the aesthetic dimension of politics not only can do without a metaphysical or cultural unity in the state, it is important precisely because of the "brokenness" of political reality. This "brokenness" refers to the inevitable gap between political representation and reality, and the corresponding necessity that all political decisions are grounded in discursive performances that can provide the stylistic coherence needed to bind people together for collective action.

10

MICHAEL LEFF

Isocrates, Tradition, and the Rhetorical Version of Civic Education

UNTIL quite recently, judgment about Isocrates has remained comfortably fixed and solidly negative. The consensus view has regarded him as an island of mediocrity within a sea of Attic genius, since, when measured against the achievement of his fourth-century contemporaries, Isocrates' work has seemed deficient—deficient in literary merit if compared to Plato, deficient in political acuity if compared to Demosthenes, and deficient in clarity and rigor of thought if compared to Aristotle. His one claim to distinction has come in the field of pedagogy, since, whatever his flaws as philosopher or politician, or literary artist, Isocrates achieved indisputable success and influence as a teacher. G. M. A. Grube (1965) has summarized this traditional attitude in a single sentence: Isocrates "was not a great thinker, a great orator, or a great writer, but he must have been a very great teacher" (44). Consistent with this assessment, Grube treated Isocrates as a figure who made little direct contribution to "literary theory and criticism," but whose "indirect influence" could "hardly be exaggerated because it was his kind of education which triumphed over all others and dominated the Greco-Roman world" (38).[1]

The essays collected in this volume clearly indicate that this attitude has now changed. All of the essays, even those that express reservations about the quality of Isocrates' thought, treat his texts directly and seriously, and none shunt Isocrates' pedagogy to the side without regard for its philosophical, literary, and political content. We find instead a concerted effort to understand Isocratean *paideia* as an important part of the culture of his time and as a lively and enduring contribution to our conception of liberal education.

The most notable sign of this revisionist attitude is a realignment of the relationship between Plato and Isocrates. In the older paradigm, the two are placed at polar extremes within the universe of Western education. Isocrates, set at one end of the spectrum, represents a thoroughly practical system of education, while Plato, at the other end, represents the idealized alternative. The more recent perspective, represented throughout the essays collected here, does not deny a major difference between the two, but it also detects an idealistic strand that runs through Isocrates' texts and places him in closer intellectual proximity to Plato than the older view would acknowledge. Thus, David Konstan begins his paper with doubts about a pervasive and sweeping dichotomy between Isocrates and Plato and announces his intention to offer an alternative that emphasizes commonalities in their thought about society and politics. Likewise, Kathryn Morgan warns against "trapping ourselves into binary oppositions" and argues for a "more nuanced approach wherein Isocrates occupies a middle ground between Athenian populist education and the rigors and exclusions of Plato." Takis Poulakos develops a somewhat similar theme when he differentiates Isocrates from the Sophists. The Sophists, on his account, treat persuasion as an amoral instrument, whereas Isocrates connects persuasion with the deliberative processes that form and sustain ethical values, and this ethical valence suggests something less than an absolute contrast with Plato. Robert Hariman also highlights the Isocratean connection between effective persuasion and the cultivation of good character, and he notes that this configuration has a distinctly idealistic tincture.

In fact, the essays in this collection express a set of overlapping, complementary arguments that combine to redefine our understanding of Isocratean *paideia*. And while it is impossible to appreciate these arguments without attention to the detailed analysis of Isocrates' speeches upon which they are based, the main tendency of this development can be condensed into seven key points: (1) Isocrates thoroughly rejects Plato's conception of abstract, objective truth, but he is equally opposed to the extreme relativism associated with Gorgias and other Sophists. He tries to position himself between these extremes and to construct a practical standard of knowledge that responds to ordinary experience, that develops within the medium of political discourse, and that generally enables us to make appropriate judgments in particular cases. (2) Good rhetoric both generates and reflects such knowledge, and it is not simply discourse that pleases or persuades an audience. (3) Good rhetoric is not produced or heeded by all people, and by adopting this view, Isocrates marks himself as an elitist. Some individuals, it follows, are capable of deliberative excellence; others are not, and in a well regulated polity, those who lack this excellence ought to defer to their better-educated fellow-citizens. (4) Rhetorical excellence requires self-restraint and a cultivated sense of the common good, and hence, it is not simply the result of technical skill but must also reflect and manifest virtues intimately connected with moral character. (5) Since popular acceptance does not determine rhetorical excellence, it cannot be based upon momentary success. It must refer to principles grounded in reasonably stable and durable conceptions of virtue. (6) Given Isocrates' theory of knowledge, such principles must have their origin within the experience of the political community. (7) Since none of the points above are, or are intended to be, descriptive of Athenian politics as actually practiced, Isocrates' educational program is an idealization.

Once these points are recognized, the distance between Isocrates and Plato seems to shrink, and we can identify enemies common to both programs. One locus of opposition comes from a narrow pragmatism that caters to the banausic interests of the student and concerns itself entirely with methods of pleasing or manipulating others. Morgan holds that this option, which she calls "polis-education," was the main rival to both Isocratean and Platonic *paideia* in fourth-century Athens. A second possibility follows from Takis Poulakos' account of fifth-century sophistic thought, and it consists in a systematic, theoretical skepticism that culminates in extreme relativism. Both these alternatives do not pretend to teach virtue, since the sheer instrumentalism of the one occludes interest in virtue, and the theoretical mechanisms of the other work to deny its possibility. Thus, if we define civic education as education into virtue, neither of them is "civic," and both can be contrasted to the Isocratean and Platonic options.

Yet while these considerations shorten the lines of disagreement between Isocrates and Plato, they do not mitigate their intensity. The two share a goal set "far beyond the limits of the traditional state, in the realm of the ideal" (Jaeger 1965: 83), but their ideals differ markedly in source and character. Plato's thought moves along an abstract, metaphysical, and mathematical trajectory, and the integrity of his philosophical system depends upon its isolation from all forms of ordinary experience—and from politics in particular. Isocrates, on the other hand, remains a thoroughly political animal. While Plato repudiates Athenian democracy, Isocrates seeks to reform it. His conception of virtue is realized in and through the *polis*, and his ideals are never completely detached from ordinary experience.

Controversies often become sharper, more dramatic, and more significant when the parties share key objectives and attitudes. Our case in hand nicely illustrates this point, for as the differences between Isocrates and Plato become better focused, they seem to grow in importance. Once we set aside a simple, totalizing dichotomy between these two versions of *aideia*, we can better appreciate their status as rival conceptions of education into virtue, since if they do not cover the whole range of pedagogical options available in fourth-century Athens, they do represent the two major main alternatives for civic education. Moreover, as Kimball (1986) has demonstrated, these options have had remarkable durability. The rivalry between the Isocratean ideal of the orator and the Platonic ideal of the philosopher has played a crucial role in the debate about liberal education from the moment of its Greek origin to the present, and the persistence of this issue lends special importance to current efforts to redefine Isocrates' place in the fourth-century and to reconsider the conceptual integrity of his educational program.

The most troublesome aspect of this project arises from the idealism that the revisionist view attributes to Isocrates' thought. It seems odd to call Isocrates an idealist, especially when we are comparing him to Plato. Plato gives us the clear case of an idealistic *paideia*, since his program identifies knowledge and virtue as abstract ideas that exist outside the realm of ordinary experience. Isocrates' "idealism" is different, less pure, and more difficult to identify and understand. If his *paideia* looks toward something better than existing political practices and opinions, it does not transcend them altogether, and he never disregards ordinary, practical experience. Since Isocrates does not contemplate "pure ideas," his thought stands in the margin between the ideal and the actual, and hence the source and character of his ideals are not immediately obvious. In dealing with Plato, we are forced to wonder how his Ideals can connect with our ordinary experience, but in the case of Isocrates, we are forced to wonder how he can establish ideals sufficiently distanced from the flux of ordinary experience to provide stable ethical principles.

The essays in this collection offer two very different responses to this problem. One response locates Isocrates' ideals in the Athenian tradition and suggests an optimistic view of how rhetorical *paideia* can generate and sustain relatively stable values. The other approach designates consistency as the key principal for Isocrates, and it eventuates in a negative judgment about Isocrates' pedagogy in particular and a skeptical attitude toward the rhetorical version of liberal education in general.

Robert Hariman, John Poulakos, Takis Poulakos, and David Konstan all argue for an intimate link between Isocratean *paideia* and the Athenian political tradition. Konstan is the most explicit in maintaining that history functions as the ground for Isocrates' political principles, and he supports his position through detailed analysis of several texts. His reading of the *Areopagiticus* offers an especially interesting insight into how the Isocratean project works.

In the *Areopagiticus,* Isocrates makes one of his typical criticisms of the existing regime and argues for a more restrained democracy in which the masses defer to the elite few who are genuinely able to make wise political decisions. Konstan explains that the justification for this principle of deference and restraint comes through an account of Athenian history anchored in the constitution of Solon. But Solon's authority is not simply an inert given; it is not embedded in an objective historical record or in the fixed memory of the Athenians. Instead it is constructed and construed by Isocrates so as to fit his own immediate political interests. Isocrates chooses Solon as his touchstone and not Theseus or some other equally plausible icon in Athenian history because that choice suits his purposes, and he explains the meaning and the effects of the Solonic reforms in terms that tilt history in the direction of his own attitudes about the present. Tradition places limits on what Isocrates can do; he is not at liberty to tell stories that have no basis in Athenian cultural memory, and he cannot construe persons or events in a way that does violence to Athenian sensibilities. Yet, these limits are broad enough for Isocrates to do his rhetorical work and to ground his argument in a plausible historical context.

On Konstan's reading, the *Areopagiticus* represents a rhetorical/ hermeneutic encounter with history.[2] The Athenian tradition frames and authorizes Isocrates' argument, but the tradition is tailored as it is used, and this process establishes a reciprocal interaction between historical understanding and the perspective on present circumstances. To the extent that it is persuasive, the representation of Solon's constitution at one and the same time alters understanding of the historic touchstone and of the immediate rhetorical situation. The text then demonstrates a rhetorical means of stabilizing values without ossifying them. Tradition surrounds and constrains the rhetorical field, but in the multivocal and constantly changing world of political rhetoric, tradition is always subject to new interpretations that allow it to "develop while still maintaining its identity and continuity" (Pelikan 1984: 58).

One other point that Konstan raises about the *Areopagiticus* deserves special notice. Konstan repeatedly and persuasively argues that Isocrates does not regard laws or constitutions as the basis for good government. These formal mechanisms are only the outward sign of the authentic source of political vitality, which consists in the character and spirit of people. Everything depends upon the capacity of the people and their leaders to govern well, and governing well requires effective deliberation about public matters, and it is the capacity to recognize and act upon political virtue that enables deliberative excellence. Konstan thus concludes: "In place of law or rights, Isocrates offers the criterion of political excellence and the moral character of the government."

These observations about Isocrates' political philosophy run parallel to the account of his educational program that Robert Hariman and Takis Poulakos develop in their papers. For both Hariman and Poulakos, the program begins with the same principles of uncertainty and contingency that inform Isocrates' conception of political wisdom. Just as there is no method, no set of absolutely fixed rules, that can regulate political judgment, so also there is no system that can guarantee persuasive success in a rhetorical encounter. So education in the art of speech must respect the flux of circumstances, the presence of competing voices, and the open-ended character of the rhetorical event. The teacher consequently should not place much faith in abstract precepts but should nurture the student's capacity for judging circumstances and audiences and for accommodating language and argument to the demands of specific occasions. This type of instruction entails learning based on material cases, and so it is developed through practice (exercises in composition that approximate real-world conditions) and imitation (the study of models of rhetorical excellence that embody strategic principles).

It was possible to deploy these methods of teaching for purely technical and utilitarian ends, and John and Takis Poulakos maintain that the Sophists practiced precisely this kind of opportunistic instruction. Isocrates, however, operated within a broader, more ethically sensitive horizon, and he insisted on connecting training in rhetorical virtuosity with education in political virtue. This commitment, as Hariman explains it, appeared most obviously in relation to imitation. The student was not to select just any text to emulate but only those that offered models of political and moral as well as persuasive excellence. He should attend to texts that were "the most illustrious and edifying, and habituating himself to contemplate and appraise such examples, he will feel their influence not only in the preparation of a given discourse but in all actions of his life" (*Antidosis* 277). In short, Isocrates' pedagogy was designed to wrap political virtue and rhetorical excellence into a single package, and these two objectives fit together so neatly because both were conceived as aspects of the same process of judgment and action.

Takis Poulakos extends the political connection to a higher level, for he finds that this attitude toward the education of the student corresponds to Isocrates' larger conception of political deliberation. The system does not simply demand that students work within the moral frame of the community; it identifies *politikos logos* with moral virtue. Isocrates' conception of rhetorical *paideia* is "political—not political in the narrow sense of party politics but in the broader sense of care and concern for general welfare." The ultimate aim is not partisan victory but the conduct of a "collective inquiry into the good" (Poulakos 1997: 4–5). This inquiry, however, must proceed along a case-by-case basis, since political values are not a priori truths but are "relative to the specific case at hand," and "choices about the preferable and the good are made with a view to a particular situation and in relation to concrete action."

It may seem that this formulation is paradoxical, since it remains focused on particular cases but aims toward the promotion of a common good that extends beyond any single case. Yet, when the arguments of Konstan, Hariman, and Poulakos are combined, Isocrates' program does seem to have a subtle coherence. Given his conviction that our knowledge is imperfect, situated, and always defeasible, and given his resistance to Sophistic relativism, Isocrates must find some source of stability for values without turning to abstract universals. He locates these values in the community, but just as the laws of the community cannot define the excellence of a government, so also communal values cannot suffer reduction to fixed axioms. Political virtue is found in the character of people who exercise proper judgment in the face of mutable circumstances and who preserve the conditions needed to sustain effective deliberation. The political tradition, therefore, is not a fixed set of norms but a living organism whose identity is constantly created, altered, and recreated; the tradition, from this perspective, is itself a rhetorical construction built up over time through the deliberative action of the community. The values in the tradition have a certain degree of stability, but they assume meaning only as they make contact with actual, constantly changing events, and so they are always subject to rhetorical adjustment.

This rhetorical process must work within the finite game of political argument, where multiple voices strive for attention and partisan differences are always at play, but if the deliberating agents are of the right moral character, they can engage in these finite contests without losing sight of the larger purpose of the exercise. Rhetorical deliberation is necessarily embedded in the particular, but in the Isocratean scheme, it should also always remain mindful of its larger purpose, which is to sustain the community as a locus of deliberative excellence. Thus when Konstan identifies tradition as the source for Isocrates' principles, he opens the way toward a complex understanding of how rhetorical *paideia* can balance the stability needed for reliable judgment with the flexibility needed for practical action.

Like David Konstan, Kathryn Morgan rejects a simple, all-encompassing dichotomy between Isocratean and Platonic *paideia*, emphasizes the idealizing strand in Isocrates' thought, and looks for values that secure his politics in something more stable than procedural democracy. But, while Konstan argues that Isocrates locates his principles in tradition, Morgan maintains that he grounds his entire project in a single intellectual principle, and that principle is consistency. "The key to sound reasoning for Isocrates," she contends, "is the principle of consistency. Inconsistency, or confusion as he would put it (*tarachē*), is both a rhetorical and political (and in the end a moral) flaw, whereas rhetorical consistency is the guarantor of moral and political consistency."

Morgan's account of consistency encompasses two different aspects of Isocrates' program. The first and most obvious of these is consistency as a standard for political judgment. A good judgment is consistent; a bad judgment is confused. Secondly, there is the more complex matter of the coherence of Isocrates' program. Morgan notes that Isocrates' program rests upon a network of seamless connections between rhetorical excellence and political virtue that rise from the individual self to the level of the *polis*, and from there to the panhellenic orbit.

In the case of the individual, excellence in speech equals excellence as a citizen and as a person, and this consistency of the rhetorical, political, and ethical is embedded within the fabric of Isocratean pedagogy. Morgan argues that, through an analogy between the city and the soul, Isocrates applies the same set of equations to the civic realm and to international relations: "The same principles must operate inside the self, within Athenian civic discourse, and in the discursive relationship of Athens with other Greek states." This alignment allows Isocrates to make assumptions that comfortably fit his interests and to avoid serious problems connected with the scope of his project.

Morgan proceeds to measure Isocrates against what she takes to be his own standard. He demands consistency from others and criticizes those who make confused judgments. But is Isocrates himself consistent? Morgan's answer is resoundingly negative. She finds internal inconsistencies within texts, external inconsistencies between texts and, in general, she charges that Isocrates succumbs to the opportunism that he denounces. In contrast to the breadth and idealism of his educational program, his rhetorical practice shifts as the mood strikes him and accommodates to the inconstant sentiment of the Athenian masses. Isocrates seems tainted by the "*polis*-education" he opposes in theory, and his whole program fails to cohere "with a centralized and governing principle. Isocrates' version of *paideia* thus falls between the Platonic rejection of the education offered by the *polis*, and the *polis'* demand that its citizens think within the boundaries it has set up. As is often the case with those who try to make a middle ground, Isocrates ends up being rejected by both sides."

As Morgan well knows, the charge of inconsistency is hardly new. It has been raised frequently against Isocrates, and there have also been some notable efforts to answer it. For example, Baynes (1960) and T. Poulakos (this volume) claim that inconsistent passages that appear in different speeches represent prudent accommodation to circumstance rather than blundering inconsistency. Harding (1973), arguing along a related but somewhat different line, maintains that some speeches in Isocrates' corpus were composed for pedagogical purposes and were intended to illustrate and embody the rhetorical process of arguing both sides of a question. Yun Lee Too (1995: 62–75) recently has supported and extended this argument, and it is consistent with Ober's observation (this volume) that Isocrates' texts consciously situate themselves in a multivocal context. Morgan acknowledges some sympathy for these ameliorative readings, but she trumps them with the demand that "we hold Isocrates to the same standards he imposes on others."

The force of this argument rests upon the clarity and accuracy of Morgan's account of consistency in Isocrates' thought, and on her reading, consistency emerges as an abstract, universal standard. She does not make this claim directly, but the language she uses and the direction of her argument indicate that this is her understanding. She characterizes consistency several times "as a guiding intellectual principle"; she asserts that "rhetorical consistency" functions as a "*guarantor* of moral and political consistency" (my emphasis), and against those who would argue that he might entertain a more flexible view of consistency, she asserts that Isocrates' criticism of Athenian policy calls for "precisely" the same behavior in different contexts; and, in a passage I have quoted above, she concludes her essay by associating consistency with a "centralized and governing intellectual principle." In short, Morgan holds Isocrates to a standard of consistency that is abstract, intellectual, formal, regulative in a precise and necessary sense, and centralized in a way that disconnects it from the sprawl of ordinary political practice.

I do not believe, however, that Isocrates' position on this matter is as simple and unambiguous as Morgan represents it. It is true that Isocrates frequently makes strong and unqualified appeals to consistency in his political arguments, but in the self-consciously rhetorical world of Isocratean texts, we cannot assume that a situated argument represents an unqualified theoretical commitment. And in those passages where he does deal with consistency directly, his remarks do not indicate that he has a formal standard in mind.

Isocrates explicitly addresses the principle of consistency in three passages, *Antidosis* 203 and 253, and *On the Peace* 114. All three express the same sentiment but, as Morgan says, the first deals with the issue in the most general terms. In it, Isocrates comments, "people who have sense should not make unequal judgments about similar matters." Nothing in the language here mandates a formal, abstract view of consistency. This definition is, in fact, proportional rather than algorithmic, and his call for judgments about similarity implies a standard embedded in the matter under consideration that cannot be exact. This looser, more practical construction of the passage, moreover, corresponds with Isocrates' general skepticism about formal rules—a skepticism that he applies specifically to the teaching of rhetoric and the impossibility of devising precepts that can encompass all the occasions for their application. "No system of knowledge," he tells us, "can possibly cover these occasions, since they elude our science" (*Antidosis* 184). In the absence of strong and direct evidence to the contrary, why should we believe that he would regard consistency as something more easily reduced to an abstract, universal standard than the strategies and structures of rhetoric?

Morgan might well respond to this question by arguing that, even if he does not explicitly endorse a formal principle of consistency, Isocrates would need to adopt one to secure the coherence of his program. If his *paideia* aspires to something higher and more rigorous than popular approval, then it must have some fixed principle to use as a standard. The only plausible candidate for this status is consistency, and so Isocrates must either regard consistency as a fixed, abstract, and guiding intellectual principle, or his program cannot sustain its ethical pretensions.

I suspect that something like this reasoning lies behind Morgan's critique of Isocrates, and from within a certain frame of reference, the position makes sense. That frame unfortunately is one that leaves no space for Isocratean rhetoric, or for any other variant of rhetorical humanism.[3] In effect, Morgan shunts aside the binary opposition between Plato and Isocrates only to accept a binary opposition between Plato and the *polis*. A coherent educational program must rest either on fixed principles or on political advantage, because nothing in between will work. One either capitulates to the demands of rhetorical expediency or transcends them through some extra-rhetorical standard. Isocrates cannot occupy a middle ground in this configuration because it allows no principles for argument or standards for consistency that fall between the extremes.

As my earlier synoptic discussion of Isocrates and tradition indicates, I believe that a middle position does exist and that it offers fertile ground for cultivating a program of liberal education. In the face of Morgan's explicit concern for fixed principles and formal consistency, this reconstruction of Isocrates' position may appear diffuse and speculative, and so it seems appropriate to consider a more recent and direct effort to deal with these issues. Specifically, the work of the Belgian philosopher and rhetorician Chaim Perelman offers an explicit basis for a rhetorical view of consistency, a view that sustains coherence without resorting to formalism.

As a young legal philosopher, Perelman set out to discover a universally acceptable definition of justice and, under the influence of formalist method, examined the definitions stated or implied in the main schools of Western philosophy. He sifted through them until he discovered features agreeable to all. The result was a principle that he called formal justice: "Beings in the same essential category should be treated in the same way." This principle, we should note, contrasts with Isocrates' notion of consistency, because it is explicitly formal. That is, Perelman's rule of justice does not call for practical judgments about similarity, but instead divides things into categories, and calls for judgments that follow deductively from this categorization.

When Perelman attempted to apply this formal principle, he made a startling discovery: it was almost entirely useless. The abstract principle and its associated method of formal entailment failed to resolve concrete cases, because actual cases always revolved around particulars and disputes about how they should be categorized. Formal justice, he concluded, "does not tell you when two objects belong to the same category; neither does it specify the treatment they should be given" (Perelman and Olbrichts-Tyteca 1969: 229). Consistent judgment, that is, cannot be mandated by formal rule, since judgment immerses us in material conditions.

As a result of this project, Perelman abandoned formal method and searched for an approach to justice more closely connected to particular cases, and eventually this effort led him to the rhetorical tradition. In that tradition, he discovered precisely what had been obscured by the dominant philosophical trends of the twentieth century—an approach to knowledge and value grounded not in formal deduction or mathematical certainty but in situated argument. This movement from formalism to Isocrateanism was not motivated by, nor did it result in, the displacement of principles and values in favor of opportunism and cynical manipulation. It represented instead an effort to generate a more realistic approach to values by understanding the interaction between principles and cases.

From Isocrates to the present, humanistic rhetoric has found its coherence in this interaction. The characteristic features of this program all suggest movement and development rather than stasis and essence. The rhetorician favors prudence rather than contemplative knowledge, argumentation rather than formal logic, and equity rather than legal formalism. These interactive and mobile resources operate within controlled limits because of one other feature of rhetorical humanism: its demand for and mode of contextualizing public affairs. Just as the rhetorician bounds a case within an occasion, so also rhetorical *paideia* places events and ideas within the history of the community. The principles arise from civic tradition.

Kathryn Morgan notes that the Athenian tradition was too adaptive and opportunistic to become the source of fixed principle. I think she is absolutely correct, and that is the reason Isocrates can make such good use of it. He can invoke the tradition as a point of reference and as a resource for discovering or inventing principles that can achieve local stability. He can also

construct the tradition even as he uses it. But if, as Morgan says, "the nature of the Athenian tradition was up for grabs," there were limits to how
it could be grabbed and for what purposes. The tradition offered a context
sufficiently stable for principled deliberation to take place, but not so rigidly
fixed that it would overwhelm the need for deliberative innovation and
adaptation. As is true of all other polities with a living tradition, fourth-
century Athens was a place where old principles and new circumstances in-
teracted in the talk of citizens and where citizens could talk about old issues
in new ways. Hence, as Ober has demonstrated, it was a place where someone could invent an audacious form of discourse and use it to promote a conservative cultural and political program.

I have now argued at some length against Kathryn Morgan's explicit critique of Isocrates and implicit critique of rhetorical *paideia* in general. But
I must also confess that both critiques have a real bite. While I believe that
Morgan's complaints about Isocrates' inconsistencies are too general and
emphatic, she does uncover discrepancies that are difficult to explain,[4] and
she reminds us that Isocrates' corpus does not open easily to the modern
reader. Many of the key concepts seem murky or alien to us, and we are
forced to do some ameliorative reading to preserve the integrity of his
thought. Most contributors to this volume believe that the effort is worthwhile, but it is important to remember, as Morgan forces us to do, that re-
furbishing Isocrates is a complex business. It cannot follow from a simple
and direct reading of his texts, and it requires a good bit of effort and good
will from those who look to him for inspiration.

Morgan also offers some very perceptive comments about the network
of correlations and assumed identities that work through Isocrates' program
and that eventuate in circular reasoning. As Morgan reviews the concepts
and levels of activity that Isocrates attempts to integrate, it appears that he
is not simply connecting the parts into consistent relationships but that he
builds them into a totalizing organic structure. Morgan treats these tendencies under the heading of consistency, but the term *organicism* might be
more appropriate. Apparent oppositions disappear as Isocrates equates rhetorical excellence with political excellence, self-interest with civic interest,
and artistic style with elevated thought. Likewise he presents a seamless
continuity that rises from the silent thought of the individual, to the voice
of the deliberating subject, to the deliberative action of the *polis*, and to the
realm of international negotiation. Isocrates justifies some of these connections, but he simply asserts the existence of others as he folds them into the

grand pattern. At the end of the process, we are confronted with a neatly wrapped package that shows no loose ends or sharp edges. All of the elements of *paideia* fit within a thoroughly idealized vision of culture.

This kind of ideal does not rest comfortably with Isocrates' pragmatism. He repeatedly insists that liberal education ought to retain connection with ordinary life and practical deliberation, and one of the most attractive features of his program is the dynamic interaction it sustains between principles and cases. Within the terms of this program, it seems fair to maintain that the partisan wrangle of specific controversies can be viewed as part of a larger process where adversarial arguments blend into a system of cooperative deliberation. But Isocrates' organicism goes well beyond a grounded balance between local friction and civic harmony, since he envelops all conflict within the ratios of a fixed equilibrium.

This organicism blunts certain problems that confront Isocratean *paideia*, since from a less thoroughly balanced and idealized perspective, the gap between the program's objectives and its limitations prove more difficult to explain. How can ethical orators persuade corrupt audiences without compromising their own integrity? How can we ensure that technical excellence in persuasion is not turned to self-interested purposes? How can an educational program designed to train an individual orator function as a mechanism for educating an entire *polis*? These questions are evaded by the organic image that Isocrates constructs as the rationale for his program. Other rhetorical humanists, Cicero most notably among them, also find this a tempting strategy. But the evasion comes at a high price, and rhetorical *paideia* might well require description in more realistic terms. Principles and cases often do not merge easily into the deliberative process; technical skill and moral purpose do not always coalesce; speakers sometimes must make excruciating decisions about whether to accommodate to an audience or to distance themselves from it; and the vision of an idealized long-range harmony of interests tends to gloss these tensions.

At the same time, however, we need to understand that the tensions are formidable and that Isocrates was hardly the only thinker to encounter troubled water when trying to cope with them. David Depew and Eugene Garver, the two authors in this collection who write about Aristotle, bring this point to light, and before closing this essay and our volume, we need to consider these two essays and how they fit Aristotle into the revisionist perspective on Isocrates.

In charting the relationship between Aristotle and Isocrates, both Depew and Garver emphasize the problem of understanding the connection between theoretical and practical wisdom. They agree that, on this issue, Aristotle diverges notably from the views of Plato and Isocrates, who both adopt totalizing attitudes. Plato totally dismisses practical knowledge and thus can imagine no intrinsic values attached to rhetoric, while Isocrates denies the possibility of theoretical knowledge and thus gives an unlimited range to practical knowledge, which he identifies with his version of the rhetorical project. Aristotle falls between these two positions. He acknowledges that both practical and theoretical knowledge exist, have value, and possess a certain range of autonomy. But while he grants them independent existence, he does not regard them as equal, for theology and metaphysics—the theoretical sciences—have priority over politics and ethics, the arena of *phronēsis*. To further complicate matters, Aristotle also distinguishes between practical and technical knowledge, and places them in a hierarchy that privileges the practical. *Praxis* (as in politics) aims toward action that is intrinsically good, whereas the various *technai* (for example, rhetoric) tend toward an instrumental goal, and for Aristotle, *praxis* is superior to *technē*, and the intrinsic standards of practical rationality should not be sullied by the instrumental preoccupations of technical reasoning.

This hierarchical arrangement, involving what Garver calls subordination without reduction, creates a problem for Aristotle in aligning politics with rhetoric. Plato dodges this problem by dissociating rhetoric from virtue, but it is as unavoidable for Aristotle as it is for Isocrates. In the case of Isocrates, as we have seen, the need to reconcile the instrumental and intrinsic values of rhetoric leads to a circular identification of deliberation with rhetorical expression and of rhetorical excellence with political virtue. Aristotle, on the other hand, resists this association and attempts to show a relationship between rhetoric and politics that allows space for the operation of the rhetorical art but that circumscribes rhetoric so that its technical ends do not contaminate politics. Rhetoric must have something to do with politics and must have the degree of autonomy needed to achieve purposes of its own, but it must do its business at some conceptual distance from genuine political deliberation. This problem, as Depew and Garver suggest, is at least as nasty as the one Isocrates encounters on the other side of the epistemological fence. And it seems to me that Aristotle is no more successful than Isocrates in resolving the tensions built into his own project.

Garver hopes to rescue the *Rhetoric* through a sophisticated and ingenious interpretation of it against the background of Aristotelian philosophy.

Aristotle, he maintains, limits artistic rhetoric to rational argument, and rhetoricians act autonomously insofar as they construct arguments in accordance with the standards of the art. So rhetoric achieves independence by restraining persuasion through argument and by providing standards of argument that are internal to the art itself; or, to use Garver's own words, Aristotle preserves the autonomy of rhetoric "by showing that even instrumental speech has internal values." But, since the intrinsic ends of instrumental speech (whatever they may be) cannot be intrinsic to politics, which must distance itself from rhetorical instrumentality, how can rhetoric connect with politics and civic education? The answer, Garver tells us, is that it cannot, at least not in any important direct sense. There is, however, an indirect nexus between Aristotelian rhetoric and civic education, and this occurs through the restraint imposed on the rhetor.

Aristotelian rhetoric, according to Garver, operates on the principle that "by being ruled politically, we learn to rule politically." By limiting itself to argument, rhetoric submits to restraint and opens space for reciprocal and mutual interaction, a balanced relationship of friendship between speaker and hearer. This reciprocity of influence, Garver adds, distinguishes Aristotelian rhetoric from the Isocratean program of hegemonic leadership, and it allows speaker and hearer to find common ground through "the reasons and argument they share." Even as rhetoric serves its own intrinsic goals, it also indirectly builds character in speakers and hearers so as to promote political friendship, one of the fundamental conditions for an intrinsically healthy polity.

This brief summary fails to do justice to the complexity and nuance of Garver's full argument, but I think it sufficient to indicate the direction of his thought and to expose some problems in this effort to reconcile the intrinsic autonomy of politics with the instrumental orientation of rhetoric. Even if we view the rhetorical generation of shared reasons and arguments as an indirect influence on politics, we might doubt how they could arise strictly from within the technical sphere of rhetoric. Rhetoric is not a formal art of discourse; its premises and arguments are always embedded in political and social circumstances, and so a rhetorician cannot produce reasons and arguments for an audience to share without entering into the political domain. And since, in Garver's view, discourse is never neutral, the value of these arguments ultimately must be referred to political ends. Even in terms of indirect effects on character, rhetorical argument still seems difficult to isolate from political *praxis.* Moreover, since shared premises and arguments cannot be disentangled easily or naturally from the images, stories, and rituals located in the culture, a categorical distinction between a "hegemonic" Isocratean rhetoric grounded in tradition and a "reciprocal" Aristotelian art grounded in argument may prove difficult to sustain. And it is not at all clear to me why rational argument necessarily offers a better ground for political friendship than does tradition.

Depew has similar reservations about the Aristotelian categories, their relevance to civic education, and their effectiveness as a basis for attacking Isocratean *paideia*. Following an analysis very similar to the one used by Garver, Depew explicates Aristotle's double subordination of *praxis* to *theōria* and of *technē* to *praxis*. Within the terms of this system, *praxis* must direct itself toward actions undertaken for their own sake, while *technai* undertake actions for some extrinsic purpose. This distinction, of course, runs against the grain of the Isocratean association between rhetorical excellence and the political good, and Depew shows that Aristotle presents an explicit indictment of Isocratean *paideia* (*EN* X.9.1181a12–19) precisely because it confuses rhetoric and politics and thus contaminates the properly intrinsic goals of politics with the extrinsic concerns of rhetoric.

Depew, however, wonders whether Aristotle's supposedly distinct and autonomous categories can withstand close scrutiny. The autonomy of politics and its superiority to rhetoric rests upon the privileging of *praxis* over *technē*, and in turn this relationship depends upon the conception of the autonomy of theory and its superiority to *praxis*. Depew contends that Aristotle justifies this exalted view of theory through "a bit of conceptual legerdemain." The Aristotelian model for intrinsically good action refers to the "leisured life of the god of philosophers," which represents a still point of theoretical calm. All actions or decisions undertaken in this rarefied atmosphere occur without resistance from external conditions or regard for external consequence, and so we find here the ultimate referent for understanding the intrinsic nature of worthy action. But on what basis does Aristotle construct this model of pure thought and action? For us, it is difficult to believe that the model devolves from an objective ontotheological vision, and Depew offers an alternative explanation. The model of a philosophical deity, Depew argues, represents a selective and idealized version of the "good and beautiful life of the Greek nobleman (*kalōkagathos*)." At the pinnacle of Aristotle's system, therefore, we come across reasoning every bit as circular as Isocrates elision between rhetorical excellence and political virtue. Selected characteristics of the ruling class are transferred to a philosophical god, and these characteristics, now given a divine aura, function as the standards for the political and ethical conduct of the ruling class.

Significantly Aristotle omits anything relevant to the instrumental actions of the *kalōkagathia* in his selection of idealized qualities. Yet, as Depew notes, the Greek nobility surely must have engaged in many of the worldly practices that Isocrates considers seriously in his version of *paideia*. Even the most ethical among them undoubtedly sought to build and maintain a reputation that would serve their instrumental purposes as they sought influence or honor or wealth. And, in contrast to Aristotle, Isocrates held that the wise could and should manage judgments about intrinsic values while thinking and acting effectively at the instrumental level. The fact that instrumental and intrinsic concerns often enter into situations simultaneously and ambiguously does not mean that they are indistinguishable or that deliberators should seek to isolate one from the other in order to exercise good judgment.

As I have noted earlier, following several of the authors in this collection, we can understand tradition as the source Isocrates uses to distinguish between immediate advantage and the long-run interests of the community. Since tradition is somewhat ambiguous, its effective invocation depends upon the skill of the deliberating agent. There is, in other words, a strong aesthetic and performative dimension to Isocratean *paideia*, and Depew, more clearly than any of our other authors, places emphasis on this point. Aristotle, he observes, reduces the performative force of rhetoric to "an empty husk." Isocrates, on the other hand, not only places it at the center of his educational program, but he also presents that program in texts that are designed to embody it. In short, as opposed to the now unfashionable metaphysical foundationalism that underpins Aristotle's theory of virtue, Isocrates offers an approach grounded in aesthetics and performance.

Depew recommends this Isocratean approach to contemporary virtue theorists, but I think his comparison and contrast between Isocrates and Aristotle also has direct application to our thinking about how to teach the liberal arts. Depew's comments about performance raise a question about whether and in what form we could translate Isocratean *paideia* to contemporary circumstances. Isocrates taught performance at the center of a curriculum designed for a small number of students who remained at his school over a period of several years. These circumstances obviously no longer exist—not even at our liberal arts colleges, let alone our research universities. How can performance center the curriculum under the conditions of mass

higher education? And even if we could overcome this institutional problem, how could we conceive and legitimate such a curriculum in an academic
context where performance outside the fine arts is viewed with suspicion
and considered to have no relationship to scholarship and research?

In a recent article, Fleming (1998) testifies to this problem when he
notes the paradox of rhetoric in the contemporary Academy. On the one
hand, he observes, we have experienced a remarkable revival of rhetorical
studies, but at the same time, rhetoric remains a "relative failure at the level
of undergraduate education; as a coherent and attractive course of study" it
is "unrevived," and the current scene presents us with "the simultaneous
rise of rhetorical theory and the continued decline of rhetorical education"
(169). Depew's reading of Isocrates supports Fleming's view that a revival
depends upon conceiving rhetoric as a practical discipline centered in performance that simultaneously radiates and absorbs theoretical and ethical
matters. This sense of direction may prove useful to contemporary advocates of a rhetorical version of civic education, but it also presents the very
serious challenge of how to implement such a program in an academic context so much different from that of the pre-modern humanists.

Secondly, and finally, I think it instructive to consider Depew's critique
of Aristotle's system for classifying the arts and sciences alongside Morgan's
critique of the linkage that Isocrates affirms between rhetoric and political
virtue. These critiques reveal the circular nature of both efforts to resolve
the tension between the instrumental and the civic dimensions of rhetoric.
Aristotle, in Depew's account, can preserve the autonomy of politics from
rhetoric only through a tautological association between theoretical knowledge and virtue. Isocrates, in Morgan's account, sustains an identity between rhetorical virtuosity and political virtue only by collapsing the two
into one another. Neither offers a coherent general account of how to merge
the self-interested and civilizing aspects of rhetoric. If Aristotle's difficulty
in resolving the issue inclines us to adopt a more tolerant attitude toward
Isocrates, it might also, and more emphatically, lead us to wonder about the
possibility of ever gaining theoretical closure on this matter. If Isocrates
proves too anxious to perfect his position, we might prefer not to correct his
theoretical error but to join Kenneth Burke in warning rhetoricians not to
become rotten with their own perfection and to hedge the tendency to dis-
solve differences within a universal aesthetic solution.

Isocratean *paideia*, like all other variants of humanistic rhetorical education, assumes the fallibility of human reason and the imperfection and

contingency of the human condition. As the essays in this volume demonstrate, these assumptions complicate the effort to justify a program that claims to impart virtue to students and to promote the public good, and even sympathetic readers of Isocrates find it difficult to explain how he solves this problem. Yet, when read as a whole, these essays do seem to clarify the nature of the problem and to underscore its relevance to contemporary interests. The great issue before us is whether we can conceive and design a program of education that is sufficiently realistic to account for the sprawl of democratic practices while it is also sufficiently idealistic to promote civic virtue. This question remains as alive for us today as it was for Isocrates and as difficult to resolve.

Notes

1. This passage from Grube's book came to my attention on reading Ford (1993: 49–50). Ford's essay presents an interesting summary and assessment of conventional views of Isocrates that nicely supplements the essays in this volume.

2. There is an interesting affinity between Konstan's view of how Isocrates uses history in the *Areopagiticus* and some recent efforts to explain the relationship between rhetoric and hermeneutics. See, for example, Jost and Hyde 1997; Mailloux 1989. For an account for the historical connections between the two, see Eden 1997.

3. On this tradition, see Lanham 1993; Sloane 1997.

4. For example, I find it hard to explain Isocrates' repeated endorsements of unified form in composition when they are set beside the passages Morgan cites where Isocrates recommends that the reader deal with the text piecemeal.

WORKS CITED

Aeschylus. 1927. *Aeschylus.* Vol. 1. Trans. H. W. Smyth. Cambridge, Mass.: Harvard University Press.

Alexiou, E. 1995. *Ruhm und Ehre: Studien zu Begriffen, Werten und Motivierungen bei Isokrates.* Heidelberg: Universitätsverlag C. Winter.

Allen, D. 2000. *The World of Prometheus.* Princeton: Princeton University Press.

Allen, J. 1994. "Failure and Expertise in the Ancient Conception of Art." In *Scientific Failure,* ed. T. Horowitz and A. Janis, pp. 81–108. Lanham, Md.: Rowman and Littlefield.

Anagnostopoulos, G. 1994. *Aristotle on the Goals and Exactness of Ethics.* Berkeley and Los Angeles: University of California Press.

Ankersmit, F. R. 1996. *Aesthetic Politics: Political Philosophy Beyond Fact and Value.* Stanford: Stanford University Press.

Annas, J. 1981. *An Introduction to Plato's Republic.* New York: Oxford University Press.

Arendt, H. 1959. *The Human Condition.* Garden City, N.Y.: Doubleday, Anchor.

Aristotle. 1926. *Nicomachean Ethics.* Trans. H. Rackham. Cambridge, Mass.: Harvard University Press.

———. 1962. *The Politics.* Trans. T. A. Sinclair. New York: Penguin.

Arnhart, L. 1995. *Aristotle and Natural Right.* Albany: State University of New York Press.

Asmis, E. 1986. *"Psychagogia* in Plato's *Phaedrus." Illinois Classical Studies* 11: 153–172.

Auerbach, E. 1953. *Mimesis: The Representation of Reality in Western Literature.* Trans. W. R. Trask. Princeton: Princeton University Press.

Bakhtin, M. 1981. "Discourse in the Novel." In *Dialogic Imagination,* ed. M. Holquist, pp. 259–422. Trans. C. Emerson and M. Holquist. Austin, Tex.: University of Texas Press.

Bakker, E. J. 1993. "Discourse and Performance: Involvement, Visualization and 'Presence' in Homeric Poetry." *Classical Antiquity* 12: 1–29.

Batstone, W. W. 1986. "Commentary on Cooper." *Proceedings of the Boston Area Colloquium on Ancient Philosophy* 1: 97–113.

Baynes, N. H. 1960. *Byzantine Studies and Other Essays.* London: Athlone.

Bennett, William. 1993. *The Book of Virtues.* New York: Simon and Schuster.

Blank, D. L. 1985. "Socratics vs. Sophists on Payment for Teaching." *Classical Antiquity* 4: 1–49.

Bledstein, B. J. 1976. *Culture of Professionalism: The Middle Class and the Development of Higher Education in America.* New York: W. W. Norton.

Bons, J. A. E. 1993. "AMPHIBOLIA: Isocrates and Written Composition." *Mnemosyne* 46: 160–171.

Boyd, J. D. 1980. *The Function of Mimesis and Its Decline*, 2d ed. New York: Fordham University Press.

Brickhouse, T. C., and N. D. Smith. 1989. *Socrates on Trial*. Princeton: Princeton University Press.

Bringmann, K. 1965. *Studien zu den politischen Ideen des Isokrates*. Göttingen: Vanderhoeck & Ruprecht, *Hypomnemata 14*.

Buchner, E. 1958. "Der Panegyrikos des Isokrates: Ein historisch-philologische Untersuchung." *Historia Einzelschrift 2*.

Burke, K. 1973. *Philosophy of Literary Form*. Berkeley: University of California Press.

Burnyeat, M. 1980. "Aristotle on Learning to Be Good." In *Essays on Aristotle's Ethics*, ed. A. O. Rorty, pp. 69–92. Berkeley: University of California Press.

Butler, J. 1997. *Excitable Speech: A Politics of the Performative*. New York: Routledge.

Buxton, R. G. A. 1982. *Persuasion in Greek Tragedy: A Study of Peitho*. Cambridge: Cambridge University Press.

Cahn, M. 1989. "Reading Rhetoric Rhetorically: Isocrates and the Marketing of Insight." *Rhetorica 7*: 121–144.

Cartledge, P. 1996. "Comparatively Equal." In *Demokratia: A Conversation on Democracies, Ancient and Modern*, ed. J. Ober and C. Hedrick, pp. 175–185. Princeton: Princeton University Press.

Christ, M. 1990. "Liturgy Avoidance and Antidosis in Classical Athens." *Transactions of the American Philological Association 120*: 147–169.

Chroust, A. 1973. *Aristotle: New Light on His Life and His Lost Works*. Notre Dame: University of Notre Dame Press.

Clark, N. 1996. "The Critical Servant: An Isocratean Contribution to Critical Rhetoric." *Quarterly Journal of Speech 82*: 111–124.

Cloché, P. 1968. "Les Hommes politiques et la justice populaire dans l'Athènes du IVᵉ siècle." *Historia 9*: 80–95.

Cmiel, K. 1990. *Democratic Eloquence: The Fight over Popular Speech in Nineteenth-Century America*. New York: William Morrow.

Cole, S. G. 1996. "Oath Ritual and the Male Community at Athens." In *Demokratia: A Conversation on Democracies, Ancient and Modern*, ed. J. Ober and C. Hendrick, pp. 227–249. Princeton: Princeton University Press.

Cole, T. 1991. *The Origins of Rhetoric in Ancient Greece*. Baltimore: Johns Hopkins University Press.

Collard, C., ed. 1975. *Euripides: Supplices*. Groningen: Bouma's Boekhuis.

Connor, W. R. 1977. "Tyrannis Polis." In *Ancient and Modern: Essays in Honor of G. F. Else*, ed. J. D'Arms and J. W. Eadie, pp. 95–109. Ann Arbor: University of Michigan Press.

———. 1992. *The New Politicians of Fifth-Century Athens*. Princeton: Princeton University Press.

———. 1996. "Civil Society, Dionysiac Festival, and the Athenian Democracy." In *Demokra-*

tia : A Conversation on Democracies, Ancient and Modern, ed. J. Ober and C. Hendrick, pp. 217–227. Princeton: Princeton University Press.

Cooper, J. 1975. *Reason and the Human Good in Aristotle*. Cambridge, Mass.: Harvard University Press.

———. 1986. "Plato, Isocrates, and Cicero on the Independence of Oratory from Philosophy." *Proceedings of the Boston Area Colloquium on Ancient Philosophy* 1: 77–96.

Coventry, L. 1990. "The Role of Interlocutor in Plato." In *Characterization and Individuality in Greek Literature*, ed. C. Pelling, pp. 174–196. Oxford: Clarendon Press.

Dahl, N. 1984. *Practical Reason, Aristotle, and Weakness of Will*. Minneapolis: University of Minnesota Press.

Depew, D. 1991. "Politics, Music, and Contemplation in Aristotle's Ideal State." In *A Companion to Aristotle's Politics*, ed. D. Keyt and F. Miller, pp. 346–380. Oxford: Blackwell.

de Romilly, J. 1959. "Le Classement des Constitutions d'Herodote à Aristote." *Revue des Etudes Grecques* 72: 81–99.

———. 1963. *Thucydides and Athenian Imperialism*. Trans. P. Thody. Oxford: Blackwell.

———. 1969. "Il Pensiero di Euripides sulla Tirannia." *Dioniso* 43: 175–187.

———. 1992. "Isocrates and Europe." *Greece and Rome* 39: 2–13.

Detienne, M. 1996. *Masters of Truth in Archaic Greece*. Trans. J. Lloyd. Cambridge: Michigan Institute of Technology Press.

Detienne, M., and J. P. Vernant. 1991. *Cunning Intelligence in Greek Culture and Society*. Trans. J. Lloyd. Chicago: University of Chicago Press.

Dillery, J. 1995. *Xenophon and the History of His Times*. London and New York: Routledge.

Dover, K. J. 1968. *Lysias and the "Corpus Lysiacum."* Berkeley and Los Angeles: University of California Press.

Dunne, J. 1993. *Back to the Rough Ground: Phronesis and Techne in Modern Philosophy and in Aristotle*. Notre Dame: University of Notre Dame Press.

Düring, I., and G. E. L. Owen, eds. 1960. *Aristotle and Plato in the Mid-Fourth Century*. Göteborg: Elanders Boktryckeri Aktiebolag.

Eden, K. 1997. *Hermeneutics and the Rhetorical Tradition: Chapters in the Ancient Legacy and Its Humanist Reception*. New Haven: Yale University Press.

Eder, W., ed. 1995. *Die athenische Demokratie im 4. Jahrhundert v. Chr: Vollendung oder Verfall einer Verfassungsform?* Stuttgart: Franz Steiner Verlag.

———. 1995a. "Monarchie und Demokratie im 4. Jahrhundert v. Chr. Die Rolle des Fürstenspiegels in der athenischen Demokratie." In *Die athenische Demokratie im 4. Jahrhundert v. Chr: Vollendung oder Verfall einer Verfassungsform?* ed. Walter Eder, pp. 153–173. Stuttgart: Franz Steiner Verlag.

Erbse, H. 1971. "Platons Urteil über Isocrates." *Hermes*. 99: 183/197.

Euben, J. P., et al., eds. 1994. *Athenian Political Thought and the Reconstruction of American Democracy*. Ithaca: Cornell University Press.

Eucken, C. 1983. *Isokrates: Seine Positionen in der Auseinandersetzung mit den zeitgenössischen Philosophen*. Berlin: Walter de Gruyter.

Farrell, T. 1993. *Norms of Rhetorical Culture*. New Haven: Yale University Press.

Farrar, C. 1988. *The Origins of Democratic Thinking: The Invention of Politics in Classical Athens*. Cambridge: Cambridge University Press.

Field, G. C. 1930. *Plato and His Contemporaries: A Study in Fourth-Century Life and Thought*. London: Methuen and Company.

Finley, M. I. 1975. "The Heritage of Isocrates." In *The Use and Abuse of History*, 193–214. New York: Viking.

Fleming, David. 1998. "Rhetoric as a Course of Study." *College English* 61: 169–191.

Flower, M. A. 2000. "From Simonides to Isocrates: The Fifth-Century Origins of Fourth-Century Panhellenism." *Classical Antiquity* 19: 65–102.

Ford, A. 1993. "The Price of Art in Isocrates: Formalism and the Escape from Politics." In *Rethinking the History of Rhetoric*, ed. T. Poulakos, pp. 31–52. Boulder: Westview.

Fornara, C. W., and L. J. Samons II. 1991. *Athens from Cleisthenes to Pericles*. Berkeley: University of California Press.

Forster, E. S. 1979. *Isocrates' Cyprian Orations*. New York: Arno.

Fussell, P. 1983. *Class: A Guide through the American Status System*. New York: Touchstone.

Gabrielsen, V. 1994. *Financing the Athenian Fleet: Public Taxation and Social Relations*. Baltimore: Johns Hopkins University Press.

Gadamer, H. G. 1975 [1965]. *Truth and Method*. London: Sheed and Ward.

Garver, E. 1994. *Aristotle's Rhetoric: An Art of Character*. Chicago: University of Chicago Press.

Gill, C. 1996. *Personality in Greek Epic, Tragedy, and Philosophy: The Self in Dialogue*. New York: Oxford University Press.

Gillis, D. 1969. "The Ethical Basis of Isocratean Rhetoric." *La Parola del Passato* 128: 321–348.

Goode, W. J. 1957. "Community within a Community: The Professions." *American Sociological Review* 22: 194–200.

González Navarro, F. 1992. *El estado social y democrático de derecho*. Pamplona: Ediciones Universidad de Navarra.

Gorgias. 1972. *Encomium of Helen*. In *The Older Sophists*, ed. R. K. Sprague, trans. G. Kennedy, pp. 50–54. Columbia: University of South Carolina Press.

Grube, G. M. A. 1965. *The Greek and Roman Critics*. Toronto: University of Toronto Press.

Guthrie, W. K. C. 1975. *Plato: The Man and his Dialogues*. Cambridge: Cambridge University Press.

Habermas, J. 1989. *The Structural Transformation of the Public Sphere: An Inquiry into a Category of Bourgeois Society*. Trans. T. Burger and F. Lawrence. Cambridge: Michigan Institute of Technology Press.

Hall, E. 1989. *Inventing the Barbarian*. Oxford: Clarendon.

Halliwell, S. 1997. "Philosophical Rhetoric or Rhetorical Philosophy? The Strange Case of Isocrates." In *The Rhetoric Canon*, ed. B. D. Schildgen, pp. 107–125. Detroit: Wayne State University.

Hansen, M. H. 1975. *Eisangelia: The Sovereignty of the People's Court in Athens in the Fourth Century B.C. and the Impeachment of Generals and Politicians.* Odense: Odense University Classical Studies 6.

Harding, P. 1973. "The Purpose of Isokrates' *Archidamos* and *On the Peace.*" *California Studies in Classical Antiquity* 6: 137–149.

Hariman, R. 1986. "Status, Marginality, and Rhetorical Theory," *Quarterly Journal of Speech* 72: 38–54.

———. 1995. *Political Style.* Chicago: University of Chicago Press.

———, ed. 2003. *Prudence: Classical Virtue, Postmodern Practice.* University Park: Pennsylvania State University Press.

Harris, W. V. 1989. *Ancient Literacy.* Cambridge, Mass.: Harvard University Press.

Haskins, E. V. 1999. "Orality, Literacy, and Isocrates' Political Aesthetics." In *Rhetoric, the Polis, and the Global Village,* ed. C. J. Swearingen and D. Pruett, 83–92. Mahwah, N.J.: Lawrence Erlbaum.

———. 2001. "Rhetoric between Orality and Literacy: Cultural Memory and Performance in Isocrates and Aristotle." *Quarterly Journal of Speech* 87: 158–178.

Havelock, E. A. 1963. *Preface to Plato.* Cambridge, Mass.: Harvard University Press.

———. 1982. *Literate Revolution in Greece and Its Cultural Consequences.* Princeton: Princeton University Press.

———. 1983. "The Linguistic Task of the Presocratics." In *Language and Thought in Early Greek Philosophy,* ed. K. Robb, pp. 7–82. La Salle, Ill.: Hegeler Institute.

———. 1986. *The Muse Learns to Write: Reflections on Orality and Literacy from Antiquity to the Present.* New Haven: Yale University Press.

Hedrick, C., Jr. 1995. "Thucydides and the Beginnings of Archaeology." In *Methods in the Mediterranean: Historical and Archaeological Views on Texts and Archaeology,* ed. D. B. Small, pp. 45–88. Leiden: Brill.

Heilbrunn, G. 1975. "Isocrates on Rhetoric and Power." *Hermes* 103: 154–178.

Herodotus. 1925. *Persian Wars.* Trans. A. D. Godley. London: William Heinemann.

———. 1942. *The Persian Wars.* Trans. G. Rawlinson. New York: Modern Library.

Hoffman, D. 2000. "Rhetoric and the Culture of Display in Hellenic Greece." Ph.D. diss., University of Iowa.

Holmes, O. W., Jr. 1962. "Speech at Dinner Given by the Bar Association of Boston, Mar. 7, 1900." In *Occasional Speeches of Justice Oliver Wendell Holmes,* ed. M. DeWolfe Howe, pp. 122–126. Cambridge, Mass.: Belknap Press of Harvard University Press.

———. 1992. *The Essential Holmes: Selections from the Letters, Speeches, Judicial Opinions, and Other Writings,* ed. R. A. Posner. Chicago: University of Chicago Press.

Irwin, T. 1977. *Aristotle's First Principles.* Oxford: Oxford University Press.

Isocrates. 1928, 1929. *Isocrates*. Vols. 1–2. Trans. G. Norlin. London: William Heinemann and Cambridge: Harvard University Press.

———. 1945. *Isocrates*. Vol. 3. Trans. L. Van Hook. London: William Heinemann and Cambridge: Harvard University Press.

Jaeger, W. 1948. *Aristotle: Fundamentals of the History of His Development*. 2nd ed. Oxford: Oxford University Press.

———. 1957. *Paideia: Los ideales de la cultura griega*. Trans. J. Xirau and W. Roces. Mexico City: Fondo de Cultura Económica.

———. 1965. *Paideia: The Ideals of Greek Culture*. Vol. 3. Trans. G. Highet. New York: Oxford University Press.

Jarratt, S. 1991. *Reading the Sophists: Classical Rhetoric Refigured*. Carbondale: Southern Illinois University Press.

Jebb, R. C. 1893. *The Attic Orators*. Vol. 2. London: Macmillan.

Jost, W., and M. Hyde, eds. 1997. *Rhetoric and Hermeneutics in Our Time*. New Haven: Yale University Press.

Kahn, C. H. 1996. *Plato and the Socratic Dialogue: The Philosophical Use of a Literary Form*. Cambridge: Cambridge University Press.

Kateb, George. 1998. "Socratic Integrity." In *Integrity and Conscience*, ed. I. Shapiro and R. Adams, pp. 77–112. New York: New York University Press, 1998.

Kennedy, G. 1963. *The Art of Persuasion in Greece*. Princeton: Princeton University Press.

———. 1972. *The Art of Rhetoric in the Roman World*. Princeton: Princeton University Press.

———. 1991. *Aristotle's On Rhetoric: A Theory of Civic Discourse*. New York: Oxford University Press.

Kenny, A. 1978. *The Aristotelian Ethics: A Study of the Relationship between the Eudemian and Nicomachean Ethics of Aristotle*. Oxford: Oxford University Press.

Kerferd, G. B. 1981. *The Sophistic Movement*. Cambridge: Cambridge University Press.

Kimball, B. A. 1986. *Orators and Philosophers: A History of the Idea of Liberal Education*. New York: Teachers College Press.

———. 1992. *The "True Professional Ideal" in America: A History*. Cambridge, Mass.: Blackwell.

Knox, R. A. 1985. " 'So Mischievous a Beaste'? The Athenian *Demos* and Its Treatment of Its Politicians." *Greece and Rome* 32: 132–161.

Konstan, D. 1994. "The Classics and Class Conflict." *Arethusa* 26: 47–70.

Kraut, R. 1989. *Aristotle on the Human Good*. Princeton: Princeton University Press.

Kurke, Leslie. 1992. "The Politics of *habrosunē* in Archaic Greece." *Classical Antiquity* 11: 91–120.

Laistner, M. L. W. 1930. "The Influence of Isocrates' Doctrines on Some Fourth Century Men of Affairs." *Classical Weekly* 23: 129–131.

Lanham, R. 1993. *The Electronic Word: Democracy, Technology and the Arts*. Chicago: University of Chicago Press.

Lanni, A. M. 1997. "Spectator Sport or Serious Politics? Hoi-periestekotes and the Athenian Law Courts." *Journal of Hellenic Studies* 117: 183–189.

Larson, M. S. 1977. *The Rise of Professionalism: A Sociological Analysis*. Berkeley: University of California Press.

Lesky, A. 1966. *A History of Greek Literature*. Trans. J. Willis and C. de Heer. London: Methuen.

Long, A. A. 1996. "The Socratic Tradition: Diogenes, Crates, and Hellenistic Ethics." In *The Cynics: The Cynic Movement in Antiquity and Its Legacy*, ed. R. B. Branham and M-O. Goulet-Cazé, pp. 28–46. Berkeley and Los Angeles: University of California Press.

Loraux, N. 1986. *The Invention of Athens: The Funeral Oration in the Classical City*. Trans. A. Sheridan. Cambridge, Mass.: Cambridge University Press.

Lord, C. 1996. "Aristotle and the Idea of Liberal Education." In *Demokratia: A Conversation on Democracies, Ancient and Modern*, ed. J. Ober and C. Hedrick, pp. 271–288. Princeton: Princeton University Press.

Luban, D. 1997. "The Bad Man and the Good Lawyer: A Centennial Essay on Holmes' *The Path of the Law*." *New York University Law Review* 72: 1547–1583.

Luschnat, O. 1970. "Thukydides." *Paulys Real-Encyclopädie der classischen Altertumswissenschaft*, suppl. 12, cols. 1085–1354.

Macintyre, A. 1981. *After Virtue: A Study in Moral Theory*. Notre Dame: University of Notre Dame Press.

Mackie, H. 1996. *Talking Trojan: Speech and Community in the Iliad*. Lanham, Md.: Rowman and Littlefield.

Mailloux, S. 1989. *Rhetorical Power*. Ithaca: Cornell University Press.

Marone, J. A. 1998. *The Democratic Wish: Popular Participation and the Limits of American Government*. New Haven: Yale University Press.

Martin, R. 1989. *The Language of Heroes: Speech and Performance in the Iliad*. Ithaca: Cornell University Press.

Marrou, H. 1956. *A History of Education in Antiquity*. New York: Sheed and Ward.

Masaracchia, A. 1995. *Isocrate: Retorica e politica*. Rome: Gruppo Editoriale Internazionale.

Mathieu, G. 1926. *Les idées politiques d'Isocrate*. 2nd ed. Paris: Les Belles Lettres.

McGee, M. C. 1985. "The Moral Problem of Argumentum per Argumentum." In *Argument and Social Practice: Proceedings of the Fourth SCA/AFA Conference on Argumentation*, ed. R. Cox, M. Sillars, and G. Walker, pp. 1–15. Annandale, Va.: Speech Communication Association.

McGlew, J. F. 1993. *Tyranny and Political Culture in Ancient Greece*. Ithaca: Cornell University Press.

Minar, E. 1949. "Parmenides and the World of Seeming." *American Journal of Philosophy* 70: 41–55.

Misch, G. 1976. "Isokrates Autobiographie." In *Isokrates*, ed. F. Seck, pp. 189–215. Darmstadt: Wissenschaftliche Buchgesellschaft.

Morgan, K. A. 1998. "Designer History: Plato's Atlantis Story and Fourth-Century Ideology." *Journal of Hellenic Studies* 118: 101–118.

———. 2000. *Myth and Philosophy from the Presocratics to Plato.* New York: Cambridge University Press.

———. 2003. "The Tyranny of the Audience in Plato and Isocrates." In *Popular Tyranny,* ed. K. Morgan, pp. 181–213. Austin: University of Texas Press.

Morris, I. 1996. "The Strong Principle of Equality and the Archaic Origins of Greek Democracy." In *Demokratia: A Conversation on Democracies, Ancient and Modern,* ed. J. Ober and C. Hedrick, pp. 19–48. Princeton: Princeton University Press.

Moysey, R. A. 1982. "Isokrates' *On the Peace:* Rhetorical Exercise or Political Advice?" *American Journal of Ancient History* 7: 118–127.

Nagy, G. 1996. *Poetry as Performance: Homer and Beyond.* Cambridge: Cambridge University Press.

Natali, C. 2001. *The Wisdom of Aristotle.* Trans. G. Parks. Albany: State University of New York Press.

Nehamas, A. 1990. "Eristic, Antilogic, Sophistic, Dialectic: Plato's Demarcation of Philosophy from Sophistry." *History of Philosophy Quarterly* 7: 3–16.

Nightingale, A. 1995. *Genres in Dialogue: Plato and the Construct of Philosophy.* Cambridge: Cambridge University Press.

Nussbaum, M. 1986. *The Fragility of Goodness: Luck and Ethics in Greek Tragedy and Philosophy.* New York and Cambridge: Cambridge University Press.

Ober, J. 1989. *Mass and Elite in Democratic Athens: Rhetoric, Ideology, and the Power of the People.* Princeton: Princeton University Press.

———. 1994. "How to Criticize Democracy in Late Fifth and Fourth Century Athens." In *Athenian Political Thought and the Reconstruction of American Democracy,* ed. J. P. Euben et al., pp. 149–171. Ithaca: Cornell University Press.

———. 1996. *The Athenian Revolution: Essays on Ancient Greek Democracy and Political Theory.* Princeton: Princeton University Press.

———. 1998. *Political Dissent in Democratic Athens: Intellectual Critics of Popular Rule.* Princeton: Princeton University Press.

Ober, J., and C. Hendrick, eds. 1996. *Demokratia: A Conversation on Democracies, Ancient and Modern.* Princeton: Princeton University Press.

Ostwald, M. 1986. *From Popular Sovereignty to the Sovereignty of Law: Law, Society, and Politics in Fifth-Century Athens.* Berkeley: University of California Press.

Parker, V. 1998. "Tu/rannoj: The Semantics of a Political Concept from Archilochus to Aristotle." *Hermes* 126: 145–172.

Pelikan, J. J. 1984. *The Vindication of Tradition.* New Haven: Yale University Press.

Perelman, C., and L. Olbrechts-Tyteca. 1969. *The New Rhetoric: A Treatise on Argumentation.* Notre Dame: University of Notre Dame Press.

Plato. 1961. *Plato: The Collected Dialogues,* ed. E. Hamilton and H. Cairns. Trans. R. Hackforth. Princeton: Princeton University Press.

———. 1977. *Protagoras.* Trans. W. R. M. Lamb. Cambridge, Mass.: Harvard University Press.

———. 1982. *Republic.* Trans. P. Shorey. Cambridge, Mass.: Harvard University Press.

Plattner, M. F. 1999. Review of *Democracy* by R. A. Dahl. *The New York Times Book Review* 7 February: 15.

Plutarch. 1914. *Lives.* Trans. B. Perrin. London: William Heinemann.

Poulakos, J. 1995. *Sophistical Rhetoric in Classical Greece.* Columbia: University of South Carolina Press.

Poulakos, T. 1987. "Isocrates' Use of Narrative in the *Evagoras:* Epideictic Rhetoric and Moral Action." *Quarterly Journal of Speech* 73: 317–328.

———. 1989. "Epideictic Rhetoric as Social Hegemony: Isocrates' *Helen.*" In *Rhetoric and Ideology: Compositions and Criticisms of Power,* ed. C. W. Kneupper, pp. 156–166. Arlington, Tex.: Rhetoric Society of America.

———. 1994. "Human Agency in the History of Rhetoric: Gorgias' *Encomium of Helen.*" In *Writing Histories of Rhetoric,* ed. V. Vitanza. Carbondale: Southern Illinois University Press.

———. 1997. *Speaking for the Polis: Isocrates' Rhetorical Education.* Columbia: University of South Carolina Press.

———. 2001. "Isocrates' Use of *doxa.*" *Philosophy and Rhetoric* 34: 61–78.

Raaflaub, K. A. 2003. "Stick and Glue: The Function of Tyranny in Fifth-Century Athenian Democracy." In *Popular Tyranny,* ed. K. Morgan, pp. 59–93. Austin: University of Texas Press.

Reeve, C. D. C. 1995. *Practices of Reason: Aristotle's Nicomachean Ethics.* Oxford: Clarendon Press.

Rhodes, P. J. 1995. "Judicial Procedures in Fourth-Century Athens: Improvement or Simply Change?" In *Die athenische Demokratie im 4. Jahrhundert v. Chr: Vollendung oder Verfall einer Verfassungsform?* ed. W. Eder, pp. 303–319. Stuttgart: Franz Steiner Verlag.

Rivier, A. 1956. "Remarques sur les Fragments 34 et 35 de Xenophane." *Revue de Philologie* 30: 37–61.

Robb, K. 1983. "The Linguistic Art of Heraclitus." In *Language and Thought in Early Greek Philosophy,* ed. K. Robb, pp. 186–200. LaSalle, Ill.: Hegeler Institute.

Roberts, J. T. 1982. *Accountability in Athenian Government.* Madison: University of Wisconsin Press.

Rosenmeyer, T. 1955. "Gorgias, Aeschylus, and Apatē." *American Journal of Philology* 76: 255–260.

Rummel, E. 1979. "Isocrates' Ideal of Rhetoric: Criteria of Evaluation." *The Classical Journal* 75: 25–35.

Schiappa, E. 1991. *Protagoras and Logos.* Columbia: University of South Carolina Press.

———. 1995. "Isocrates' *Philosophia* and Contemporary Pragmatism." In *Rhetoric, Sophistry, Pragmatism.* ed. S. Mailloux, pp. 33–60. Cambridge: Cambridge University Press.

—————. 1996. "Toward a Predisciplinary Analysis of Gorgias' *Helen*." In *Theory, Text, Context*, ed. C. L. Johnstone, pp. 65–86. Albany: State University of New York Press.

—————. 1999. *The Beginnings of Rhetorical Theory in Classical Greece*. New Haven: Yale University Press.

Schofield, M. 1999. *The Stoic Idea of the City*. Chicago: University of Chicago Press.

Schrader, C., trans. 1979. *Herodoto: Historia, libros III–IV*. Madrid: Editorial Gredos.

Schwarze, S. 1999. "Performing *Phronesis:* The case of Isocrates' *Helen*." In *Philosophy and Rhetoric* 32: 78–95.

Sedley, D. 1991. "Is Aristotle's Teleology Anthropocentric?" *Phronesis* 36: 179–195.

Segal, C. 1962. "Gorgias and the Psychology of the Logos." *Harvard Studies in Classical Philology* 66: 99–155.

Sloane, T. 1997. *On the Contrary: The Protocol of Traditional Rhetoric*. Washington, D.C.: Catholic University Press.

Smethurst, S. E. 1953. "Cicero and Roman Imperial Policy." *Transactions and Proceedings of the American Philological Association* 84: 216–226.

Sprague, R. K., ed. 1972. *The Older Sophists*. Columbia: University of South Carolina Press.

Steiner, D. T. 1994. *The Tyrant's Writ: Myths and Images of Writing in Ancient Greece*. Princeton: Princeton University Press.

Stocks, J. L. 1929. "Moral Values." *Journal of Philosophical Studies*.

Svenbro, J. 1988. *Phrasikleia: Anthropologie de la lecture en Grèce Ancienne*. Paris: Editions de la découverte.

Taylor, C. 1975. *Hegel*. Cambridge: Cambridge University Press.

Timmerman, D. M. 1998. "Isocrates' Competing Conceptualization of Philosophy." *Philosophy and Rhetoric* 31: 145–159.

Too, Y. L. 1995. *The Rhetoric of Identity in Isocrates*. Cambridge: Cambridge University Press.

Treming, David. 1999. "Rhetoric as a Course of Study." *College English* 61: 169–191.

Trevett, J. C. 1996. "Aristotle's Knowledge of Athenian Oratory." *Classical Quarterly* 46: 371–379.

Tuplin, C. 1985. "Imperial Tyranny: Some Reflections on a Classical Greek Political Metaphor." In *Crux: Essays Presented to G. E. M. de Ste. Croix on his 75th Birthday*, ed. P. Cartledge and F. D. Harvey. Exeter: University of Exeter Press. *History of Political Thought* 6: 348–375.

Usener, S. 1994. *Isokrates, Platon und ihr Publikum: Hörer und Leser von Literatur im 4. Jahrhundert v. Chr. Tübingen:* Gunter Narr Verlag. *ScriptOralia* 63.

Usher, S. 1973. "The Style of Isocrates." *Bulletin of the Institute of Classical Studies* 20: 39–67.

Veysey, L. R. 1965. *The Emergence of the American University*. Chicago: University of Chicago Press.

Vidal-Naquet, P. 1996. "Foreword." In *The Masters of Truth in Ancient Greece*, ed. M. Detienne, trans. J. Lloyd, pp. 7–14. Cambridge: Michigan Institute of Technology Press.

Vitanza, V. 1997. *Negation, Subjectivity, and the History of Rhetoric.* Albany: State University of New York.

Vlastos, G. 1983. "The Socratic Elenchus." *OSAP* 1: 27–58.

Wallace, R. W. 1994. "Private Lives and Public Enemies: Freedom of Thought in Classical Athens." In *Athenian Identity and Civic Ideology,* ed. A. Boegehold and A. Scafuro, pp. 127–155. Baltimore: Johns Hopkins University Press.

———. 1997. "Poet, Public, and 'Theatocracy': Audience Performance in Classical Athens." In *Poet, Public, and Performance in Ancient Greece,* ed. L. Edmunds and R. Wallace, pp. 97–111. Baltimore: Johns Hopkins University Press.

Walzer, M. 1988. *The Company of Critics: Social Criticism and Political Commitment in the Twentieth Century.* New York: Basic.

Wardy, R. 1996. *The Birth of Rhetoric: Gorgias, Plato, and Their Successors.* London and New York: Routledge.

Welch, K. 1999. *Electric Rhetoric: Classical Rhetoric, Oralism, and a New Literacy.* Cambridge: Michigan Institute of Technology Press.

White, E. 1987. *Kaironomia.* Ithaca: Cornell University Press.

Wilcox, Stanley. 1942. "The Scope of Early Rhetorical Instruction." *Harvard Studies in Classical Philology* 53: 121–155.

Wilms, H. 1995. *Techne und Paideia bei Xenophon und Isokrates.* Stuttgart and Leipzig: B. G. Teubner.

Wolin, S. 1966. "Transgression, Equality, and Voice." In *Demokratia: A Conversation on Democracies, Ancient and Modern,* ed. J. Ober and C. Hedrick, pp. 63–90. Princeton: Princeton University Press.

Yunis, H. 1996. *Taming Democracy: Models of Political Rhetoric in Classical Athens.* Ithaca: Cornell University Press.

Zeitlin, F. I. 1990. "Thebes: Theater of Self and Society in Athenian Drama." In *Nothing to Do with Dionysus? Athenian Drama in Its Social Context,* ed. J. J. Winkler and F. Zeitlin, pp. 130–167. Princeton: Princeton University Press.

CONTRIBUTORS

TAKIS POULAKOS is Associate Professor of Rhetoric at the University of Iowa. He has published several essays on classical rhetoric, is the author of *Speaking for the Polis: Isocrates' Rhetorical Education* (South Carolina, 1997), and editor of *Rethinking the History of Rhetoric: Multidisciplinary Essays on the Rhetorical Tradition* (Westview, 1993).

DAVID DEPEW is Professor of Communication Studies and Rhetoric of Inquiry at the University of Iowa. He has published a number of papers on Aristotle's political theory, and is at work on a book entitled *Biology, Society, and Philosophy in Aristotle's Politics*. He is editor of *The Greeks and the Good Life* (Hackett, 1980). He has also written, with Bruce H. Weber, *Darwinism Evolving: Systems Dynamics and the Genealogy of Natural Selection* (MIT Press/Bradford Books, 1994), and, with Marjorie Grene, *Philosophy of Biology: An Episodic History* (Cambridge University Press, 2004).

JOSIAH OBER is Magie Professor of Classics at Princeton. He is the author of several books on Greek democracy and politics, including: *Political Dissent in Democratic Athens* (Princeton, 1998); *The Athenian Revolution: Essays on Ancient Greek Democracy and Political Theory* (Princeton, 1996); *Mass and Elite in Democratic Athens: Rhetoric, Ideology and the Power of the People* (Princeton, 1989). He is also the editor of volumes linking ancient and contemporary politics, including: *Demokratia: A Conversation on Democracies, Ancient and Modern* (Princeton, 1996); *Athenian Political Thought and the Reconstruction of American Democracy* (coeditor, Cornell, 1994).

JOHN POULAKOS is Associate Professor of Communication Studies at the University of Pittsburgh. He has written extensively on classical rhetoric and the Sophists, including *Sophistical Rhetoric in Classical Greece* (South Carolina, 1995) which won the Winans-Wichelns Award for Distinguished Scholarship in Rhetoric and Public Address, and the Everett Lee Hunt Award.

EKATERINA HASKINS is Assistant Professor of Communication Studies at Boston College. She has published several essays on classical and contemporary rhetoric, one of which received the Charles Kneupper Award from the Rhetoric Society of America. Her book *Logos and Power in Isocrates and Aristotle* (South Carolina, in press) offers a reading of Isocrates and Aristotle as two distinct paradigms of thinking about public discourse, education, and democracy. She is interested in how the intersection of aesthetics and power in classical philosophy and rhetoric may inform contemporary humanistic debates about democracy and civic identity.

DAVID KONSTAN is John Rowe Workman Distinguished Professor of Classics and the Humanistic Tradition at Brown University. He has written extensively on classical literature including *Pity Transformed* (Duckworth, 2001); *Friendship in the Classical World* (Cambridge, 1997); *Greek Comedy and Ideology* (Oxford, 1995); *Sexual Symmetry: Love in the Ancient Novel and Related Genres* (Princeton, 1994); he is the translator of *The Greek Commentaries on Aristotle's Nicomachean Ethics 8 and 9* (Cornell, 2001); *Simplicius on Aristotle's Physics 6* (Cornell, 1989), which won the Choice Award for Outstanding Academic Books.

KATHRYN MORGAN is Associate Professor of Classics at the University of California, Los Angeles. She has written several essays on Greek literature and rhetoric. She is the author of *Myth and Philosophy from the Presocratics to Plato* (Cambridge, 2000) and the editor of *Popular Tyranny: Sovereignty and Its Discontents in Ancient Greece* (Texas, 2003).

EUGENE GARVER is Regents Professor of Philosophy at Saint John's University. He has written extensively on classical and contemporary philosophy, including *For the Sake of Argument: Practical Reasoning, Character, and the Ethics of Belief* (Chicago, forthcoming, 2004); *Aristotle's Rhetoric: An Art of Character* (Chicago, 1994); *Machiavelli and the History of Prudence* (Wisconsin, 1987). He is also coeditor of *Pluralism in Theory and Practice: Richard McKeon and American Philosophy* (Vanderbilt, 2000).

ROBERT HARIMAN is Levitt Professor of Rhetoric at Drake University. He is the author of *Political Style: The Artistry of Power* (Chicago, 1995); coeditor of *Post-Realism: The Rhetorical Turn in International Relations* (Michigan State, 1996); and editor of *Prudence: Classical Virtue, Postmodern Practice* (Pennsylvania State, 2003).

MICHAEL LEFF is Professor at the University of Memphis. He has published extensively on rhetoric in national and international journals devoted to the history, criticism, and theory of rhetoric. His work has been repeatedly awarded, including the Winans-Wichelns Award for Distinguished Scholarship in Rhetoric and Public Address, the Charles Woolbert Award for Scholarship of Exceptional Originality and Influence, and the International Society for the Study of Argumentation Award for Distinguished Scholarship. He has coauthored *Reading Texts Rhetorically* (Houghton-Mifflin, 1998), and coedited *Rhetoric and Pedagogy* (Erlbaum, 1995).

INDEX

Academy, 11, 26–27, 29, 118, 129, 132, 157, 159, 165, 167, 179, 184n.7, 212n.15, 253

Achilles, 94

Aeschines, 21, 28, 36, 92, 111

Aeschylus, 88, 101–102, 108

Agamemnon, 94–95, 149

agōn, 9, 32

Alcibiades, 138, 157

Alcidamas, 78

alētheia, 46–47, 85–88

Alexiou, E., 123n.22

Allen, D., 42n.23

Allen, J., 52

Althusser, L., 23, 39

amphibolia, 149, 154n.44

Anagnostopoulos, G., 184n.8

Anaxagoras, 43n.28

Andocides, 41n.13

Ankersmit, F., 234nn.24,31

Annas, J., 153n.30

Antalcidas, 143, 147, 149

anthrōpina, 158, 162–164, 178, 183

antidosis, 32–33, 36, 42nn.16–17

Antiphon, 122n.10

Anytus, 128

apatē, 46–47

apologia, 7, 32, 36, 42n.21

Arendt, 42n.25

aretē, 129, 172, 190–191

Aristophanes, 109, 122n.11

Aristotle: Constitution of the Athenians, 122n.10, 176; De Anima, 183n.5; Eudemian Ethics, 163, 165, 167–168, 172, 183nn.5–6, 184n.6, 206; Gryllus, 158; Metaphysics, 162, 183n.5, 197; Nicomachean Ethics, 1,

14, 48, 158–159, 162–177, 182, 183nn.5–6, 184nn.9–10, 185n.15, 190, 197–198, 201, 204, 207, 209, 213n.18; Poetics, 158, 162, 182, 193, 196, 211n.10, 251; Politics, 1, 102, 158, 160–162, 165, 176, 178–179, 184n.8, 192–193, 201, 203–207, 209; Protrepticus, 158, 167; Rhetoric, 15, 41n.13, 100, 158, 174, 182, 190, 193, 196–198, 201–205, 207–210, 211nn.7,10, 232n.11, 249; Topics, 167

Arnhart, L., 185n.12

Arnold, M., 15–16

Asmis, E., 11

Aspasia, 113

Athena, 186

Auerbach, E., 231n.3

Austin, J. L., 23

Bakhtin, M., 85–86

Bakker, E., 86, 93

Batstone, W., 152nn.18–19,22

Baynes, N., 243

Bennett, W., 1

bia, 10, 87

Blank, D., 152n.6, 231n.5

Bledstein, B., 220, 231n.6

Bons, J., 154n.44, 233n.21

bouleusis, 166

Boyd, J., 231n.3

Brickhouse, T., 8, 43nn.29,31

Bringmann, K., 41n.14, 123nn.17,24,30

Buchner, E., 41n.14

Burke, K., 99, 253

Burnyeat, M., 171–172

Butler, J., 23, 39, 40n.1

Buxton, R., 103n.5

White, E., 65n.4
Wilcox, S., 83n.8
Wilms, H., 123n.25
Wolin, S., 212n.15

Xenophanes, 47
Xenophon, 41n.13, 122n.10
Xerxes, 102

Yunis, H., 3, 41n.13, 152nn.3,17,
 154n.40, 234n.28

Zeitlin, F., 123n.16